The Poetry and Music of Joaquín Sabina

The Poetry and Music of Joaquín Sabina

An Angel with Black Wings

Daniel J. Nappo

LEXINGTON BOOKS
Lanham • Boulder • New York • London

Published by Lexington Books
An imprint of The Rowman & Littlefield Publishing Group, Inc.
4501 Forbes Boulevard, Suite 200, Lanham, Maryland 20706
www.rowman.com

6 Tinworth Street, London SE11 5AL, United Kingdom

Copyright © 2021 The Rowman & Littlefield Publishing Group, Inc.

All rights reserved. No part of this book may be reproduced in any form or by any electronic or mechanical means, including information storage and retrieval systems, without written permission from the publisher, except by a reviewer who may quote passages in a review.

British Library Cataloguing in Publication Information Available

Library of Congress Control Number: 2020947187

ISBN: 978-1-7936-1577-0 (cloth)
ISBN: 978-1-7936-1579-4 (pbk)
ISBN: 978-1-7936-1578-7 (electronic)

Para Adrián y Daphne, por guapos.

Contents

Acknowledgments		ix
Introduction: Joaquín Sabina and the Question of Song Lyrics as Poetry		1
	Who Is Joaquín Sabina?	1
	Song Lyrics and Poetry	12
	Title and Organization of This Book	16
1	Essential Biography and Musical Trajectory	25
	Ubeda	25
	Granada	29
	London	34
	Madrid	39
2	The Poetics of Joaquín Sabina's Lyrics	65
	Sabina as Poet	65
	Lexical Antithesis	68
	Antithesis of Imagery	72
	Structural Antithesis	78
3	"Los cuentos que yo cuento" ("The Stories That I Tell")	93
	Sabina as Narrator	93
	Structuring Narrative	95
	The Fantastic	109
	Sabina as "Huelebraguetas"	116

Conclusion: The Poetry of Joaquín Sabina and Bob Dylan	131
An Anxiety of Influence?	131
Harmony	138
Dissonance	148
Boots of Spanish Leather	158
Bibliography	171
Index	179
About the Author	189

Acknowledgments

I feel very fortunate to have written what I believe to be the first English-language book about Joaquín Sabina and his music. Curiously, my research for this book began long before I had the inspiration to write it. My first exposure to Sabina's music occurred during the mid-1990s at Michigan State University. A Spanish classmate played a recording of "Así estoy yo sin ti" for me and I marveled at the beauty of the song's similes, its unexpected adjectives. A few years later I was living in Mexico City and listening more frequently to Sabina's music. I can remember some "ambiguas horas" of the early morning there, driving south on Amores, running red lights after the perfunctory tap of the horn, while enjoying the cassette of *19 días y 500 noches*. A few years later, after moving back to the States, I recall longer, lonelier road trips up and down US 45E, now listening to the compact discs of *Mentiras piadosas*, *Física y química*, and *Esta boca es mía*. By that time, I was no longer a *sabinero* but an amateur *sabinista*.[1] This progress was reflected in my activities. For example, when I traveled to Spain, I made a point of not only purchasing Sabina's albums but also visiting places mentioned in his songs.[2] During my last trip to Madrid, I visited La Mordida, his Mexican restaurant located on Calle de las Fuentes near the Puerta del Sol. Not only was the selection of tequila outstanding, when I went to use the "servicios" in the basement, I noticed that the toilet seat and lid had been removed, leaving only the gaping, open bowl. Everyone knows of Sabina's love of Spanish America, but here, I thought, was evidence of a man with a truly profound appreciation of "México lindo y querido." I half expected "Viridiana" to make an appearance at the bar.

My fascination with Sabina's music has proven beneficial to me. As is the case with most students who try to learn a foreign language, my initial understanding of Spanish was woefully literal. But by listening repeatedly to Sabina's songs, I began to appreciate subtleties and connotations. It occurred to me, for example, that in "¿Quién me ha robado el mes de abril?" he sang of "el marido de mi madre" (*"the husband of my mother"*) instead of "mi padrastro" (*"my stepfather"*). It also struck me that the first lyric of "Contigo," a love ballad, was "Yo no quiero un amor civilizado" (*"I don't want a civilized love"*). As I looked more closely at his lyrics, I noticed that Sabina employed many of the literary techniques once used by the poets I was reading in graduate school, luminaries as Rubén Darío, César Vallejo, and Federico García Lorca. Simile and alliteration figure prominently in his lyrics, but Sabina also employed less-common devices such as enjambment, polysyndeton, and synesthesia. Like just about every sabinista or sabinero I have known, I went through several periods where his albums were nearly all that I listened to—occasionally to the dismay of those who were with me. I even learned to play some of my favorite Sabina songs on guitar. My interest (the Spanish *afición* is a more precise word) led me to present two papers about Sabina's lyrics at national conferences dedicated to popular culture, where I usually found myself on panels with other scholars presenting their research on Portuguese *fado* or J-pop. Because Sabina's poetic expression is difficult to classify, being an exceptional sophistication in the vernacular mode of rock music, I was neither surprised nor disappointed to be on such panels.

 A number of people have helped me so much with this project, I feel compelled to call them out by name. Antón García-Fernández, my friend and colleague, was the first person to suggest that I write this book. Earlier, after I had asked him the meaning of a dozen or so *cheli* words I had heard in Sabina's songs, he gave me a copy of the *Diccionario de argot español* by Víctor León so I would no longer have to keep inquiring about words such as "peluco," "cutre," and "chungo." (In spite of the dictionary, I have continued to ask Antón countless questions.) Antón's father, the poet Antonio García Teijeiro, also conversed at length with me about Spanish musicians and other topics related to this book. José F. Colmeiro, one of my favorite professors from my grad-school days, gave me some helpful suggestions for resources on Spanish popular music. Another outstanding professor of mine, Joseph Snow, helped me with the bureaucratic side of this project and, when he wasn't in the reading room of the Biblioteca Nacional de España, provided updates about Sabina's activities that he gleaned from newspapers. I also extend my gratitude to Jeremy L. Cass, of Furman University, for sending me the copy of a difficult-to-obtain article in about forty-eight hours, and to Richard F. Thomas, of Harvard University, for his advice concerning my use of Bob Dylan's lyrics. I would also like to thank writers Julio Valdeón and Maurilio de Miguel for taking the time to speak with me and tell me so much more about the "genio y figura" of Sabina. I am also indebted to *cantautor* Joaquín

Carbonell for answering questions about Sabina's legendary performances at La Mandrágora. As the final manuscript of this book was being prepared, don Joaquín was in the ICU of a Zaragoza hospital, fighting valiantly against COVID-19. He died on September 12. A talented musician, poet, and writer, he will be sorely missed. I feel very fortunate to have made his acquaintance.

The former chair of my department, David Carithers, was generous with support for my research, whether it was facilitating a conference presentation or approving a course reduction. I thank my colleague in English, Neil Graves, for helping me to identify a literary device I discuss in the final chapter. I would also like to thank my colleague Julie Hill, of the department of Music, for patiently answering questions about rhythms and arrangements featured in some of Sabina's songs. Two other colleagues in the department of music, Doug Owens and Roberto Mancusi, helped with different questions of a technical nature. Dana Breland, of the Paul Meek Library, receives my gratitude for obtaining so many resources for me through interlibrary loan. On the subject of libraries, I would also like to extend my most heartfelt appreciation to Paula Covington, the Latin American and Iberian bibliographer at Vanderbilt University, for all the invaluable assistance she gave me during my research. Not only did Paula obtain several books for me, she also gave me an illuminating crash course on the wealth of databases available through Vanderbilt's libraries. On the publishing end of this enterprise, I would especially like to thank Courtney Lachapelle Morales, of Lexington Books, for approaching me in the spring of 2019 about the opportunity to write this book. Courtney understood that even those of us managing 4/4 teaching loads at small state universities have something to offer in the way of scholarship. I would also like to thank my family for being who they are and for sharing this period of research and composition—as well as the much longer period of listening to the music of "el Flaco de Úbeda"—with me. Finally, I would like to send my love and gratitude to my mother, Mary Beth, because more than anyone else she is responsible for my scholarly inclinations and interest in music.

I am also grateful to David Beal, of Special Rider Music, for helping me to obtain the permission to reprint some of the lyrics from the following songs in my final chapter:

1. "The Lonesome Death of Hattie Carroll," written by Bob Dylan. Copyright © 1964, 1966 by Warner Bros. Inc.; renewed 1992, 1994 by Special Rider Music. All rights reserved. International copyright secured. Reprinted by permission.
2. "Just Like A Woman," written by Bob Dylan. Copyright © 1966 by Dwarf Music; renewed 1994 by Dwarf Music. All rights reserved. International copyright secured. Reprinted by permission.

3. "My Back Pages," written by Bob Dylan. Copyright © 1964 by Warner Bros. Inc.; renewed 1992 by Special Rider Music. All rights reserved. International copyright secured. Reprinted by permission.
4. "Fourth Time Around," written by Bob Dylan. Copyright © 1966 by Dwarf Music; renewed 1994 by Dwarf Music. All rights reserved. International copyright secured. Reprinted by permission.
5. "You're Gonna Make Me Lonesome When You Go," written by Bob Dylan. Copyright © 1974 by Ram's Horn Music; renewed 2002 by Ram's Horn Music. All rights reserved. International copyright secured. Reprinted by permission.
6. "Tombstone Blues," written by Bob Dylan. Copyright © 1965 by Warner Bros. Inc.; renewed 1993 by Special Rider Music. All rights reserved. International copyright secured. Reprinted by permission.
7. "The Times They Are A-Changin'," written by Bob Dylan. Copyright © 1963, 1964 by Warner Bros. Inc.; renewed 1991, 1992 by Special Rider Music. All rights reserved. International copyright secured. Reprinted by permission.
8. "Like A Rolling Stone, written by Bob Dylan. Copyright © 1965 by Warner Bros. Inc.; renewed 1993 by Special Rider Music. All rights reserved. International copyright secured. Reprinted by permission.
9. "Leopard-Skin Pill-Box Hat," written by Bob Dylan. Copyright © 1966 by Dwarf Music; renewed 1994 by Dwarf Music. All rights reserved. International copyright secured. Reprinted by permission.
10. "I Shall Be Released," written by Bob Dylan. Copyright ©1967, 1970 by Dwarf Music; renewed 1995 by Dwarf Music. All rights reserved. International copyright secured. Reprinted by permission.
11. "Only A Pawn In Their Game," written by Bob Dylan. Copyright © 1963, 1964 by Warner Bros. Inc.; renewed 1991, 1992 by Special Rider Music. All rights reserved. International copyright secured. Reprinted by permission.
12. "George Jackson," written by Bob Dylan. Copyright © 1971 by Ram's Horn Music; renewed 1999 by Ram's Horn Music. All rights reserved. International copyright secured. Reprinted by permission.
13. "Chimes of Freedom," written by Bob Dylan. Copyright © 1964 by Warner Bros. Inc.; renewed 1992 by Special Rider Music. All rights reserved. International copyright secured. Reprinted by permission.
14. "Mr. Tambourine Man," written by Bob Dylan. Copyright © 1964, 1965 by Warner Bros. Inc.; renewed 1992, 1993 by Special Rider Music. All rights reserved. International copyright secured. Reprinted by permission.
15. "Dear Landlord," written by Bob Dylan. Copyright © 1968 by Dwarf Music; renewed 1996 by Dwarf Music. All rights reserved. International copyright secured. Reprinted by permission.

16. "Hurricane," written by Bob Dylan. Copyright © 1975 by Ram's Horn Music; renewed 2003 by Ram's Horn Music. All rights reserved. International copyright secured. Reprinted by permission.
17. "Ballad of a Thin Man," written by Bob Dylan. Copyright © 1965 by Warner Bros. Inc.; renewed 1993 by Special Rider Music. All rights reserved. International copyright secured. Reprinted by permission.
18. "Tangled Up In Blue," written by Bob Dylan. Copyright © 1974 by Ram's Horn Music; renewed 2002 by Ram's Horn Music. All rights reserved. International copyright secured. Reprinted by permission.

NOTES

1. A *sabinista* is someone who enjoys Sabina's music and studies it in an organized manner; a *sabinero* is a more casual fan. See Guillermo Laín Corona's entertaining preface, "Sabinero, sabiniano y sabinista," in *Joaquín Sabina o fusilar al rey de los poetas*, ed. Guillermo Laín Corona (Madrid: Visor, 2018), 9–11.

2. See Rocío Ortuño Casanova, "Atlas de lugares sabinianos," in *Joaquín Sabina o fusilar al rey de los poetas*, ed. Guillermo Laín Corona (Madrid: Visor Libros, 2018), 161–201.

Introduction

Joaquín Sabina and the Question of Song Lyrics as Poetry

WHO IS JOAQUÍN SABINA?

At the beginning of a book such as this one, it may prove beneficial to address two questions. First, who is Joaquín Sabina? Second, why write a book in English about him? To answer the first, Sabina is a Spanish singer-songwriter who has sold well over ten million records, making him one of the best-selling Spanish-language music artists of all time.[1] And, if popularity is any justification for a book-length study, from Buenos Aires to Mexico City, and from the Caribbean to his homeland of Spain, hundreds of millions of people listen to his music and admire his ability to express himself poetically. The approximately 400 songs,[2] the majority of which are from his fifteen studios and three live albums,[3] are as meaningful to his Spanish-speaking fans as the songs of the Beatles are to millions of English-speaking fans. It has been said that Sabina is the greatest songwriter in the history of Spanish rock music.[4] Admiration of this scope and intensity, generated by an individual at the far end of a forty-year career in music, is uncommon. Today's music industry hardly functions on the level of the personal and careers as long as Sabina's are the exception rather than the norm. Powerful, multinational recording corporations exercise far too much control over artists and—as it is well understood—tend to prioritize quantity over quality.[5] The remarkable critical and commercial success Sabina has enjoyed working within such an industry is one of many improbable aspects of his career.

An upside to the multinational state of the business, however, may be the ability of the modern music industry to introduce artists to different markets around the world, for without mega-companies such as Sony Music Entertainment, Warner Music Group, or Universal Music Group, many living outside the United States and Great Britain would never have heard of Patti Smith or Tom Waits. For Joaquín Sabina, however, this kind of promotion has not worked in the opposite direction: among music lovers in the non-Spanish-speaking world, he is largely unknown. For this reason, the primary goal of this book is to help introduce the brilliance of Joaquín Sabina to English-speaking music enthusiasts, especially those who enjoy listening to talented lyricists such as Lou Reed, Ray Davies, Joni Mitchell, Leonard Cohen, and (of course) Bob Dylan. Highly regarded authors, from Chinua Achebe to Émile Zola, have always benefited from careful translations to other languages, and Joaquín Sabina is no different. Being a popular recording artist, Sabina has acquired many nicknames. Because of the poetic sophistication of his song lyrics, perhaps the most common is the "Spanish Dylan."[6]

Among Spanish musicians, Sabina is unique because many of his best songs demonstrate a deep familiarity with classic rock performed by the Rolling Stones, the Beatles, J. J. Cale, and other famous Anglophone artists. Having lived as a *"squatter"* in London during the 1970s, Sabina's six-year exile[7] has informed and enhanced his musical development. This experience also served to make his songs more commercial and helped him to evolve beyond his original and somewhat confining identity as a «cantautor» who brandishes a guitar and chants lyrics committed to social change. Undoubtedly thinking of Dylan, a respected Spanish music journalist observed that Sabina is "el mejor representante en España del cantautor eléctrico norteamericano" (*"the best representative in Spain of the electric, North American singer-songwriter"*).[8] It is for this potent combination of intelligent lyrics and rock music that Joaquín Sabina—rather than other Spanish performers such as Miguel Ríos, Luis Eduardo Aute, or even Joan Manuel Serrat—had the greatest potential to appeal to listeners in English-language markets. That such a crossover never occurred for Sabina probably has more to do with timing and a lack of promotion than his music. In recent years, talented performers such as Shakira, Alejandro Sanz, and Luis Fonsi have successfully crossed over, demonstrating that language is not necessarily a barrier when that language is Spanish.

While the respective careers of Dylan and Sabina share some similarities, the single aspect of their work that compels millions of their fans to purchase their albums or download their songs is their uncommonly high standards for song lyrics. To say that "Dylan has always had a way with words"[9] amounts to a bit of an understatement; by the same token, to claim that Sabina's songs are *"full of . . . a poetry that is often more brilliant and profound than that which one can find in the better part of poetry books"*[10] does not fully recognize his achievement as a lyricist, either. Dylan's recent Nobel Prize in Literature has helped to increase the prestige of song lyrics such as his, Sabina's, and those of other singer-songwriters. The late Sara Danius, secretary of the Nobel Prize Committee, seemed to presage the new valorization of song lyrics when she announced, "The Nobel Prize in Literature for 2016 is awarded to Bob Dylan for having created new poetic expressions within the great American song tradition."[11] In Spanish and with less fanfare, Sabina has accomplished a similar feat by crafting lyrics that draw comparisons to the most celebrated Spanish poetry. In fact, the fundamental premise of this book is that Sabina's work is best understood as poetry that has been put to music.

Since Dylan became a Nobel laureate, there has been a surge in the amount of research dedicated to his music, a growing field of scholarship that at least one journalist has referred to as "Dylanology."[12] Like his American counterpart, Sabina has inspired a modest but growing amount of critical attention devoted to his lyrics. The past ten years have seen an increase of general books about Sabina and his music, although few of them have been scholarly in nature. The most notable books have been biographies and, in this regard, Sabina has been fortunate to have had three outstanding writers dedicate themselves to this important endeavor. Prior to 2000, there had been only one biography, the illuminating early portrait, *Joaquín Sabina* (1986), written by journalist Maurilio de Miguel for the Los Juglares series. Indisputably, the most prolific *sabinista* has been another journalist, Javier Menéndez Flores, who has written a best-selling biography (now into an expanded second edition), a wide-ranging book-length interview with Sabina, and most recently an attractive coffee-table book discussing Sabina's musical influences, journalistic endeavors, biographical highlights, and major literary techniques of the lyrics. Julio Valdeón's *Sabina. Sol y sombra* (2017) is an engrossing investigation of the circumstances in which Sabina's songs were inspired and recorded. Written with verve and featuring some of the best information about the artist's exile in London, Valdeón's book is an indispensable reference for Sabina's fans. The past few years have also witnessed an appreciable increase in the amount of academic research dedicated to Sabina and his *oeuvre*, with researchers from prestigious institutions such as the University of Salamanca producing books and articles of the variety normally devoted to the work of Lope de Vega or Rubén Darío.[13] In 2018, the University of La Rioja organized a series of scholarly presentations about Sabina's lyrics entitled "Pongamos que hablo de Sabina."[14]

On a general (or even generic) level, "singer-songwriter" may be used to describe Sabina's profession.[15] However, a more precise term that lends itself more easily to some of the themes developed in this book is a Spanish version of "singer-songwriter," «cantautor» (hereafter not put between guillemets). The Royal Spanish Academy of the Language's definition of the term is both concise and functional: "*A singer, most commonly a soloist, that tends to be the author of his or her own compositions, in which a message of critical or poetic intention is prevalent over the music.*"[16] While today the term is often understood among Spanish speakers as any musical artist who writes and sings his or her own songs (a definition oblivious to the quality of the lyrics), beginning in the 1960s cantautor invoked that variety of folk balladeer best exemplified by American artists such as Woody Guthrie, Joan Baez, Phil Ochs, Tom Paxton, and the pre-electric Bob Dylan. In other words, the classic cantautor is the epitome of the "poet and a one-man band" described by Paul Simon in the song "Homeward Bound" (1966).

Sabina began his career in the 1970s as a cantautor and, even if his first musical compositions were mostly unremarkable, it was clear that serious thought went into his lyrics. As time passed and the influence of American and British popular music became greater in Spain, the concept of a cantautor broadened to encompass the modern music performer who enters a recording studio to produce albums featuring a variety of instruments and arrangements. Nevertheless, song lyrics that demonstrate literary qualities and deep introspection still define the cantautor's repertoire. Writing about Dylan, Carl Eric Scott has provided the useful term "literary pop song" to describe the genre that the Minnesotan legend pioneered in the early 1960s.[17] We could easily modify the term to "literary rock song" without a substantive change in its scope. Indisputably this is the genre in which Sabina has worked over the course of his career.

A comparison between the previously mentioned American artists and the Spanish cantautors (from whom Sabina eventually distinguished himself) is appropriate at this point, not simply in terms of chronology, but because of the respective political contexts that helped to produce them. In the United States, "[t]he roots of the protesting sixties run into the loam of the fifties, when conservatism and self-interest dominated American youth. Criticizing the American way of life then was not only unfashionable, but downright dangerous . . . Censorship was rampant, orthodoxy ascendant."[18] In other words, a stifling conservatism existed in the United States that tried to thwart the Civil Rights Movement and was quick to identify every political dissident as a communist sympathizer. In Spain, during the same era, we observe an even more oppressive political regime headed by General Francisco Franco, who ruled as dictator from 1939 to 1975. Because of this sociopolitical setting, a more conscious commitment to progressive, liberal, or left-wing political causes was expected from the Spanish cantautor, even at the beginning of Sabina's musical career. The cantautors opposed the dictatorship and Spain's isolation from the rest of the world; they also wished to preserve unique regional identities that were threatened by Franco's centralist government based in Madrid. Above all, these musicians were committed to crafting thoughtful lyrics to express their emotions and beliefs. Their lyrics were consciously poetic and the composition of them took precedence over that of the music which, more often than not, was simply a vehicle to deliver the words to listeners, serving much the same purpose as an envelope to a letter. The respected Spanish chronicler of this genre, Fernando González Lucini, describes the Spanish cantautors as having been born with "la voluntad explícita de hacerse voz de la realidad y de los problemas, más o menos conscientes, de los hombres y de las mujeres de nuestros pueblos" (*"the explicit intent to give voice to the reality and to the problems, more or less apparent, of the men and of the women among our people"*).[19]

At least one other researcher has determined the product of the cantautor, the «canción de autor», to be a more radicalized artistic creation, a «canción de protesta» (*"protest song"*).[20] There is no shortage of examples to substantiate a more subversive view of the cantautor and his or her songs, since many of them experienced censorship in one form or another, were exiled from Spain, or were even detained by Francoist authorities. The amount of censorship or persecution leveled at a cantautor was a reliable indicator of the artist's *bona fides*: during the Eurovision Song Contest of 1968, Joan Manuel Serrat famously insisted on singing the Dúo Dinámico song "La, la, la" in Catalonian, in defiance of the Francoist authorities, and was thus expelled from the competition;[21] in 1973, Víctor Manuel and Ana Belén were exiled for half a year for allegedly defaming the Spanish flag during a performance in Mexico; in that same year the brilliant Chilean cantautor, Víctor Jara, was arrested and murdered shortly after the *coup d'état* orchestrated by Augusto Pinochet and the CIA.[22] The ideology of the cantautors became particularly influential—even transformational—in the years immediately after the death of Franco, on November 20, 1975, and prior to the approval of the Spanish Constitution in December 1978. These two events frame the decisive historical period known as "the Transition."[23] Socially committed cantautors were one of several important forces advancing a progressive cultural and political agenda, on a national scale, in the late 1970s. As José F. Colmeiro explains, the cantautors "played a very significant part in the collective assertion and acceptance of new ideas that would be of crucial importance . . . such as the multicultural and multilingual reality of Spain, and the legitimization of the democratic system."[24]

But once the successful transition to a democracy was accepted as a foregone conclusion, Spanish cantautors simply did not have as much subject matter against which they could react. Sabina, benefiting in no small way from his exile in the progressive London of the early seventies,[25] evolved from being a(nother) pre-Transition cantautor to a master of the more commercial rock or pop genres that would flourish in the liberating environment of Madrid during the eighties, a mythologized cultural setting known as the «movida» (*"Madrid scene"*). Although his participation in anti-Franco rallies and a dubious incident involving a branch of the Banco de Bilbao and a Molotov cocktail would be factors leading to his exile,[26] Sabina was never as consistently or militantly political as many of his well-known predecessors and contemporaries. Nevertheless, as biographer Maurilio de Miguel points out, Sabina always believed that there existed the possibility of a combination between the more cerebral art of the cantautor and the expressive possibilities of pop-rock music.[27] The commitment to poetically inspired, contemplative lyrics remained a shared characteristic among him and the cantautors, even as he became more of a rock star. More recently, Sabina has stated that today's version of rock music is a more highly evolved artistic medium, capable of expressing themes much more sophisticated than, for example, the urge to dance or wanting to hold someone's hand.[28] Of course Sabina's achievement—to compose what we have dubbed "literary rock songs"—has been attempted by others. Nevertheless, it is an uncommon endeavor because the creative minds of popular music have deliberately tried to steer clear of what Scott calls "the intellectual and fine arts side of life."[29] If song lyrics become too heady, they do not appeal to the popular taste. Sabina's music—like that of other, poetically inclined songwriters—is intended for a more select subset of the broad demographic that enjoys pop or rock music.

What are, then, some of the recurring themes of Sabina's music? As alluded to earlier, when one examines his body of work since the debut album *Inventario* (1978), there is very little in the way of the political or topical. In fact, his albums with the most references to the era in which they were recorded are *Hotel, dulce hotel* (1987), with its memorable evocation of "el telón de acero" ("*the Iron Curtain*") and the Chernobyl nuclear accident; *Mentiras piadosas* (1990), where "el muro de Berlín" ("*the Berlin Wall*") and Christina Onassis, Mickey Rourke, and Kim Basinger are mentioned; and *Física y química* (1992), where he sings about the actresses of Pedro Almodóvar's films. His subject matter, for the most part, has been that great theme of world literature: human beings and their at-times amorous, at-times conflictive relationships with one another. Specific recurrent themes of Sabina's songs include nostalgia, personal freedom and pleasure, the bohemian lifestyle, the stagnation of passion that can occur when love becomes domesticated,[30] and the many unpleasant paradoxes of life.[31] In an interview from 1985, Sabina stated that there were "*three or four*" themes that obsessed him and invariably appeared on his albums: that of the marginalized urban hero—typically depicted by Sabina with unflinching detail; that of "*intimate introspection*"; and that of the night and nocturnal activities.[32] The decision concerning subject matter is crucial for the artist who wishes his or her songs to endure in collective memory. Regardless of how noble the sentiments they contain may be, most songs written with political messages have a limited shelf life. On the other hand, songs that are free of topical references and deal with the complexities of the human heart can become timeless—an achievement that Sabina realized with his albums of the nineties. Such a transition to a more personal subject matter was made famous, of course, by Dylan, the singer-songwriter to whom Sabina is most often compared. Dylan understood the limitations of being labeled a "political singer" by about 1965. By going electric at the Newport Folk Festival that summer, he effectively unfettered himself from Hootenanny circuit and the protest movements in which he had previously participated. By his own estimation, Dylan had evolved from finding inspiration in the rhetoric of a collective movement to finding it within individuals. When asked during a 1968 interview how he could be ambivalent about the Vietnam War after having written the song "Masters of War" only a few years earlier, Dylan replied:

> That was an easy thing to do. There were thousands and thousands of people just wanting that song, so I wrote it up. What I'm doing now isn't more difficult, but I no longer have the capacity to feed this force which is needing all these songs. I know the force exists but my insight has turned into something else. I might meet one person now, and the same thing can happen between that one person (and myself) that used to happen between thousands.[33]

What Dylan expressed, in essence, is tapping into what may be seen as a universal sentiment as a source of inspiration; but it may be found by listening to an individual (including to oneself), rather than by subscribing to the collective opinion of the masses. In *Chronicles: Volume One*, Dylan elaborated on searching for and discovering a new creative process in the late 1960s when he wrote, "Creativity has much to do with experience, observation and imagination, and if any one of those key elements is missing, it doesn't work."[34] In terms of where Sabina finds his inspiration to write songs, a similar transformation occurred to him shortly after his return to Spain in 1976. Still struggling to earn a living as a musician, Sabina discovered that he could no longer play to popular expectations in the Madrid of the late 1970s, but instead had to look within himself for the raw material of his songs: "es que en Londres cantaba canciones mexicanas o canciones de Dylan, y en España, en los momentos de la premovida y de la Transición, no podía ir por ahí cantando canciones mexicanas. De esa forma comencé a escribir canciones" ("*it's that in London I used to sing Mexican songs or Dylan songs, and in Spain, in the moments of the pre-Movida and Transition, I wasn't able to go around singing Mexican songs. In that way I started to write songs*").[35] Like Dylan, Sabina no longer found that inspiration in an external "force" that had previously compelled him; he, too, had to look elsewhere. In the concluding section of Esther Pérez-Villalba's *How Political Singers Facilitated the Spanish Transition to Democracy, 1960–1982* (2007), a scholarly examination of selected lyrics by Sabina (as well as those by Víctor Manuel and Ana Belén), the author notes the "depoliticisation" of Sabina's work after 1978 and his turn to "more personal politics."[36] With Spain's transition to democracy nearly complete, Sabina was unable to pick up where he had left off ideologically prior to his exile. Furthermore, he was no longer the provincial young man he had been when he left Spain, and so he had to reinvent himself as a performer.[37]

In one sense, Sabina's transformation into the recording artist he became was relatively simple, because his literary inclinations and poetic ability had long been established apart from his development as a musician. At the start of his university days in Granada, already touched by melancholy as a teenager, he wrote his first collection of poems, *No es fácil ser joven* (*It's Not Easy Being Young*).[38] In the late 1960s he was loosely associated with the Granada-based *Poesía 70* group, which produced a journal and a long-running radio program. In this same period of time and into the early seventies, Sabina published poems in literary journals such as *Tragaluz*, *Caracola (revista malagueña de poesía)*, and the aforementioned *Poesía 70*.[39] In April 1976, while living in London, he published his first collection of poems, *Memoria del exilio* (*Memory of Exile*), the initial thousand copies of which he paid for out of his own pocket.[40] Many of *Memoria*'s poems would become the lyrics for his first studio album, *Inventario*. Upon his return to Spain—and even when he was completing his obligatory military service in Palma de Mallorca—Sabina's ability as a writer resulted in additional income when he submitted articles to magazines and daily newspapers such as *Última hora*. His journalistic endeavors have continued into the present, writing for major newspapers and composing satirical poems of a topical nature for the weekly news journal *Interviú*. In 1986, the Council of Granada published Sabina's second book of poems, *De lo cantado y sus márgenes* (*From the Sung and Its Margins*), as part of the "Maillot Amarillo" collection under the direction of poet Luis García Montero. Most of the poems in *De lo cantado y sus márgenes* were the lyrics of songs he had recorded to that point of his career. Years later, Sabina also published a collection of sonnets entitled *Ciento volando de catorce* (2001). Alongside collections written by Mario Benedetti and Pablo Neruda, *Ciento volando de catorce* is one of the best-selling works of Spanish poetry ever published and is already into a sixteenth edition.[41] Sabina has also published other collections of less serious poetry, such as the satiric verses of *Esta boca es mía* (2005) and *Esta boca sigue siendo mía* (2007); similarly, he has collected many of his drawings and paintings in *Muy personal* (2013) and *Garagatos* (2016). In regard to his song lyrics, Temas de Hoy has published a compilation of them entitled *Con buena letra*, which is now into its third edition (2002, 2005, and 2010); the latest edition of *Con buena letra* contain all Sabina's lyrics except those from his most recent studio album, *Lo niego todo* (2017), and his recent collaborations with Joan Manuel Serrat.

These publications show quite clearly that Sabina is much more than a songwriter and recording artist. Guillermo Laín Corona, a professor of Spanish literature, has scrutinized Sabina's credentials as a poet, at times questioning them; eventually, however, he concludes that in time there will no longer be room to question Sabina's status, especially if he should receive a prestigious literary award, such as one from the publishing giant Grupo Planeta or the Premio Miguel de Cervantes.[42] While a few academics may continue debating the literary value of Sabina's lyrics, many celebrated writers do not. Argentinian novelist and poet Mario Benedetti was an admirer of Sabina, calling him a "cuentista de fuste" (*"short story writer of importance"*) among other compliments.[43] Sabina was also a close friend of Gabriel García Márquez, Colombian novelist and Nobel Prize laureate, to whom the cantautor dedicated the book *Sabina en carne viva. Yo también sé jugarme la boca* (2006). Sabina's reputation as a poet and man of letters reveals itself in other unexpected ways. The Gran Café de Gijón, or simply "el Gijón," located on Paseo de Recoletos between Calle de Prim and Almirante, is the most celebrated literary locale in Madrid. It can boast of a regular-clientele-to-literary-celebrity ratio far smaller than that of other historically literary locales, such as City Lights Bookstore in San Francisco or the Shakespeare and Company bookstore in Paris. Among the hundreds of famous *tertulianos* of the Gijón—including writers and artists such as Federico García Lorca, Ernest Hemingway, Picasso, Miguel de Unamuno, and Orson Welles—one finds the name "Joaquín Sabina."[44] As a final testament to his literary interests and fascination with the Spanish language, Sabina was included among the *Experts and Creators* who attended the Eighth International Congress of the Spanish Language, held in Córdoba, Argentina, in March 2019, and organized by the Royal Spanish Academy of the Language.[45] During the Congress, Sabina read two poems and a short, autobiographical text expressing his intense devotion to his native language;[46] his lecture cited lyrics from songs spanning his career and those in attendance applauded enthusiastically.[47] Beyond his indisputable credentials as a singer and songwriter, Sabina is also a champion of the Spanish language, a journalist, an illustrator, and—most importantly—a poet.

In regard to Sabina's personality—because, after all, we should not simply describe his musical and literary talents—he is generous, gregarious, witty, famously unpunctual, and alternatingly crude or elegant. Sabina loves cats, playing billiards, and devotes a few hours of each day to reading the newspaper. He does not know how to drive and does not carry a cell phone.[48] He also has a strong aversion to television. Sabina's longtime personal secretary, María Ignacia Magariños, describes him as having "una inteligencia deslumbrante . . . No es un ser de este siglo, es un tipo del siglo XIX con un lenguaje del Siglo de Oro. Es una mezcla extraña de muchas gentes y de muchos tiempos" ("*a brilliant intelligence . . . He is not a person of this century, but a guy from the nineteenth century with the language of the [Spanish] Golden Age. He's a strange mix of many people and many eras*").[49] Unfortunately, after having been fired without warning, Magariños may also be an authority on the cantautor's mercurial temperament.[50] In his relations with other people, one observes an unusual intensity of both his friendships and enmities. Being so outspoken, Sabina has often been involved in acrimonious disputes, waged face-to-face or in the media, with notable people such as the writer Alfonso Ussía and musicians Manolo Tena, Ramoncín, and Fito Páez. It is important to observe, however, that the cantautor subsequently had a sincere reconciliation with each of them. Sabina's romantic relationships, with the exception of his current one, have generally been brief. In his own words, "Soy muy mal novio, un pésimo amante y peor marido. Pero soy un estupendo amigo" ("*I'm a bad boyfriend, an abysmal lover and a worse husband. But I'm a wonderful friend*").[51]

Politically, Sabina is a complicated case. Menéndez Flores is correct in his assertion that Sabina has been more political outside his songs than within them.[52] Even accepting this, Sabina has often made it difficult to understand his positions since he usually opts for paradoxical or ironic explanations in his public statements. For example, citing the Basque philosopher Fernando Savater, Sabina called himself "*an anarchist that respects stoplights.*"[53] Ultimately, this statement is about as viable as a description of his politics as anything else he may have said publicly. Early in his career, when he was more easily categorized as a classic cantautor, Sabina embraced leftwing causes and even worked a little social commentary into his songs. The debut album, *Inventario*, and the live album, *La Mandrágora* (1981), both feature several songs that may be understood as political in nature, for example "1968," "Mi vecino de arriba" ("My Upstairs Neighbor"), "Canción para las manos de un soldado" ("Song for the Hands of a Soldier"), and "Adivina, adivinanza" ("Guess this Riddle"). The first of these examples is a humorous (but undeniably sexist) critique of the stereotypical, intolerant, Francoist male, making him out to be someone like a fascist Archie Bunker. "Canción para las manos de un soldado" offers an especially poetic cross-section of Spaniards from several walks of life, with the ones performing manual labor more noble than those with "manos finas" ("*fine hands*"), such as the mayor. Finally, in "Adivina, adivinanza," Sabina sings one of his most outrageously crude political songs: in a vertiginous slew of satirical verse, Sabina depicts Franco's funeral, attended by dozens of historical figures, and ridicules the Generalissimo, his senescent regime, and the Catholic Church: "[m]il años tardó en morirse, / pero por fin la palmó" ("*took a thousand years [for him] to die, / but [he] croaked at last*").[54] But even in these early songs, it is not easy to discern a serious political message because Sabina usually opts for comic or irreverent depictions that dyed-in-the-wool cantautors would frown upon. For example, Pérez-Villalba acknowledges the politically incorrect character of Sabina's "Mi vecino de arriba" in that near the end of the song he exults in having "*made out*" with the Francoist neighbor's daughter. When the bullying, ultraconservative "*upstairs neighbor*" overhears his daughter telling the longhaired musician/poet to take off his pants in the elevator of their apartment building, Sabina feels like he has given him his just deserts. Pérez-Villalba explains that in her study she did not want to interview the subjects about this particular song for fear of skewing their opinions from the outset.[55]

It is indisputable that Sabina was a pro-democracy activist and showed solidarity with other expatriate Spaniards during his London exile. In the 1980s, too, when his career was gathering momentum, he performed at rallies for the Communist Party of Spain and protested against Spain's membership in NATO. In the 1990s, Sabina took to the streets to protest the Gulf War and, ever since, has lent his celebrity in support of different leftwing causes. During appearances in Mexico, he has advocated the legalization of drugs in order to diminish the power of cartels. Sabina identifies himself politically as a "rojo" ("*red*"), but in the sense as it was understood by many Republicans during the Spanish Civil War: an ardent believer in liberty, equality, and fraternity.[56] But as Pérez-Villalba explains, Sabina's political activism—particularly that in which he participated during his lengthy exile in London—should not be mythologized because, in parallel with his advocacy of Spanish democracy, "he enjoyed a much more frivolous and easy-going lifestyle, as he himself acknowledged . . . Sabina always belonged to the 'izquierda traviesa' ('*naughty left*') rather than to the 'ultraizquierda' ('*ultra left*').[57] Nowhere is this better exemplified than one of the cantautor's most celebrated sayings, "Yo he sido siempre un marxista de la tendencia pro grouchiana" ("*I have always been a Marxist of pro-Groucho [Marx] tendencies*").[58]

In general, Sabina has supported revolutions and, after having been invited to Cuba by cantautor Pablo Milanés, actually met with Fidel Castro at the president's home. Somewhat surprisingly, the communist leader was a fan of Sabina and the two enjoyed each other's company. In *Sabina en carne viva*, the cantautor described several of the positive accomplishments of the *castrista* regime, especially in regard to health care and public education.[59] However, at other times, Sabina has shown little or no consideration of political matters. For example, in 2012, Sabina, alongside fellow cantautor Joan Manuel Serrat, gave a concert in Tel Aviv, in spite of the vehement protest of many fans. More recently, Sabina has been an outspoken critic of Catalonian independence, denouncing—again, alongside Serrat—the results of the October 2017 referendum.[60] Sabina has also made no secret of his love of *tauromaquia*, the Iberian cultural tradition which is usually mistranslated in English as "bullfighting." These viewpoints have occasionally resulted in Sabina being called a "facha" (*"fascist"*) by a few Spaniards of the extreme left.

SONG LYRICS AND POETRY

A third question to pose at the beginning of this book is, perhaps, unnecessary if one accepts Sabina to be a poet: Can song lyrics be understood to be poetry? To put the question another way, are song lyrics as rich as poems are in terms of their literary merit? A few lyricists, for example Vinícius de Moraes, never doubted for a moment that their lyrics should be understood as poetry.[61] Yet the analysis of song lyrics as if they were the kind of poetry found in a Norton anthology remains, for many, a misguided endeavor. In terms of the subject matter of this book, the first important consideration of song lyrics as poetry was Richard Goldstein's paperback from the late 1960s, *The Poetry of Rock*, which discussed Dylan's lyrics among those of many other artists. But even much later, when Dylan received his Nobel Prize in Literature, there was no shortage of critics contending that his work did not deserve such recognition.[62] In no uncertain terms, Spanish novelist Alberto Olmos stated that Dylan's Nobel Prize heralded the *"end of literature."* According to Olmos, to bestow the Nobel Prize on a musician is the same as if *"your mother gave a party to your best friend on the day of your birthday."*[63] Olmos' thinking reflects a widely held, qualitative assessment between what is written and what is sung. Albert Lord, in a classic study of the oral narrative tradition, noted that one of the difficulties in comprehending the shift from oral to written style lies in the fact that we always think of the latter as being better: "We assume without thinking that written style is always superior to oral style, *even from the very beginning*."[64]

In short, the argument against song lyrics runs like this: Words that are sung do not attain the sophistication of those that are printed on a page, even if they convey as much emotion and move the hearts of many more people. One could creatively employ the metaphor of wine and suggest that the best may only be found gathering dust in a cool cellar, select and inaccessible to most, just as the best poetry should be found on the pages of long undisturbed books in the furthest recesses of a library. If one accepts the superiority of the printed word, it could perhaps be said that the custom of some musical artists to include the lyrics among the liner notes of their albums is an unconscious acknowledgement of that medium's supremacy.[65] However, if what is written were truly superior, then we could propose, *reductio ad absurdum*, that the very finest poetry would have to be concrete poetry, which cannot exist apart from the printed page. But, to be sure, few would consider the major practitioners of concrete poetry among the greatest poets. To blur even further the boundary between oral and written poetry, one may consider that the English word, *lyric* (often plural), is more thoroughly embedded in the oral tradition since its Greek etymon refers directly to the musical instrument, the *lyre*.[66] The Spanish word for the same thing, *letra*, is Latinate and springs from the same etymon as the words *letter* and *literature*.[67] Consequently, depending on the language, there may be more or less controversy in the consideration of a song lyric as poetry. Would it have made more sense for Dylan to have been awarded a Nobel Prize in "Lyricature"?

For many, the transition from the oral poetic style to the written (or vice-versa) is ultimately irrelevant. As music critic Bill Wyman asked, "Why discount what has been written because of where it ends up?"[68] In other words, why should lyrics not be considered poetry simply because they are eventually sung? The debate hinges largely on two points: first, an insistence that poetry exist on a written page and an arbitrary, lofty definition of what poetry should be. The expectation that poetry should exist on a written page is relatively easy to dismiss for, long before Johannes Gutenberg rolled out his printing press in the mid-fifteenth century, poetry had indeed been sung. Going back to the very origins of world literature, we observe rich traditions of oral narrative; in the Western canon, for example, we have the Homerian epics and several from the Middle Ages. In the wake of the printing press, some of the finest poetry—including that written by Shakespeare, William Blake, and Federico García Lorca—was still best appreciated when it was sung. So, again, why should poetry be dismissed as inferior simply because it is adapted to music? As pointed out earlier, primordially, verse *was* sung and only got around to being written when literacy was sufficiently widespread; later it was regularly printed only when the technology to do so came into existence. By pointing this out there is no intention to dismiss fundamental, indisputable differences between what is written and what is performed;[69] it is simply to say that with varying degrees of success what is originally committed to print may be sung, and what is originally sung may be printed.

The argument against analyzing lyrics as poetry also becomes less convincing when the lyrics manage to convey powerful emotions and concepts. This is nothing unusual, for there have been many singer-songwriters from a range of countries, more or less contemporary with Dylan and Sabina, whose lyrics are considered to be poetry: George Brassens (France), Jacques Brel (Belgium), Chico Buarque (Brazil), Jean-Patrick Capdevielle (France), Leonard Cohen (Canada), José Alfredo Jiménez (Mexico), Silvio Rodríguez (Cuba), and Joan Manuel Serrat (Spain). (At one time or another, Sabina has invoked each of these singer-songwriters as an influence on his work.) The lyrics of these singer-songwriters (and those of many others) are admired for the deep sentiments, vivid imagery, and careful composition they so clearly demonstrate. Sabina has stated repeatedly that a great song is a combination of five elements: a good lyric, good music, a good interpretation, a good arrangement, "y algo más que nadie sabe lo que es, y que es lo único que importa" ("*and something more that no one knows what it is, and yet it is the only important thing*").[70] Although the literary merits of song lyrics and most poetry are commensurate, Sabina himself is careful to point out that a good lyric is not a poem or vice versa. Furthermore, during the composition of a song, he first writes the lyrics which have to be sung "*inside*" his mind; if this is not possible, the product is not the verses of a song, but of a poem, perhaps more specifically of a sonnet.[71]

Earlier it was stated that the debate over song lyrics as poetry hinged mostly on a widely held belief that what is written is superior to what is only sung, and then that argument was deconstructed and largely dismissed. But there should not be a broad equivalency drawn between these modes of expression, because it is true that song lyrics and poetry are not always one and the same. A few poetic devices and visual possibilities due to the medium of print do not translate to performed song lyrics; some examples include enjambment, italics, acrostics, clarity with regard to homonyms, and the understanding of a text's length prior to reading (e.g., one can immediately observe that a poem is a pair of quatrains, a sonnet, or a sequence of free verse). An example of a widely admired lyric that—once separated from the music—could not sustain its comparison to poetry was provided by Robert Christgau in 1967. In his piece "Rock Lyrics Are Poetry (Maybe)," the estimable critic argues that Dylan's "My Back Pages" is crammed with metaphors, epithets, and examples of "using a noun for a verb to spice things up." Christgau concludes his essay by saying that "My Back Pages" makes for a bad poem but "a good song, supported by a memorable refrain which couldn't possibly bear the weight of a whole poem."[72]

On the other hand, sung verse offers its own unique possibilities. Some important aspects of the text, such as rhyme and assonance, are highlighted in a manner that is impossible to appreciate as fully through a silent reading. Alliteration, for example, is more fully expressed. Rhythm, which is crucial to the ways in which we use and understand language, is more clearly established with aural (re)presentation, especially through rhetorical devices such as anaphora.[73] Other rhetorical devices, such as antithesis, are realized more effectively through song and speech. John F. Kennedy's famous call to fellow Americans near the end of his inaugural address—"ask not what your country can do for you—ask what you can do for your country"—must be among the most famous examples. Once again, referring to the oral narrative tradition, Lord explains that the singer's "manner of composition differs from that of the writer in that the oral poet makes no conscious effort to break the traditional phrases and incidents,"[74] which is to say that, unlike the poets who compose on paper, there is not the same consideration of the visual structure of lines, stanzas, and sections. Clearly, this observation is not entirely relevant to the cantautor or lyricist such as Sabina, but the fact that there is more structural flexibility in oral performance with no less of a responsibility to establish the correspondence of rhyme (in couplets or even more complex arrangements) demonstrates that the challenge facing lyricists and conventional poets is comparable. Free verse is much more commonly the product of poets than of lyricists.

The distinction of style—oral or written—is not the only source of controversy in this debate. As philologist Emilio de Miguel Martínez explains, much of the poetry we most admire today existed at the margins of official taste when it was written.[75] Similarly, we can perhaps appreciate how song lyrics can be found at the margins of what constitutes poetry for many people today. After all, when our subject is popular music, the fact that their meanings are readily appreciable by the masses is what makes such lyrics popular. In his best-selling paperback, Richard Goldstein expresses this idea perfectly when he responds to the oft-made accusation that rock and pop lyrics are "illiterate": "Of course they were; that was their greatest virtue."[76] Sabina himself seems to acknowledge such popular appeal with the song "El rocanrol de los idiotas" ("The Rock and Roll of the Idiots"). Eventually, such a fringe assessment of song lyrics may change and there will be a clear acknowledgment of their value, as has been the case with Dylan and perhaps, eventually, also with Sabina. One of Dylan's earliest biographers, music critic Robert Shelton, addressed the question of interpreting song lyrics as literature thirty years before his subject became a Nobel laureate, noting the many dissertations and academic papers that had been written about Dylan's lyrics to that point in his career.[77] In spite of these academic investigations, as late as 2003 it proved difficult getting an infrequently offered, freshman seminar on Dylan added to the curriculum of Harvard University. Professor Richard F. Thomas, author of *Why Bob Dylan Matters* (2017), reports that some members of a faculty committee scoffed at his course proposal, asking in effect, "What's he going to do, sit there and listen to 'Highway 61 Revisited' with his students?"[78]

Sabina, the subject of this book, is keenly aware of the often overlooked musicality of words: "Me parece completamente absurdo que los cantantes no se den cuenta de que las palabras ya llevan su música" ("*It seems to me completely absurd that singers do not realize that the words already carry their [own] music*").[79] To be fair, poets and writers also overlook the musicality of words at times. Since it is clear that words carry their own music within them, discussing song lyrics in the same manner as poetry should be no less valid an endeavor as discussing poetry as if it were music. In *Joaquín Sabina. Concierto privado* (2008), Emilio de Miguel Martínez selects dozens of Sabina's songs (in particular the thirteen from *19 días y 500 noches* [1999], judged by many to be the artist's finest album), and conducts a careful analysis of the lyrics. In the introductory chapter the author, a philologist and professor of Spanish literature, defends the subject of his scholarship by concluding, "*Nos sobran los motivos* . . . para centrarnos en la producción letrística de Sabina con el más estricto enfoque filológico" ("*We have an abundance of reasons . . . to direct our attention to the lyrical production of Sabina with the most strict philological focus*").[80] This book adopts a similar approach, analyzing the song lyrics of Sabina so that the complexity and artistic brilliance of his body of work may be better appreciated.

TITLE AND ORGANIZATION OF THIS BOOK

The title of this book is drawn from the image of Sabina on the cover of his best-known and most critically acclaimed album, *19 días y 500 noches*. There, and also on the reverse side of the compact disc's jewel case, we see Sabina in a long black coat, wearing dark sunglasses and smoking, but also sporting enormous black wings fixed to his back. He is pictured on the streets of Madrid, most likely in the oldest quarter of the city somewhere around the Plaza Mayor. The portrait of the artist in this manner recalls the decadent *poète maudit* (Spanish, "maldito poeta," "*accursed poet*"), the name given by French poet Paul Verlaine to himself and a few of his fellow Symbolists because of their bohemian, marginalized, and transgressive lifestyles. At least one investigator of the musician's work has noted that, by associating himself in this manner to the *poètes maudits*, Sabina has effectively underscored his self-identification as a poet—in this case, as a decadent one, a scoundrel roaming the urban landscape of the Spanish capital.[81] Significantly, Sabina chose that particular image of himself as an "ángel con alas negras" ("*angel with black wings*") as the first of several he rejects at the very beginning of the revisionist title track of his most recent album, *Lo niego todo*:

Ni ángel con alas negras	*Neither an angel with black wings*
ni profeta del vicio.	*nor a prophet of vice.*
Ni héroe en las barricadas	*Neither a hero in the barricades*[1]
ni ocupa, ni esquirol.	*nor a squatter, nor a scab.*[2]
Ni rey de los suburbios	*Neither the king of the suburbs*
ni flor del precipicio.	*nor a flower at the precipice.*
Ni cantante de orquesta	*Neither an orchestra singer*
ni el Dylan español.	*nor the Spanish Dylan.*[3]

[1] Undoubtedly a reference to "A las barricadas," a popular song sung by Anarchist fighters during the Spanish Civil War (1936–1939).
[2] A "*scab*" in the sense of an employee that goes to work during a labor strike.
[3] "Lo niego todo" (lyrics cowritten with Benjamín Prado), from the liner notes of *Lo niego todo*, Sony Music, 889854133221, 2017 (compact disc).

But the brilliant results of over forty years of recording and performing live are not so easily renounced. For this author, the image of Sabina as an angel with black wings seems an appropriate one to begin a wide-ranging study of his music such as this; after all, given the enormous success of *19 días y 500 noches*, it may be the image most often associated with him. Once readers come to appreciate more fully the best songs and lyrics from throughout his career, a more accurate and nuanced appreciation of Sabina will undoubtedly develop.

For many, a careful translation to English is necessary in order to appreciate Sabina's lyrics. Much thought and consultation has gone into the translations featured on the following pages, especially with regard to obscure and colloquial words and phrases. In most cases, the original Spanish is presented and then followed by the English translation, italicized between parentheses. The translation of proper names and song titles are not italicized. Since the titles of novels and collections of poems are generally not translated in most studies of Spanish or Spanish American authors, I have not translated most titles of Sabina's albums. This book is organized in a manner that first attempts to provide the essential biographical information about Joaquín Sabina in order to inform the discussion of his musical and poetic achievements. That portion of the book, chapter 1, also devotes attention to his musical development, especially that which is exhibited in albums of the late 1980s and 1990s, a feverishly productive period in which Sabina worked closely with musicians Francisco "Pancho" Varona and Antonio García de Diego. Chapters 2 and 3, which constitute the core of the book, are where I analyze Sabina's song lyrics as one would analyze poems. The second chapter examines the use of traditional rhetorical and poetic devices in selected songs; the third considers Sabina's remarkable talent for storytelling. The concluding chapter turns its attention to the oft-made comparison between Sabina and the American singer-songwriter, poet, and Nobel Prize laureate, Bob Dylan. I understand that a scholarly book about Sabina's music may not be for everyone. Many (if not most) fans of Sabina have a deeply personal connection with his songs and, for that reason, may be inclined to dismiss an academic's opinion of them out of hand. But I also have a personal connection with many of Sabina's songs, which I do not think becomes irrelevant or is diminished to any extent because of the professional research that I conduct. Because of that personal connection, my hope has always been that this scholarly endeavor will be uniquely inspired. I am confident that the following pages will feature something to enrich just about any fan's appreciation of Sabina's lyrics.

From the mid-1980s forward, Sabina consistently attained a level of commercial success unknown to nearly all his cantautor contemporaries, but at the same time maintaining what Menéndez Flores has called *"high-caliber literature"* in his songs.[82] This is not to say that Sabina has not written a few *ripios*—a colloquial term that can mean lyrical doggerel, or poorly rhymed verses. Sabina himself has criticized some of his work, in particular a few of the albums that bookend his career: *Inventario, Alivio de luto* (2005), and *Vinagre y rosas* (2009). But in spite of the occasional *ripio*, there is an extraordinary consistency in terms of the poetic quality of Sabina's lyrics, especially from the late eighties through the 1990s. That and the fact that Sabina is capable of making critical admissions about his work serve as evidence of the seriousness with which he has understood his vocation as lyricist. He has always understood himself as a poet who happened to become a musician and songwriter. In the lively series of interviews, *Sabina en carne viva. Yo también sé jugarme la boca* (2006), Menéndez Flores asks Sabina provocatively if his work has not been *"undervalued"* vis-à-vis other Spanish-language cantautors.[83] After some deliberation and (perhaps feigned) reluctance to admit the poetic qualities of his lyrics, Sabina finally agrees that he has an exceptional talent for *"literature in song,"* and that he would give anyone *"a run for their money"* in that relatively select category.[84] This book will carefully evaluate Sabina's assertion by analyzing the lyrics of selected songs composed throughout his career. By its conclusion, it will be clear that Sabina is not only one of the finest rock or pop music lyricists in any language, but also one of the most accomplished Spanish poets of the past fifty years.

NOTES

1. Julio Valdeón, *Sabina. Sol y sombra* (Valencia: Efe Eme, 2017), 15.

2. An estimate given by Sabina during the interview with Julio Valdeón, "Tirso de Molina, julio de 2016," in *Sabina. Sol y sombra* (Valencia: Efe Eme, 2017), 486.

3. Only Sabina's studio albums, recorded as a solo artist or with his mid-1980s band Viceversa, will be the subject of this book; the collaborative albums, *Enemigos íntimos* (1998), recorded with Fito Páez, and his more recent collaboration with Joan Manuel Serrat, *La orquesta del Titanic* (2012), will not be discussed. Sabina's major live albums will also be discussed, albeit in less detail: *La Mandrágora* (1981), *Joaquín Sabina y Viceversa en directo* (1986), and *Sabina y Cía. Nos sobran los motivos* (2000). For Sabina's complete discography, see Valdeón, *Sabina. Sol y sombra*, 501–6.

4. Valdeón, *Sabina. Sol y sombra*, 498.

5. As Van Morrison famously said, "Music is spiritual. The music business is not." Quoted in Steve Turner, "Spirit Dealers," *The Times (London)* (July 6, 1990), 17. Sabina made a similar statement when he pointed out the conflicting interests of musicians and those on the marketing side of the music industry: "Yo creo que ellos saben vender chorizos y nosotros escribir canciones. Entonces es muy difícil ponerse de acuerdo un escritor de canciones con un vendedor de chorizos" (*"I believe that they*

know how to sell sausages and we write songs. So it's very difficult for a songwriter to come to an agreement with a sausage vendor"). Quoted in Maurilio de Miguel, *Joaquín Sabina* (Madrid: Ediciones Júcar, 1986), 137.

6. Sabina himself mentions this flattering sobriquet—and rejects it unequivocally—in the title track of his last studio album, *Lo niego todo* (2017).

7. Although the topic will be discussed in more detail in the subsequent chapter, there is inconsistency among Sabina's biographers about the duration of his exile in the United Kingdom. Two of them—Maurilio de Miguel and Javier Menéndez Flores—state that it was an exile of seven years. Valdeón, however, indicates that the exile began either in late 1970 or early 1971 and that Sabina returned to Spain on July 8, 1976, which constitutes an exile of only five or six years (*Sabina. Sol y sombra*, 24–25, 37–38). Sabina himself has said on several occasions that his exile lasted seven years.

8. Matías Uribe, quoted in Esther Pérez-Villalba's *How Political Singers Facilitated the Spanish Transition to Democracy, 1960–82: The Construction of a New Identity* (Lewiston: Edward Mellen Press, 2007), 4.

9. Christopher Ricks, *Dylan's Visions of Sin* (New York: HarperCollins, 2003), 11.

10. "[S]us canciones... están llenas de poesía, de una poesía a menudo mucho más brillante y profunda de la que uno puede encontrar en una buena parte de los libros de poemas." Benjamín Prado, "Cómo olvidar una canción de Joaquín Sabina," prologue of Joaquín Sabina, *Con buena letra* (Madrid: Ediciones Temas de Hoy, 2002), 16.

11. "Announcement of the Nobel Prize in Literature 2016," *YouTube* (October 13, 2016), https://www.youtube.com/watch?v=RZDPKYuI6DQ (accessed November 12, 2019).

12. Matt Damsker, "Something's Missing in Why Dylan Matters," *USA Today* (November 28, 2017): 4D.

13. For example, Emilio de Miguel Martínez, *Joaquín Sabina. Concierto privado* (Madrid: Visor, 2008); and Guillermo Laín Corona, ed., *Joaquín Sabina o fusilar al rey de los poetas* (Madrid: Visor, 2018). De Miguel Martínez is a professor of Spanish medieval literature at the University of Salamanca and Laín Corona is a professor of Spanish literature at the National Distance Education University, based in Madrid. See also the recently published book by Justo Zamarro, *Ciudad Sabina: guía básica para sabineros* (Madrid: Europa Ediciones, 2019). Zamarro is a professor of Spanish literature and history who lives in Austria.

14. For the full program, see: https://www.unirioja.es/apnoticias/servlet/Noticias?codnot=5811&accion=detnot (accessed December 12, 2019).

15. Sabina himself prefers to be called, simply, a "*songwriter*." He detests being called an "*artist*" and views the term «cantautor» (which will be used throughout this book) as "*horrible*" and "*very ugly*." Sabina, quoted in Joaquín Carbonell, *Pongamos que hablo de Joaquín. Una mirada personal sobre Joaquín Sabina* (Barcelona: Ediciones B, 2011), 127. Sabina often uses "cantante" ("*singer*") to describe himself, but since this book is focused on the compositional side of his talent, it does not seem an appropriate term to use here. Instead, the term «cantautor» will be used throughout this book, mostly because it is not nearly as clunky as "singer-songwriter." The most suitable alternative, "songwriter," usually denotes someone who composes songs for others but does not perform them.

16. Real Academia Española, "cantautor," *Diccionario de la lengua española*, 23rd edition (online version 23.3), https://dle.rae.es (accessed October 10, 2019).

17. Carl Eric Scott, "What Dylan Means to Literature, and to Song," *Modern Age* 59, no. 2 (Spring 2017): 76.

18. Robert Shelton, *No Direction Home. The Life and Music of Bob Dylan* (New York: Beech Tree Books, 1986), 137.

19. Fernando González Lucini, *Crónica cantada de los silencios rotos. Voces y canciones de autor, 1963–1997* (Madrid: Editorial Alianza, 1998), 32.

20. See Roberto Torres Blanco, "«Canción protesta»: definición de un nuevo concepto historiográfico," *Cuadernos de la Historia Contemporánea* 27 (2005): 223–46.

21. Joan Manuel Serrat, "Serrat" (n.d.), http://jmserrat.com/biografia/ (accessed November 13, 2019).

22. González Lucini, *Crónica cantada de los silencios rotos*, 142.

23. According to some historians, the Spanish Transition was not fully completed until the constitutional government survived the feeble, attempted *coup d'état* of Lieutenant Colonel Antonio Tejero in 1981; others view the victory of the Spanish Socialist Workers' Party (PSOE) in the 1982 elections as the definitive conclusion of the Transition.

24. See José F. Colmeiro's "Review of Esther Pérez-Villalba's How Political Singers Facilitated the Spanish Transition to Democracy, 1960–82: The Construction of a New Identity," *Bulletin of Hispanic Studies* 86 (2009): 449–50.

25. Sabina admits as much during his interview with Valdeón: "Me libré de ser un cantante progre coñazo porque había vivido en Londres, había visto a los Rolling, había escuchado discos de Dylan, había visto en el Hammersmith Odeon a Duke Ellington" (*"I got away with not being a boring, liberal songwriter because I had lived in London, I had seen the Rolling Stones, I had listened to Dylan's albums, I had seen Duke Ellington at the Hammersmith Odeon"*). Sabina. *Sol y sombra*, 485.

26. In the biographies and the extended interview, *Sabina en carne viva. Yo también sé jugarme la boca*, it is reiterated that Sabina and some fellow students used a Molotov cocktail against a bank, in protest of the "Proceso de Burgos," and then he fled the country to avoid being captured by authorities. The verb that is usually used to describe the incident is «colocar», which means, vaguely, *"to place."* Valdeón seems to be the only author of a book about Sabina to use the noun «lanzamiento» (*"throw"*) in the description of what seems to have happened. Sabina. *Sol y sombra*, 24.

27. Miguel, *Joaquín Sabina*, 126.

28. See the interview "DE PROFESIÓN POETA Joaquín Sabina," *YouTube* (July 26, 2014), https://www.youtube.com/watch?v=OhIyqYEsIbM&t=179s (accessed December 26, 2019).

29. Scott, "What Bob Dylan Means to Literature," 80.

30. Sabina encapsulates this theme with the pithy observation, "El bienestar anestesia" (*"Well-being anesthetizes"*). Quoted in Carbonell, *Pongamos que hablo de Joaquín*, 365.

31. See Javier Menéndez Flores, *Sabina. No amanece jamás* (Barcelona: Blume Editorial, 2016), 13.
32. Quoted in Javier Menéndez Flores, *Perdonen la tristeza* (Barcelona: Libros Cúpula, 2018), 97.
33. Bob Dylan, interview with John Cohen and Happy Traum, *Sing Out!*, in *Bob Dylan. The Essential Interviews*, ed. Jonathan Cott (New York: Wenner Books, 2006), 137.
34. Bob Dylan, *Chronicles: Volume One* (New York: Simon & Schuster, 2004), 121.
35. Joaquín Sabina and Javier Menéndez Flores, *Sabina en carne viva. Yo también sé jugarme la boca* (Barcelona: Ediciones B, 2006), 111.
36. Pérez-Villalba, *How Political Singers Facilitated the Spanish Transition*, 357.
37. See the brief chapter "En pro y en contra de cantautores" in Miguel, *Joaquín Sabina*, 71–78.
38. Miguel, *Joaquín Sabina*, 24.
39. For an interesting treatment of Sabina's earliest poetry, see Margarita García Candeira's "La importancia de llamarse Martínez. Sabina, poeta del 68 (cuatro poemas)," in *Joaquín Sabina o fusilar al rey de los poetas*, ed. Guillermo Laín Corona (Madrid: Visor, 2018), 203–50.
40. Miguel, *Joaquín Sabina*, 60.
41. Sabina and Menéndez Flores, *Sabina en carne viva*, 293–94. See also Menéndez Flores, *Sabina. No amanece jamás*, 212. According to Julio Neira, by 2016 *Ciento volando de catorce* was into a nineteenth edition and had sold 250,000 copies. See his article, "Los sonetos de Sabina," in *Joaquín Sabina o fusilar al rey de los poetas*, ed. Guillermo Laín Corona (Madrid: Visor, 2018), 251.
42. Guillermo Laín Corona, "Sabina ¿no? es poeta," in *Joaquín Sabina o fusilar al rey de los poetas*, ed. Guillermo Laín Corona (Madrid: Visor, 2018), 85.
43. Mario Benedetti, "Joaquín Sabina," in *Joaquín Sabina: Calle melancolía y otras canciones* (Buenos Aires: Espasa-Calpe, 1995), 6.
44. José Esteban, et al., *Café Gijón. 100 años de historia. Nombres, vidas, amores y muertes* (Madrid: Ediciones Kaydeda, 1988), 311.
45. Real Academia Española, "El VIII Congreso Internacional de la Lengua Española se presenta en Córdoba (Argentina)" (October 23, 2018), https://www.rae.es/noticias/el-viii-congreso-internacional-de-la-lengua-espanola-se-presenta-en-cordoba-argentina (accessed November 12, 2019).
46. "Aunque no nos gusta, creo que yo podría la pena de muerte a todos los hispanos que cantan en inglés" ("*Although we do not like it, I believe I would impose the death penalty on all the Hispanics who sing in English*"). Quoted in Carbonell, *Pongamos que hablo de Joaquín*, 165.
47. "Sabina, 'el impostor' y su poema imperdible en el Congreso de la Lengua," *YouTube* (March 29, 2019), https://www.youtube.com/watch?v=ywGL8TV8Cms (accessed December 23, 2019).
48. Joaquín Sabina, "Uno no puede mentirle a su gente y fingir que es un rockerito de 25 años," Interview with Carmen Lozano, *Diario Córdoba*, (April 15, 2018)

online edition, https://www.diariocordoba.com/noticias/cultura/uno-no-puede-menti rle-gente-fingir-es-rockerito-25-anos_1218720.html (accessed May 15, 2020).

49. Quoted in Carbonell, *Pongamos que hablo de Joaquín*, 137.

50. After four years of working for Sabina in the late nineties, Magariños admitted, "No sé que le pasó. De un día para el otro se blanqueó los dientes, se quitó de los dedos las manchas de tabaco, se dejó crecer una barba tipo candado, se tiñó el pelo y me despidió" ("*I don't know what happened to him. From one day to the next he whitened his teeth, got rid of the tobacco stains on his fingers, let himself grow a moustache and goatee, dyed his hair, and fired me*"). Quoted in Luis Cardillo, *Los tangos de Sabina* (Buenos Aires: Grupo Editorial Olimpia, 2003), 134.

51. Quoted in Menéndez Flores, *Perdonen la tristeza*, 409.

52. Menéndez Flores, *Sabina. No amanece jamás*, 137.

53. Sabina and Menéndez Flores, *Sabina en carne viva*, 81.

54. According to Maurilio de Miguel, Sabina performed this song at La Mandrágora one night when the dictator's granddaughter, Carmen, was in attendance. She apparently finished her drink but did not applaud. *Joaquín Sabina*, 110–12.

55. Pérez-Villalba, *How Political Singers Facilitated the Spanish Transition*, 102.

56. Menéndez Flores, *Sabina. No amanece jamás*, 139.

57. Pérez-Villalba, *How Political Singers Facilitated the Spanish Transition*, 304.

58. Menéndez Flores, *Perdonen la tristeza*, 408.

59. Sabina and Menéndez Flores, *Sabina en carne viva*, 194–95.

60. Mar Centenera, "Sabina: 'los independentistas han hecho un mundo de mejores y peores catalanes, es diabólico'," *El País*, online edition (October 30, 2017), https://elpais.com/internacional/2017/10/30/actualidad/1509391363_472148.html (accessed February 29, 2020).

61. Ruy Castro, *Bossa Nova. The Story of the Brazilian Music That Seduced the World*, trans. Lysa Salsbury (Chicago: A Cappella Books, 2000), 127.

62. Some even accused Dylan of plagiarizing parts of his Nobel Prize lecture. See Ben Sisario, "Accusations About Bob Dylan's Nobel Prize Lecture Rekindle an Old Debate," *The New York Times* (June 14, 2017), online edition (accessed May 6, 2019).

63. "¿Un Premio Nobel para Bob Dylan? Es el fin de la literatura," *El Confidencial* (October 13, 2016), https://blogs.elconfidencial.com/cultura/mala-fama/2016-10-13/bob-dylan-premio-nobel-fin-literatura_1274692/ (accessed May 10, 2019).

64. Albert B. Lord, *The Singer of Songs* (New York: Atheneum, 1976), 134 (italics in the original).

65. Sabina has been especially diligent about publishing his lyrics, whether among the liner notes with each album (even the double album of live performances, *Joaquín Sabina y Viceversa en directo*, recorded at the Teatro Salamanca of Madrid in 1986, includes nine pages of lyrics), or his best-selling compilation of his complete lyrics, *Con buena letra*. Regarding that compilation of song lyrics, Laín Corona notes the subtle double meaning of "buena letra" (as "*good song lyrics*," but also related to the word "*literature*") and concludes that *Con buena letra* represents "*a process of institutionalization of [Sabina's] songs as literature and, specifically, as poetry, through*

a change of form: from album to book." "Sabina ¿no? es poeta," *Joaquín Sabina o fusilar al rey de los poetas*, 45.

66. "lyric, adj. and n.," *OED Online* (Oxford University Press, December 2019), https://www.oed.com/view/Entry/111676?rskey=UAeFN4&result=1 (accessed February 26, 2020).

67. Real Academia Española, "letra," *Diccionario de la lengua española*, 23rd edition (online version 23.3), https://dle.rae.es (accessed February 26, 2020).

68. Bill Wyman, "Knock, knock, knockin' on Nobel's Door," *The New York Times*, online edition (September 29, 2013), https://www.nytimes.com/2013/09/29/opinion/sunday/knock-knock-knockin-on-nobels-door.html (accessed November 19, 2019).

69. Ricks, *Dylan's Visions of Sin*, 11–17.

70. Sabina and Menéndez Flores, *Sabina en carne viva*, 106. See also Carbonell, *Pongamos que hablo de Joaquín*, 188.

71. Sabina and Menéndez Flores, *Sabina en carne viva*, 108–9.

72. Robert Christgau, "Excerpt from 'Rock Lyrics Are Poetry (Maybe)'," in *Studio A. The Bob Dylan Reader*, ed. Benjamin Hedin (New York, NY: Norton, 2004), 62–63.

73. "One of the devices of REPETITION, in which the same expression (word or words) is repeated at the beginning of two or more lines, clauses, or sentences." From C. Hugh Holman and William Harmon, *A Handbook to Literature*, 6th edition (New York, NY: MacMillan, 1992), 21. Through its repetition, anaphora may suggest the passage of much time or even a sense of timelessness; anaphora can also be a useful device for setting up an especially powerful verse that suddenly does not follow the established pattern.

74. Lord, *The Singer of Songs*, 4.

75. Miguel, *Joaquín Sabina*, 15.

76. Richard Goldstein, ed., *The Poetry of Rock* (New York: Bantam, 1969), xi.

77. Shelton, *No Direction Home*, 225–35.

78. Richard F. Thomas, *Why Bob Dylan Matters* (New York: Dey St. Books, 2017), 9.

79. Quoted in Valdeón, *Sabina. Sol y sombra*, 497.

80. Miguel Martínez, *Joaquín Sabina*, 15 (italics in the original).

81. Laín Corona, "Sabina ¿no? es poeta," 54–64.

82. Sabina and Menéndez Flores, *Sabina en carne viva*, 289.

83. Ibid., 119–23.

84. Ibid., 359.

Chapter 1

Essential Biography and Musical Trajectory

"Yo soy del Sur, / como andaluz / tengo el alma alegre, triste y callada, / sé llorar entre risas / y reír entre mis lágrimas."[1]

UBEDA

That song lyric, written by the cantautor Antonio Mata, could also describe Joaquín Sabina, who was a slightly younger contemporary during the late 1960s. Like Mata, Sabina is Andalusian and given to both exuberant laughter and profound sadness; and, as we will see in the following chapter, Sabina is also fond of structuring antithesis in his song lyrics. In order to inform the subsequent chapters devoted to his music and song lyrics, this chapter will provide the essential biographical information about Sabina. Since his mature recording career—that which dates from the mid-1980s to his last studio album of 2017—features most of the textual material under analysis in the pages to come, less attention will be given to that period in this chapter. Nor is it necessary to describe in great detail the release and reception of each album. Instead, this chapter aspires to be something of a concise, carefully researched *bildungsroman* of the Spanish cantautor. Few lives worthy of being examined can be split up into convenient parts. Sabina's extremely interesting life, however, can be divided into four sections with a kind of Borgesian precision and sequential order rooted in four different cities: Ubeda, Granada, London, and Madrid.

Joaquín Ramón Martínez Sabina was born in Ubeda, the first of those four cities, during the leanest years of Franco's fascist dictatorship on February 12, 1949. This particular period of the late 1940s would be reimagined by Sabina much later, in a most vivid poetic language, in the song "De purísima y oro" ("Of Sky Blue and Gold"), from the album *19 días y 500 noches* (1999). Ubeda is located in the region of Andalusia known as "the Upper Guadalquivir" where a significant portion of Spain's olive oil is produced. There is also much tourism to the region, thanks to the proximity of Granada and Cordoba, larger cities that feature UNESCO World Heritage Sites. Jaen, the province in which Ubeda is located, is famous for its ceramics and still produces the traditional varieties, in spite of the fact there are no more than a handful of family-owned potteries still in operation, many fewer than the one hundred or more that existed at the turn of the twentieth century. Jaen was the first Spanish province to mine a fine, red clay used for a variety of earthenware; the *jienenses*, or people of Jaen, once boasted of having more quarries of that material than any other province in the country.[2] With approximately 30,000 inhabitants, Ubeda faces the rugged Sierra de Cazorla mountain range. Historically, Ubeda has been more isolated than many Andalusian towns of comparable size. A popular Spanish expression, "irse por los cerros de Úbeda" (*"to wander off in the hills of Ubeda,"* meaning *"to wander away"* or *"to be distracted"*), was perhaps inspired by the feeling of solitude that pervades the city.[3] On two occasions Miguel de Cervantes mentions the "cerros de Úbeda" in the second part of his great novel.

In spite of Sabina's fame, if he recorded another ten critically acclaimed albums, he still would not be the most famous musician to hail from Jaen. That distinction belongs to the classical guitarist Andrés de Segovia who, in 1893, was born in Linares, a larger city about thirty kilometers to the west of Ubeda. Probably not unlike the virtuoso's experience as a child, as a boy Sabina must have absorbed the sounds of the guitar—that most Spanish of musical instruments—especially the quick *rasgueos* (vigorous strumming) of guitarists performing at weddings and other social gatherings. Throughout Andalusia, "the guitar was clearly associated with spontaneous music-making, with song and dance."[4] Apart from his passion for the acoustic guitar, Sabina has shown himself to be thoroughly Andalusian in other cultural matters. He has stated that the *zarzuelas* he used to hear as a child, performed during September festivals, represent some of his earliest exposure to music.[5] Sabina is also a devoted *aficionado* of bull fighting, as well as a connoisseur of Spanish cuisine, calling himself "más castizo" (*"purer"*) than others who, like his long-time girlfriend (and now, wife) Jimena Coronado, enjoy foreign dishes such as *sushi*.[6] Somewhat surprisingly, however, Sabina reveals that he was never introduced to *flamenco* music until his university years in Granada.[7]

In terms of his considerable reputation as a poet, Sabina could publish several more best-selling collections of sonnets and still not be the most famous writer from his hometown. That distinction belongs to Antonio Muñoz Molina, the celebrated novelist and member of the Royal Spanish

Academy of the Language, who was born in Ubeda seven years after Sabina. Muñoz Molina's early novel, *Beatus Ille* (1986), describes a Spanish town that closely resembles Ubeda, to the point of describing the venerable Church of Saint Peter, the nearby Casa de las Torres, and the trains, departing from the station and heading north to Madrid, that would take such a powerful hold of the cantautor's imagination. One of Sabina's earliest published poems is written from the perspective of a young man traveling on a train between his hometown and Granada, the larger city of the subsequent chapter of his life.[8]

In Ubeda, Sabina lived a comfortable yet somewhat austere childhood. He grew up in a stable household with a loving family that attended Catholic mass every Sunday. In spite of being a police inspector in town, Sabina's father, don Jerónimo, was by no means wealthy. His mother, doña Adela, was a homemaker. The musician also has an older brother named Francisco, who followed the example of their father and became a police officer. Sabina himself describes his family and upbringing best: "Yo pertenezco a una de esas familias honestas, avaras y cristianas hasta la médula que no son chicha ni limoná, y que se quitan dinero de la comida para que el hijo vaya a un colegio decente" ("*I belong to one of those families, honorable, miserly, and Christian to the bone, not easy to categorize, that will spend less money on food so that the son goes to a good school*").[9] Don Jerónimo wrote poetry in his spare time and encouraged his youngest son's literary endeavors. As the local police inspector, don Jerónimo was admired and respected by everyone in town. In spite of the candid acknowledgment that his father was Francoist,[10] the artist had a close relationship with him. Sabina's cousin has even suggested that don Jerónimo was very proud of his "*poet son,*" although he never admitted it.[11] Sabina credits his grandfather, don Ramón, as the person who ignited his musical aspirations.[12] According to Menéndez Flores, the young Sabina was an excellent—even brilliant—student.[13] And from the beginning he was interested in the arts. At fifteen he made his initial trip to Madrid and the first place he visited was the Prado Museum, where he stood transfixed in front of Diego Velazquez's masterpiece, *Las meninas* (1656).[14] Sabina began writing poetry by the age of fourteen and, at sixteen, was modeling his verse on that of canonical Spanish poets such as Fray Luis de León, Jorge Manrique, and José Hierro.[15] Sabina attended Catholic schools, including a Salesian preparatory in his hometown. At a young age, he became familiar with the works of celebrated foreign authors such as William Faulkner, James Joyce, and Marcel Proust, which he read in translation.[16]

Spain's popular music scene of the late fifties was dull—even insipid—in comparison with what was happening on the other side of the Atlantic. The songs of Elvis, Chuck Berry, and Bill Haley and the Comets were virtually unknown in Spain. As one critic explains, Spanish children sang Falangist hymns in school, while on the radio songs with "*traditional, racial virtues*" were heard; it was clearly not an auspicious setting for rhythm-and-blues inspired vocals and electric guitars.[17] On the radio, Sabina occasionally heard the songs of Cuban composer Antonio Machín, tangos by Carlos Gardel, and, more frequently, examples of that most Andalusian of genres, the *copla* or *canción popular*, performed by singers such as Sara Montiel, Miguel de Molina, and Concha Piquer. These songs, often telling stories of forbidden love and fallen women, were extremely popular during the first twenty years of the Franco dictatorship.[18] Manuel Vázquez Montalbán writes that well-known coplas, such as "No te mires en el río" ("Don't Look in the River") and "Que no me quiero enterar" ("I Don't Want to Find Out"), have Shakespearian elements—lovers, tragic deaths, atavisms—but often suffer from a "*subnormal logic*," with which the protagonists would rather continue dreaming than confront reality.[19] Although the subject matter of most coplas could not be more dissimilar to that of Sabina's mature songs, their clever storytelling techniques undoubtedly had an influence on his development as a songwriter.

About the time Sabina was writing his first poems, his parents were preparing to present him with a wristwatch for passing his standardized exams prior to high school, a long-standing tradition in the Martínez family. But young Joaquín asked instead for a guitar and his parents obliged. Shortly thereafter, he and three of his friends formed a rock-and-roll band called the Merry Youngs. At fourteen, Sabina fell in love for the first time, with a local girl affectionately nicknamed "Chispa." After her father moved with her to Granollers, Sabina made a precipitous journey to the Catalonian city and actually lived for a time in a tent outside her house; later, he and Chispa escaped to the Aran Valley, in the province of Lleida, and spent several days and nights living idyllically in the wild.[20] His insubordinate behavior sometimes earned him a beating from his father, but apart from those moments or the occasional fight with his brother, Sabina never participated in a fistfight or experienced violence in his youth.[21]

To this point in his life, the most important contributions to Sabina's musical education were the previously mentioned zarzuelas, coplas, sundry forms of Spanish popular music, and the relatively infrequent broadcast of an American or British Invasion pop song performed by the original artists. In the early 1960s, the rock-and-roll music of Elvis, Chuck Berry, and Little Richard began trickling into Spain from the United States. Much more American popular music came to Iberia—distilled and translated—through Spanish performers such as Los Llopis, Los Brincos, and El Dúo Dinámico, two aeronautical engineering students from Barcelona who topped the national charts several times with songs intended to accompany popular dances such as the "Twist" and the "Madison." After those pioneers, the Rolling Stones and (especially) the Beatles created a sudden *tsunami* of popularity from which even Franco's culturally insulated Spain could not easily resist.[22] After completing his basic education, the teenage Sabina enrolled at the University of Granada, one of the largest and most prestigious Spanish universities, and began his studies in Romance philology.

GRANADA

In his late adolescence, Granada provided a broadening of Sabina's interests, as much in terms of music as in literature. He likely began his university studies in the Andalusian city in 1967, at the age of eighteen.[23] For the personal freedom the young artist suddenly enjoyed in Granada, it is perhaps the most important city in which he ever lived. As Sabina himself reveals, "Granada no sólo no me defraudó, sino que fue un subidón" (*"Granada not only did not disappoint me, it was a high"*).[24] Home to the dazzling Alhambra, an Arab citadel and palace, Granada is one of the most beautiful cities in Spain; it is also the birthplace of one of the country's most beloved poets, Federico García Lorca (1898–1936). Through the sequential and specialized curriculum of the university, Sabina read widely and broadened his understanding of the expressive possibilities of the Spanish language. At least as important as what he learned in the classroom was what he learned during his extracurricular activities in and around Granada. At eighteen, Sabina felt liberated of his hometown and could come and go as he pleased for the first time in his life. Maurilio de Miguel, Sabina's first biographer, writes extensively of the young student's initial nocturnal pursuits and experiences.[25] Among his most interesting extracurricular activities, on at least one occasion Sabina performed as a university minstrel—known as a *tuno*—and serenaded pedestrians in Granada wearing the distinctive, sixteenth-century outfit known as the *grillo* (*"cricket"*).[26]

Sabina also made the acquaintance of influential colleagues and friends. Of special importance was Pablo Del Águila (1946–1968), a prodigiously talented and charismatic student from Granada who also played guitar. In recurring descriptions Sabina has described this dear friend from his university days as his Pygmalion, Dorian Grey, and García Lorca.[27] Del Águila was very likely one of the first Andalusians of his age to perform songs of Joan Baez, Atahualpa Yupanqui, and Pete Seeger.[28] Apart from his ability as a musician, Del Águila excelled as a poet and his collected works have recently been published.[29] Sabina has declared that if he had never met Del Águila, he never would have become a music artist or written a word of poetry.[30] As a manner of tribute, Sabina incorporated some verses by his friend into the lyric of the song "Amor se llama el juego" ("The Game is Called Love") from the album *Física y química* (1992).

It is during his Granada years that Sabina is formally and informally introduced to the work of poets who have never ceased to serve as sources of inspiration. In his coursework he read the canonical works of Spanish literature. However, two of the most influential poetic works for Sabina were composed by Spanish Americans: Pablo Neruda's *Versos del Capitán* (1952) and César Vallejo's *Poemas humanos* (1939), both of which were recommended to him by Del Águila.[31] Neruda's *Residencia en la tierra* (1933) was another favorite during his university days. Sabina also read and admired several poets whose work was circulating on university campuses in spite of the censorship imposed by Francoist authorities: Gabriel Celaya, Blas de Otero, and León Felipe.[32] In *Poesía 70*, a literary journal based in Granada, Sabina published one of his earliest poems alongside those of more established poets such as José Heredia Maya, Carmelo Sánchez Muros, the aforementioned Pablo Del Águila, and Juan Loxa, the poet and intellectual who started *Poesía 70* as a radio program.[33] This early poem, "Todas las tardes de domingo muere una flor amarilla en los tejados" ("Every Sunday Afternoon a Yellow Flower Dies on the Rooftops"), was published in the first issue of the journal and, approximately ten years later, would form the basis of the lyric for "Tango del quinielista" ("Tango of the Soccer Bettor"), one of the selections from his first album, *Inventario* (1978).[34] Apart from its literary vocation, the group of artists and intellectuals that coalesced around de Loxa's project featured many notable musicians who, in 1968, founded the "Manifiesto Canción del Sur" movement, which sought to revitalize the poetic language of cantautors and the rich tradition of the Andalusian copla. Some of those musicians include Carlos Cano, Enrique Moratalla, Raúl Alcover, and the previously cited Antonio Mata. Multitalented cantautor Luis Eduardo Aute also contributed poetry and artwork to *Poesía 70*. Sabina was delighted to be a younger colleague in this vibrant «tertulia», even if he did not participate regularly.[35] Margarita García Candeira has argued that Sabina's poems from this period provide ample evidence of an *"ambitious process of apprenticeship and intertextual assimilation."*[36]

In the late 1960s, university students the world over became galvanized into political action. From Berkeley to Paris, they stepped up to podiums and took to the streets to challenge the authority of their parents' generation. During his university days, Sabina was fully committed to the great convulsion of student activism. As recounted to his first biographer, Sabina started cutting out and taping to the wall of his room photos from *Triunfo*, a weekly journal read avidly by intellectuals who opposed the dictatorship; in his own words, *"we thought something magical was happening."*[37] The cantautor expressed almost identical thoughts about the historical moment about ten years later in the song "1968": "La poesía salió a la calle, / reconocimos nuestros rostros, / supimos que todo es posible / en 1968" (*"Poetry went out into the streets, / we recognized our faces, / we found out everything is possible / in 1968"*).[38] With his friends he engaged in energetic debates about capitalism, the works of Herbert Marcuse, and the fall of the Spanish dictatorship. In fact, if we are to interpret the pervasive reticence concerning his university studies as any indication of his activities, he seems to have earned more of a reputation as a "subversive" than he did as a scholar.

In 1968, there occurred one of the most memorable anecdotes about the young Sabina, one in which his antiestablishment stance afterward was actually hardened rather than softened. After some subversive activity by individuals not formally affiliated with the Communist Party of Spain (PCE),[39] activity which led to a round-up of some of his colleagues by police, Sabina decided to return to Úbeda and avoid arrest.[40] The next day, however, his father the police inspector was contacted by regional authorities and ordered to bring his son to the headquarters in Granada for an interrogation. If the young Sabina did not feel he was the poet García Lorca had been, in that particular moment he certainly must have felt he was his equal in terms of the situation. There, in police custody, he was subjected to the "good cop / bad cop" routine, but with his father waiting just outside in the hallway. As one of the interrogators told him, they would have *beaten [his] face in*" if his father had not been nearby.[41] Shortly after his release, Sabina joined the PCE and would not cease his political activism in spite of the alarming experience in Granada.

More important than his activism—and perhaps more important than even his formal education—in Granada the young Sabina becomes better acquainted with the music of the Spanish cantautors of the sixties: Raimon, Francesc Pi de la Serra, Víctor Manuel, Joan Manuel Serrat, Lluís Llach, and others. As explained in the previous chapter, these artists usually performed only with their voice and a guitar, and wrote songs advocating for democracy and personal freedom. Unlike his *Poesía 70* colleagues in Granada, however, these cantautors were already famous throughout the country. The work of these artists was often labeled "canción protesta" ("*protest song*") or "canción de autor" ("*singer-songwriting*"); occasionally, rather than being identified as cantautors they were called "cantantes políticos" ("*political singers*").[42] González Lucini describes the different regional manifestations of this movement: the "Nova cançó" ("New Song") of Catalonia; the "Ez dol amairu" ("There are Not Thirteen") of the Basques; the "Canción del Pueblo" ("Song of the People") of Castilla; and the "Voces Ceibes" ("Free Voices") of Galicia, among others.[43] In many ways—but without the explicitly separatist bent—the *Poesía 70* circle could be viewed as an Andalusian version of the Catalonian "Els Setze Jutges" ("The Sixteen Judges") group that was key to the "Nova cançó" movement of the same period.

Aspiring musicians such as Sabina listened mostly to these national cantautors, not only because the dictatorship worked to prevent the intrusion of culture and politics from beyond Spain's borders but because their music was quite popular on university campuses. Nevertheless, a few international versions of the cantautor—brilliant artists such as Georges Brassens, Léo Ferré, Atahualpa Yupanqui, Violeta Parra, and Jacques Brel—also managed to make an impression on young Spaniards like Sabina who sang and played guitar.[44] Sabina has said that the first foreign cantautors he studied were Brassens and Yupanqui.[45] There in Granada, Sabina probably played guitar into the early morning hours with his friends, laughing, drinking wine, and performing loose renditions of the songs they most enjoyed. As Valdeón's research has uncovered, Sabina was also listening to the music of Chilean cantautor Víctor Jara years before his albums were introduced to Spain—proof, as Valdeón explains, that the *"hardcore repertoire of the resistance song"* was in Sabina's blood before many of his Spanish contemporaries adapted it from the same foreign sources.[46] As for the music of Bob Dylan—who had already recorded most of his classic sixties albums by the time Sabina began his university studies—the Andalusian would not know of his songs until his English (or Scottish) girlfriend put *John Wesley Harding* (1967) on a turntable for him, toward the end of 1970 or in early 1971.[47]

The national and international cantautors provided an important example for the young Spanish musicians because they prioritized the composition of passionate, intelligent lyrics. Furthermore, because of their advocacy of democracy, personal freedom, and free expression, they were similarly influential in a political sense. The cantautors had a receptive audience with the young Spaniards for, vis-à-vis the oppressive Franco dictatorship, they could easily find causes against which they too could protest. During this exciting period of Spanish popular culture and activism, the young people who attended performances of cantautors would "light candles, matches, [and] cigarette lighters in a simple symbol of hope and anticipation of the end of the long dictatorship, which found an easy and communicable symbol in the darkness."[48] While the degree of political activism varied between the Spanish cantautors, there existed between them the shared attribute of writing intelligent lyrics, at times aspiring to a kind of oral poetry. In the years leading up to the ratification of the Constitution of 1977, any young Spaniard with a guitar, an interest in songwriting, and the ability to carry a tune was practically obligated to demonstrate his leftist bona fides. Many aspiring cantautors like Sabina looked to emulate Luis Eduardo Aute, Víctor Manuel, and above all the Catalonian Joan Manuel Serrat.[49] The literary quality of their songs must have made a deep impression on Sabina, who at the time still dreamed of becoming a writer rather than a musician.[50]

Two years after the interrogation in Granada, Sabina would commit his most serious subversive act. Following the "Proceso de Burgos" ("Judgment of Burgos") in December 1970, in which numerous members of the leftist

Basque separatist group ETA (Euskadi Ta Askatasuna, or "Basque Homeland and Freedom") were sentenced to death by the increasingly anachronistic national government, there was another surge of student activism throughout Spain. Accompanied by some fellow students, Sabina apparently threw a Molotov cocktail at a branch of the Banco de Bilbao located in Granada. With its headquarters in Madrid, the Banco de Bilbao is the second-largest bank in Spain. No one was injured during this alleged act of violence and Sabina managed to escape the scene, although the authorities began investigating and closing a dragnet around suspected perpetrators. Shortly afterward, Sabina made the acquaintance of Mariano Zugasti, a comrade from the PCE, and explained to him his desperate situation and wish to travel to the United Kingdom with his girlfriend at the time, Lesley, who was a student from the United Kingdom wrapping up her studies at the university. Making Zugasti's acquaintance was a stroke of good fortune, for, in a remarkable act of generosity and altruism, Zugasti gave the young cantautor his passport. Once he had carefully replaced Zugasti's photo with his own, Sabina had a functional passport and was able to depart Spain with Lesley, first by train from Madrid to France, and then by airplane to England.[51] For this reason, Sabina sings in the autobiographical song, "Me pido primer" ("Me First!"), that his first passport was called "Mariano."[52] In February 1971 there appears the first documented evidence of Sabina's exile when he officially requests residency in the United Kingdom, which he would receive.[53] Sabina would remain with Lesley at her home in London for the first few months of his exile.

Although Sabina never earned his degree, the three and a half to four years he spent at the University of Granada were extremely important during this especially formative period of his life. As he admits to Menéndez Flores:

> Todo lo que he sido luego, todo lo que he hecho luego, todo lo que me ha interesado luego, todo lo que he escrito luego, todo lo que he follado luego, todo lo que he bebido luego, todo lo que he soñado luego, todo lo que he imaginado y todo lo que no he podido ser luego, el germen de todo eso cristalizó en los cuatro años que pasé en Granada. En aquellos cuatro cursos que hice de Filosofía y Letras en la Universidad de Granada.

> *Everything that I have been afterward, everything that I have done afterward, everything that has interested me afterward, everything that I have written afterward, everything that I have fucked afterward, everything that I have drank afterward, everything that I have dreamed afterward, everything that I have imagined and everything that I have not been able to become afterward, the seed of all that crystallized during those four years that I spent in Granada. In my four years of Philosophy and Letters at the University of Granada.*[54]

LONDON

Sabina's exile in the United Kingdom—for the vast majority of its duration, in London—is the part of his biography subject to the most conjecture. In the first place it is not immediately clear when, precisely, Sabina left Spain; nor is it entirely clear if he was interrogated by authorities in Granada after the Molotov cocktail incident, having taken place in 1968, or if it happened toward the end of 1970. If the second possibility is the truth—which, indeed, seems most likely to be the case—then perhaps he intended to leave Spain to escape the authorities, taking advantage of his girlfriend at the time and her return trip to the United Kingdom in early 1971. In *Sabina en carne viva*, the cantautor explains to Menéndez Flores that his father was ordered to arrest him after a group of protestors loosely affiliated with the PCE had thrown "*a Molotov cocktail at a bank in Granada.*" Shortly afterward, Sabina admits, "*we did it.*" To be fair, before recounting the story Sabina quips that he may not be up to the task as a result of his mild stroke of 2001.[55] For his part, Maurilio de Miguel writes about Sabina's arrest by his father and the Molotov cocktail as two separate events, explaining that the attack on the bank occurred in 1970 and was the unprofessional work of "*idealists*" rather than "*strategists.*" In the aftermath of the incident, Sabina found himself faced with certain capture and imprisonment because he had to turn himself in for obligatory military service in a matter of weeks; as a result, he decided to go into exile "*with all his war medals.*"[56]

The lack of clarity regarding Sabina's departure for the United Kingdom, his return to Spain, and the motives for his exile are the consequence of conflicting information from the four major sources of biographical information: Miguel's *Joaquín Sabina*, Menéndez Flores' *Perdonen la tristeza* and the extended interview, *Sabina en carne viva*, and Valdeón's *Sabina. Sol y sombra*. For example, there is little agreement on the total amount of time Sabina spent in the United Kingdom. In *Perdonen la tristeza*, Menéndez Flores observes "siete largos años" and indicates 1977 as the year of his return to Spain.[57] But in his most recent book, *Sabina. No amanece jamás*, in a section of called "Las cuatro fechas clave de su carrera" ("*The Four Key Dates of His Career*"), Menéndez Flores indicates Sabina's return to Spain as having occurred in "1977/1978"[58]—although he may be combining the year of his return with the year of Sabina's first album, *Inventario*, which was recorded and released in 1978. Valdeón provides what seems to be a more thoroughly researched timeline of five or six years in exile, with July 8, 1976, as the date of Sabina's return to Spain as indicated by a diary kept at the time.[59] Thanks to Valdeón's research, there are also more details about Sabina's activities in exile. For his part, Joaquín Carbonell corroborates the date of Sabina's return to Spain as July 8, 1976, but incorrectly calculates the length of his exile as seven years.⁶⁰ Sabina himself has said during different interviews that his exile lasted seven years, but on at least one occasion that it lasted six.⁶¹

While the true duration of his exile amounts to little more than a minor detail, more important are Sabina's motives for departing Spain. Some have surmised that he went into exile to escape the police dragnet that was closing in on him,⁶² but by his own admission his reasons were more personal than political. In the biographical section of *Sabina. No amanece jamás*, Menéndez Flores lists the following four reasons for leaving Spain: "para vivir una aventura digna de ser contada a los nietos, para no separarse de la escocesa a la que había conocido en la universidad, Lesley, y de la que se enamoró ... y para librarse del servicio militar" (*"to live an adventure worthy of being told to grandchildren, to stay with Lesley, the Scottish woman he had met at the University of Granada, and with whom he fell in love, [. . .] and in order to avoid military service"*).⁶³ There is no mention here of escaping the Francoist authorities after the Molotov cocktail incident. In the most recent biography of the artist, the second edition of Menéndez Flores' *Perdonen la tristeza*, Sabina explains that he took advantage of a return to the United Kingdom by his girlfriend at the time (who had worn the *"first and most glorious miniskirt in Granada"*), accompanying her, only to return to Spain seven years later.⁶⁴ There seems to be more consensus among the cantautor and his biographers that Lesley wore her miniskirt fetchingly than what her nationality may have actually been.

The Molotov cocktail incident and his subsequent exile are pillars of the mythology that partially obscures Sabina's early biography. No attempt will be made here to confirm the *"pseudo-terrorist act"*⁶⁵ or determine whether or not it was the principal motive of Sabina's exile. But the London exile was fortuitous for Sabina, for not only did it postpone his military service until after the death of Franco and the end of his repressive regime, he lived for several years in a more cosmopolitan environment that broadened his horizons and benefited his art. What can be concluded of the Molotov cocktail incident is that it most likely did occur, but Sabina—far from being the ringleader—was probably only among those who orchestrated the attack.⁶⁶ For my part, I do not believe he committed the deed himself because Sabina's values are, without exception, humanistic, and he would never harm another person, much less for political motives. As he sings in one of his early songs, "nunca entiendo el móvil del crimen a menos / que sea pasional" (*"I never understand the motive of a crime unless / it's a crime of passion"*).⁶⁷ One of the artist's closest friends during his exile in London, Spanish photographer Publio López Mondéjar, expresses the skepticism that anyone who loves Sabina's music would have about the incident:

> Joaquín se fue de España porque estaba detrás de Leslie [sic], y de paso se forjaba una leyenda de rojo, porque, la verdad, no me imagino a Joaquín participando

en un acto violento. Lo del cóctel molotov, mmm, no sé . . . Pondría la mano en el fuego a que no participó. Él es un hombre de izquierdas, con cultura de izquierdas, pero, ¿un acto violento? No me lo imagino. Joaquín tiene muchas virtudes, pero el coraje no está entre ellas . . . y la violencia, menos. Y no digo que fuera mentira, pero creo que se fue detrás de Leslie, y además se libraba de la mili, que le horrorizaba.

Joaquín left Spain because he was following Leslie, and afterwards there was forged the legend of being a red, because, truth be told, I don't imagine Joaquín participating in a violent act. That business of the Molotov cocktail, hmmm, I don't know . . . I would be willing to bet anything that he didn't participate. He's a leftist, from the culture of the left, but a violent act? I can't imagine it. Joaquín has many virtues, but courage is not one of them . . . and violence, even less. I'm not saying that it was a lie, but I believe that he left with Leslie and at the same time was getting out of the military service, which horrified him.[68]

Sabina himself admits as much in the *Rolling Stone* interview he conducted with Spanish film critic Carlos Boyero, stating unequivocally, "*I am someone who profoundly detests violence.*"[69]

Sabina stays with Lesley and her father in London for the first few months of his exile. In fear of being arrested and returned to Spain, and with little ability in English, he relies on his girlfriend for nearly all his needs. Sabina quickly tires of this dependency. In early April 1971, after a stay in Edinburgh, Scotland, Lesley and he return to London where, according to Maurilio de Miguel, Sabina "*takes a French leave*" during the night and disappears. Lesley looks for him in vain and, although they would speak briefly on the phone a few years later, they never see each other again.[70] And so begins Sabina's legendary exile in London.

Fellow *jienense*, novelist Antonio Muñoz Molina, observes that Sabina's residence in London provided him a double aura of political persecution and cosmopolitanism.[71] As an outsider in an enormous metropolis—a situation in which he was subject to detention and deportation at any moment—Sabina developed a greater political awareness. Maurilio de Miguel views the period from 1972 to 1975 as being especially important in terms of this development, observing that his performances from that time feature songs depicting the "*struggles and problems of Spain and South America.*"[72] Sabina makes friends and connections in the community of exiled Hispanics living in London. There he meets Chileans and Argentinians escaping their own repressive regimes. In his own words he quickly becomes "*hippified*" and often lives as a squatter, sleeping in the abandoned rooms of empty buildings. During the later years of his exile, he lives in an apartment in the Camden Town District. Sabina acknowledges the importance of photographer López Mondéjar during his stay in London for, not only did he host Sabina at his apartment, he kept him in contact with other Spaniards.⁷³ During this period Sabina also participates in cultural activities hosted by the Club Antonio Machado, a Communist group founded by exiled Spanish Republicans living in London.

In order to make ends meet, Sabina works various odd jobs washing dishes, serving food, lugging stretchers, and even putting cadavers into freezers in a hospital morgue.⁷⁴ Eventually, however, he rediscovers his musical ability and begins earning a little money by performing at Hispanic-themed establishments around London. After countless *mariachi* performances of songs such as "Cielito lindo" and "Guantanamera," Sabina becomes a more seasoned performer and eventually something of a local star in the Latino bars and restaurants of London.⁷⁵ On one occasion, at an establishment called the Mexicano-Taverna, Sabina performed at George Harrison's birthday party and the former Beatle tipped Sabina a £ 5 note—an invaluable bit of memorabilia that the Spaniard has kept to this day. On other occasions, Sabina sang for actor Richard Chamberlain and serenaded Elizabeth Taylor. After his performances, he would often visit clubs along King's Road and other locales in West London where he would see live performances of such acts as the Rolling Stones and J. J. Cale.⁷⁶

In *Sabina en carne viva*, the singer concurs with Menéndez Flores that London never appears in his songs in spite of his years of trying to scrape out a living in the great city.⁷⁷ But the absence of London in his lyrics is only half the story, for although he was there in the exact historical moment when reggae was helping to inspire punk rock, his music is almost entirely free of the tempos and arrangements of those genres. Living as a squatter for a time in what must have been the ground zero of the reggae (and punk) scenes—the international districts around King's and Portobello Roads—it is remarkable that Sabina's first full-on reggae, "¿Qué estoy haciendo aquí?" ("What Am I Doing Here?"), would not be recorded until his 2017 album, *Lo niego todo*.⁷⁸ As for punk rock, in spite of his admiration and acknowledgment of it as the last important "*alternative*" movement with which he was familiar,⁷⁹ Sabina has no punk music in his repertoire. This is evidence, perhaps, that his pedigree as a Spanish cantautor could not be entirely erased. In other words, "you can take the boy out of Spain, but you can't take Spain out of the boy." In spite of the absence of references to London in his songs, Sabina has nothing but superlatives to say in regard to his experience living in that great metropolis:

> Me dio unas oportunidades que no hubiera tenido nunca. Por ejemplo, vivir como un pajarito: sin construir nada, sin almacenar nada, sin coleccionar nada, sin sentar las raíces de nada y sin saber nunca dónde y con quién iba a dormir . . . Era fantástico. Le recomiendo a todo el mundo que se exilie un ratito.

> It gave me opportunities that I never would have had. For example, to live like a little bird: without constructing anything, without storing anything, without collecting anything, without laying down roots on anything, and without ever knowing where and with whom I was going to sleep . . . It was fantastic. I recommend to everyone that they go into exile for a little while.[80]

The London exile is decisive for the manner in which it shapes Sabina's subsequent musical development. In *Perdonen la tristeza*, Sabina describes the influence by saying that rather than remaining in Spain: "en Londres empecé a escuchar a Dylan y a los Stones, lo cual creo que le dio a lo que compuse después un aire más roquerito, callejero, anglosajón. Una cosa más turbia, mezcla a la que nunca he renunciado" (*"in London I began to listen to Dylan and the Stones, which I believe gave a more rock-n-roll, street, Anglo-Saxon feel to what I composed afterward. A blurrier thing, a mixture that I have never renounced."*).[81] But no one—not even Sabina himself—has described the influence of the London sojourn on his later musical development as well as Julio Valdeón. Summarizing his years of exile, he posits that Sabina was inspired to imagine how the Rolling Stones' *Exile on Main Street* (1972)—the band's eclectic, double-album masterpiece—might be fused with the poetry of César Vallejo.[82] The influence of English-language rock music is conspicuous in a recent list of the singer-songwriter's favorite songs for, of the eight listed, three are by English-language artists: Leonard Cohen, Bob Dylan, and Lou Reed.[83] One other important result of the London exile is the way it would later encourage Sabina to isolate himself—sometimes traveling to other regions in Spain for months at a time—to write songs or even record a new studio album. Once fame made privacy next to impossible in and around his usual haunts in Madrid, Sabina needed to find the semi-solitude outside the capital that would permit him to compose but without shutting himself away entirely.[84] The London exile seems to be the occasion in which Sabina discovered the benefits of an occasional stint of anonymity.

Once Franco dies on November 20, 1975, Sabina immediately begins planning his return to Spain. He publishes his first collection of poems, *Memoria del exilio*, in April 1976, only three months before returning to his homeland. The collection is published independently, with money out of his own pocket and with a cover illustration by another Spaniard, Aurelio Díaz, "el Buly," with whom Sabina was living at the time. According to Sabina, he manages to sell all the copies by hawking them up and down Portobello Road. Eight of the poems from *Memoria* would be put to music and become part of his first album, *Inventario* (1978). Sabina has admitted that these early attempts at writing song lyrics—first by writing poetry and then trying to put the verses to music—cost him *"sweat and tears."*[85] And the results were less-than-successful. But he would return to the vocation of songwriter with better results after completing the mandatory period of military service postponed by his lengthy exile.

In 1976, Sabina returns to Spain with his first authentic passport, leaving behind in London a *"library"* of some 500 books.[86] An essential part of his preparation for military service is, apparently, marriage to a Catalonian woman from an Argentine family named Lucía Inés Correa Martínez because, once married, he does not have to remain in the military barracks at night and could return home to his wife. Sabina met Lucía in London and their marriage ceremony takes place on February 18, 1977. Sabina and Lucía would remain together for the next several years, but separate and eventually divorce in 1989. Upon reporting for duty, Sabina is stationed in Palma de Mallorca. In the evenings Sabina earns extra money working as a reporter for the daily newspaper, *Última hora*.[87] Once his military service is completed in 1978, and with Franco dead and no further obstacles or obligations facing him, Sabina is free to move with Lucía to the Spanish capital.

MADRID

"Un Madrid absurdo, brillante y hambriento" (*"an absurd, brilliant, and starving Madrid"*) is the memorable description of the capital by another artist who went there to make it his home, the poet and dramatist Ramón María del Valle-Inclán.[88] Sabina and Lucía rent a tiny apartment on Calle Tabernillas, in the bustling La Latina neighborhood of the city. There, Sabina becomes a professional musician at night while Lucía works in an office building during the day, an arrangement depicted memorably by Sabina in the early single, "Caballo de cartón" ("Cardboard Rocking Horse"), from 1984. Through connections made in London, Sabina's first album, *Inventario*, is recorded by Movieplay in 1978. Because his musical experience to that point in his career was mostly performing live with only his guitar, he was largely unprepared for the opportunity and recorded a disappointing debut album, full of pretentious orchestration and little evidence of the distinctive qualities of his music. *Inventario* sold poorly and, had Sabina not become famous, it may have been entirely forgotten. He admits that during the sessions for the album, "*I didn't ask anyone who the musicians were or what arrangements there were, nothing. I didn't have a serious, rigorous plan to be a singer.*"[89] Because he was discouraged by the recording process, Sabina admits that after the sessions for *Inventario* he doubted that he would ever enjoy a career as musician.[90] In fairness, many of the lyrics of the album are quite good and show many of the tendencies that would be more fully developed in his subsequent work: unexpected and memorable adjectives, potent metaphors, and subtle allusions to the work of his favorite poets. *Inventario* also features some of Sabina's satiric humor ("Tango del quinielista"), his penchant for paradoxical narratives ("Tratado de impaciencia número 10"), and the most deliberate criticism of Francoist society and values of his entire *oeuvre* ("Mi vecino de arriba"). Nevertheless, Sabina himself dislikes the album intensely and is reluctant to discuss it.[91] *Inventario* was not included in a 2015 Sony boxset of his albums and the cantautor himself has been known to purchase copies of *Inventario* and burn them.[92]

In hindsight the release of *Inventario* turned out to be beneficial for Sabina, in spite of the album's quality, because it encouraged him to rededicate himself to his profession in different ways and force a transition from being simply an entertaining live performer to a successful recording artist. *Inventario* was a fortuitous misstep at a moment in the late 1970s when, had the album been successful, he may have continued along the path of the conventional cantautor, which would not have been a fruitful professional decision. As alluded to in the previous chapter, Sabina launched his career in a turbulent historical moment that straddled two key events: the end of Francoist Spain with its cultural and political hegemony and the national transition to democracy, achieved largely by 1977 with the ratification of a liberal constitution.[93] At the beginning of the transitional period, the cantautors enjoyed their greatest success because their messages started to reach an audience beyond that of intellectuals and students. But once the establishment of a more progressive society and government was nearly complete, young Spaniards were suddenly presented with a much greater variety of musical genres and cultural possibilities. With Franco dead and the country democratic, the Spanish cantautor simply did not have the same urgency or motivation to compose the politically charged material that had been popular since the 1960s; when they continued doing so in the late 1970s and early 1980s, they must have seemed like troubadours of a lost age. This pivotal moment has been described by one investigator as "*the crisis of the cantautor*,"[94] but it hardly requires scholarly analysis: as a pithy Spanish popular expression states, "Muerto el perro, se acabó la rabia" ("*Once the dog is dead, no more rabies*"). Had Sabina charged ahead at this juncture, with nothing but his guitar, poetic lyrics, and leftwing *bona fides*, he would have become an anachronism before his career ever took off. Because of his unique experience of living in London for six years, upon his return to Spain he had an important decision to make: continue along the path he had been on prior to the exile, or channel his individual experiences and influences into becoming a different kind of performer. Sabina was sufficiently savvy to have opted for the second possibility.

After his disappointing first album, Sabina understood that it was imperative to become an original songwriter, if only to earn a living as musician in a challenging yet opportune moment in Spain's history. In an interview from 1978, Sabina recalls a moment near the end of his London exile when he cloistered himself in his room until he finished composing his first song, which he described as "muy mala, muy larga, muy autobiográfica . . . de esas canciones de adolescente en las que uno echa todo lo que lleva dentro" (*"very bad, very long, very autobiographical . . . one of those adolescent songs into which one throws everything they're carrying inside"*).[95] With much hard work and no small leap of faith, Sabina managed to become an exceptional songwriter and lyricist shortly after returning to Spain. His decision in the late seventies to dedicate himself to becoming a performer of original songs featuring poetic lyrics was *"the first mortal leap without a net"* of his career.[96] Miguel observes insightfully that, although Sabina is no slouch on the guitar, he could have become a virtuoso with more dedication to the musical side of his art. Instead he decided to make better use of words than melodies, because in this way he could more creatively depict the world around him.[97]

Further changes were occurring in Spain, especially in some areas of Madrid just to the northeast of where Sabina lived and often performed. A cultural movement was percolating in the city—a wave of hedonic creativity expressed through music, fashion, and cinema—and the neighborhoods just north of the Gran Vía were its ground zero. In the eighties the Spanish capital was a metropolis of graffiti, liberated youth, post-punk fashion, sexual promiscuity, and recreational drug use. Known as the «movida madrileña» (*"the Madrid scene"*), the movement has been defined in innumerable ways and is undoubtedly associated most often with the films of Spanish director Pedro Almodóvar. But rather than a movement with masses of people conscious of their collective participation in something, the movida could be viewed more persuasively as an exuberant expression of freedom in the wake of decades of dictatorship, as well as a reaction vis-à-vis the explosion of New Wave music from England and the United States. The enormous cultural liberation sparked by the movida had far-reaching effects; in 1984, even the conservative Royal Spanish Academy of the Language included, for the first time, obscene words in the twentieth edition of its dictionary.[98] In his fascinating book about the movida, José Gallero asks:

> ¿Pero qué se entiende por movida? En rigor, no puede hablarse de un movimiento, pues, de entrada, no existe conciencia de serlo, como no existe ningún tipo de coherencia teórica, programa o incluso pretensiones, a no ser que consideremos como tales la intensidad, la pasión y la capacidad de divertirse.

> *But what does one understand with [the term] movida? In all honesty, one cannot speak of a movement, for, to start with, there is no consciousness of it being one, as there does not exist any kind of coherent theory, project or plans, unless we can consider intensity, passion, and the capacity to enjoy oneself.*[99]

During the 1980s, the movida spread through the bars of Malasaña and Chueca and into the live-music venues such as Martín and Alfil, where bands such as Kaka de Luxe, Radio Futura, Alaska y los Pegamoides, and Antonio Vega's Nacha Pop performed. Certain discotheques, such as the Rock-Ola and El Sol, also became epicenters of the movement.[100] There remains much debate about the historical importance of the movida,[101] but for many, including the pop-music chronicler Jesús Ordovas, "Los años 80 fueron una puerta abierta a la imaginación. Todo era posible. Ya no había barreras sociales, políticas ni económicas. Lo que habían sido los 60 para los americanos, eran los 80 para nosotros. Nuestra *Movida* fue el equivalente a su *Verano del Amor*" ("*The eighties were an open door to the imagination. Everything was possible. There were no longer any social, political, or economic barriers. What had been the sixties for the Americans was the eighties for us. Our Movida was the equivalent of their Summer of Love*").[102]

The advent of the movida would exert a considerable but indirect influence on Sabina's music because it encouraged him to create a more popular, radio-friendly sound. At the same time, his poetic and rock influences led him to create music that was vastly different from the New Wave sounds of movida acts. Sabina's pedigree was exceptional—a Spanish cantautor with a passion for English-language rock music of the 1960s and 70s. But his songs needed to be fresh and appealing because, apart from the throngs of mohawked and ear-ringed youths who partied intensely around Madrid, there were even larger legions of young Spaniards whose musical tastes had not been influenced by the work of cantautors. An important point to remember is that Sabina was three days short of his thirty-first birthday on February 9, 1980, the night of Los Secretos' Canito Memorial Concert, the event usually understood as the inauguration of the movida. In other words, just as Sabina was too young to be the archetypal cantautor of the sixties, he was too old to be a true movida act of the 1980s.

The product of this uncertain moment is Sabina's first album of which he was proud: *Malas compañías* (1980). With it, Sabina first became a modern, electrified cantautor performing rock songs with a heavy dose of poetic inspiration. *Malas compañías* is also his first recording for Epic / CBS, which at the time was the largest recording company in Spain. As Menéndez Flores observes, even though the album is Sabina's second, it could very well be considered his musical debut.[103] Were it not for Sabina's friendship with a young protégé and some unexpected good fortune, this pivotal album probably would not have been recorded and his successful career would not have been launched.

Just as it was incredibly fortunate to have met someone willing to hand over their passport nearly ten years earlier, a younger musician and friend of Sabina nicknamed "Pulgarcito" ("*Little Flea*") provided perhaps an even greater service to the cantautor in 1979. What transpired could not have happened to Sabina himself. Miguel notes that although he often associated with street singers, especially those that performed on Calle Preciados, at this juncture of his career he was on the margins of the group and never busked in the subway or on the streets of Madrid.[104] Pulgarcito, however, regularly performed on the street, usually at the entrance of a mega-department store near Metro Callao. One day Tomás Muñoz Romero, the executive director of CBS España and a legendary discoverer of talent, happened to hear Pulgarcito singing Sabina's "Qué demasiao" ("Awesome!"), a sympathetic portrait of a well-known Spanish delinquent who had died—shot to death—on the streets of the capital.[105] When Muñoz asked Pulgarcito about the song, he confessed to the music executive that Sabina had written it.[106] Shortly thereafter, Sabina was contacted by the record company and, with superior folk and folk-rock arrangements by Hilario Camacho, recorded *Malas compañías* in a matter of days. The album featured poetic lyrics and an eclectic range of styles, from Latino-flavored music ("Círculos viciosos"), rock and roll ("Pasándolo bien"), and two of the enduring classics of his entire catalog: "Calle melancolía" ("Melancholy Street") and "Pongamos que hablo de Madrid" ("Let's Say I'm Talking about Madrid"). Even on the less memorable songs such as "Bruja" ("Witch") and "Mi amigo Satán" ("My Friend Satan"), Sabina's charisma and wit are on full display. Unlike *Inventario*, *Malas compañías* established a modest following for Sabina; his new fans appreciated the electrification he brought to the vocation of cantautor, to say nothing of his imaginative lyrics about life in the capital and the profound melancholy it can inspire.

During this period of the late 1970s and early 1980s, Sabina begins to perform regularly in the basement of a small club called the Café La Mandrágora, located at Calle de la Cava Baja 42. Accompanied by cantautors Alberto Pérez and Javier Krahe, Sabina sings and plays guitar, harmonica, and kazoo. There, in the vibrant *barrio* of tapa bars and popular markets, the three performers create an enormously entertaining and often hilarious live act. Born in Sigüenza, Pérez played the Spanish guitar and often sang with improvisational, jazzy flourishes; unlike the other two musicians, however, Pérez did not compose original music.[107] Slightly older than the other two and born in Madrid, Krahe became an important mentor for Sabina. Like Sabina, Krahe became a professional musician later than most; he also had literary inclinations and wrote songs with comic lyrics. Valdeón describes the affinity between the two cantautors with the observation: "Nadie ha entendido mejor la obsesión de Sabina por la coma y el adjetivo, por encontrar la palabra perfecta, la imagen exacta, la medida quirúrgica del idioma, que su amigo [Krahe]" (*"No one has better understood Sabina's obsession with the comma and the adjective, with finding the perfect word, the exact image, the surgical precision of the language, than his friend [Krahe]."*[108] Sabina has repeatedly referred to Krahe as *"wise"* and has said that if he has not sold very many records, it speaks poorly of Spain's taste in music.[109] No stranger to controversy, Krahe earned the distinction of being the first Spaniard to utter the expletive "gilipollas" during a televised performance of "Marieta," with Sabina and Pérez, on the program *Esta noche*.[110] Krahe was also the first Spanish artist censured since the resaturation of democracy, for his song "Cuervo ingenuo" ("Naive Crow"), which ridicules the prime minister at the time, Felipe González. With their clever improvisation and witty lyrics, Sabina and Krahe become the nucleus of the act with Pérez often relegated to providing back-up harmony, or extemporizing melodies while one of the other two stepped offstage for a drink. The trio's La Mandrágora music is clearly a reimagining of the cantautor repertoire and has little or nothing to do with the movida; rather, it is a post-Transition reemergence of the «canción de autor», with irreverent humor replacing the earnest political message. Other artists such as Luis Eduardo Aute, Chico Sánchez Ferlosio, Joaquín Carbonell, and Teresa Cano often joined Sabina, Krahe, and Pérez on the diminutive stage in the cellar of the legendary establishment, which is now a popular restaurant.

The success of the performances at La Mandrágora, coupled with his improbable discovery by a major record company, would yield Sabina his third recording: an entertaining live album of the trio performing thirteen songs, named after the venue and released in 1981. On the *La Mandrágora* album, listeners get a taste of the Spanish troubadour that had made a precarious living in London. With the exception of Sabina's magical performance of "Pongamos que hablo de Madrid," the music on the album is spirited, unadulterated absurdity. With no subject off limits on the album, Sabina also pokes fun of the *"hard rock"* of Krahe before the elder cantautor's performance of "El cromosoma" ("The Chromosome"). That Sabina would make such a joke is interesting—perhaps even prophetic—because he himself would shortly turn decisively to rock music as the genre in which he would record and perform.

The album *La Mandrágora* sells more than 100,000 copies and Krahe, Sabina, and Pérez make memorable appearances on Spanish television.[111] Having attained some measure of fame, especially in Madrid, the trio dissolves and each artist strikes off on his own. It must be said that although Pérez and Krahe could have continued to perform at La Mandrágora and other venues in Madrid for small crowds, Sabina was ready to step up to a larger stage, with its correspondingly larger audience. He no longer needed to share the spotlight. Consequently, it was at this point Sabina made the decision to turn to rock music—not hard rock, but pop-rock or AOR (Adult-oriented Rock)—the broad genre in which he would record his music going forward. While maintaining the same high standard for his lyrics, Sabina more fully immersed himself in this listener-friendly version of rock, crafting songs that were closer in sound to those of younger contemporaries than those of Aute, Serrat, and Krahe. As further evidence of this change—considered an apostasy by many diehard fans of the cantautors—Sabina even cut his hair and shaved his beard.

It was for these reasons he gave the title *Ruleta rusa* (*Russian roulette*) to his next album, which was released in 1984. If the album's title did not effectively convey the risky career move Sabina was taking, the cover photograph shows Sabina holding a revolver to his temple. Valdeón believes *Ruleta rusa* to be an important work in the history of Spanish music, not merely for Sabina's commitment to his new musical direction but because for the first time he fully assumes the personality he would project for the rest of his career. Although the songs of *Ruleta rusa* lack the seriousness and profundity of his later work, Sabina's basic persona is established: the rock-and-roll cantautor, with a *"suitcase full of books,"* prowling the nocturnal haunts of the Spanish capital.[112] No one has ever depicted this persona better than fellow cantautor, the late (great) Luis Eduardo Aute: "Degenerado y mujeriego, / con cierto aspecto de faquir / anda arrastrando su esqueleto / por las entrañas de Madrid" (*"Degenerate and womanizer, / with [that] particular look of a faqir / he moves about dragging his skeleton / through the bowels of Madrid"*).[113] Indicative of the activities of this persona is the lyric of "Noche negra" ("Black Night"): "La noche que yo amo tiene dos mil esquinas / con mujeres que dicen «¿me das fuego, chaval?» . . . La noche que yo amo no amanece jamás" (*"The night that I love has two thousand corners / with women that say, 'Will you give me a light, young man?' . . . / The night that I love never sees the dawn"*).[114] With this lyric, Sabina seems to be embarking on an endless night of carousing and sex, possibly a metaphor for his mature career.[115] The album also features "Eh, Sabina," a colorfully narcissistic ditty in which he complains of people advising him to stop smoking, drinking, and cavorting with multiple women. With such themes, one may observe a near total transformation from the performer he had been only five years earlier.[116] But these stylistic changes would not come without a cost, and Sabina ran the professional risk of being labeled a "vendido" (*"sell-out"*). As he explained in a recent interview, however, his decision was ultimately the correct one: "El poquito rechazo que noté de culturetas rojos estuvo compensado porque vino una avalancha de gente más joven, fantástica" (*"The little rejection I noted on the part of red posers was compensated because an avalanche of young people came, fantastic"*).[117]

Though highly entertaining, *Ruleta rusa* is an uneven album. A few of the deep cuts, such as "Ring, ring, ring" and "Guerra Mundial" ("World War," featuring lyrics by Manolo Tena), are mostly forgettable. On the songs with rock or power-pop arrangements, for example, "Eh, Sabina" and "Juana la loca," Sabina records with musicians who would later form the bands

Alarma!!! and Viceversa. Largely because of the programmed drumbeats, much of the music on *Ruleta rusa* has the flat, repetitive, machine-generated sound so common during the 1980s. A few tracks, such as "Guerra Mundial" and "Juana la loca," feature fiery solos courtesy of Jaime Stinus, one of Spain's finest electric guitarists. But in spite of the fact the album indicates further development for Sabina, from the first track to the last *Ruleta rusa* sounds very much like a product of its era.

After *Ruleta rusa*, Sabina would go on to record two albums with Viceversa: the studio album *Juez y parte* (1985), and a double album of live performances, *Joaquín Sabina y Viceversa: En directo* (1986). These albums are his first two recordings with the BMG-Ariola label, with which he would continue to record throughout the 1990s. The live album sold extremely well in Spain, with some observers viewing it as Sabina's earliest breakthrough. *Juez y parte* is an especially important studio album in Sabina's trajectory because, according to Valdeón, it is the first in which he finds his *"musical identity"* in addition to the persona of the gregarious, scoundrel troubadour he established on the previous album; in other words, all the songs on his album are strong with no gimmicky or partially conceived tracks.[118] Of equal importance is the fact that *Juez y parte* is Sabina's first album in which the production is outstanding throughout. His songs, rather than sounding like cultural artifacts from the mid-1980s, begin to feature a more distinctive music. Several of them, most notably "Cuando era más joven" and "Princesa," feature some of his most memorable lyrics. The first single from the album, "Güisqui sin soda" ("Whisky No Soda"), seems at first glance to be an irreverent anthem of carousing, an "Eh, Sabina" reboot. Upon closer scrutiny, however, the lyric is actually quite intelligent and stands as one of the clearest, most succinct expressions of the cantautor's personal philosophy. Sabina himself states that beginning with *Juez y parte*, he assumes full ownership of his work, with all its *"errors and successes."*[119] Miguel also observes that Sabina, accompanied by Viceversa, achieves for the first time *"a high level of professionalism,"* not merely with their approach to studio recording but also with live performances.[120] Álvaro Feito, a respected music journalist, declared that Sabina became *"up to date"* with important trends in popular music through his brief collaboration with the band.[121]

With these two Viceversa albums, Sabina became a leader of a rock band and thus aligned himself more closely with acts such as Manolo Tena's Alarma!!!, Radio Futura, Antonio Vega, and Los Secretos. This change is much more than a simple career decision because Sabina casts his lot with the more commercial musical acts of the movida, in spite of his age and artistic background, though it must be said he does not continue down this path for long. Shortly after these successes with Viceversa, the artistic visions of the band and its leader begin to diverge. One night in 1987, Sabina invites the band to dinner at Lhardy, Madrid's historic restaurant (as well as one of the most expensive). What he tells the musicians is something like a soft ultimatum: *"You all want to leave, and I want you all to leave."* But Pancho Varona, the guitarist, decides to continue working with Sabina, not merely as a musician but also, in some instances, as a songwriting collaborator.[122] These decisions show Sabina to be a savvy, forward-thinking music artist. By the mid-1980s he had effectively established an identity and creative space for himself. This metamorphosis from cantautor to *roquero* is described in a most ingenious manner by Sabina in the final stanza of *Juez y parte*'s "El joven aprendiz de pintor" ("The Young Painter's Apprentice"). Anticipating critics who might accuse him of being a "sell-out," Sabina turns retrospective: *"¿Y qué decir del crítico que indignado me acusa / de jugar demasiado a la ruleta rusa? / Si no hubiera arriesgado tal vez me acusaría / de quedarme colgado en calle melancolía"* (*"And what about the indignant critic who accuses me / of playing too much Russian roulette? / If I hadn't taken a chance maybe he would accuse me / of staying broke on melancholy street"*).[123]

In 1987, Sabina releases his true breakthrough album, *Hotel, dulce hotel* (*Hotel, Sweet Hotel*). Its first single, "Así estoy yo sin ti" ("This Is How I Am Without You") is one of the classic songs of Spanish popular music and the album, Sabina's fifth, sells over 400,000 copies in a few months.[124] But even this watershed moment does not represent the highest point of Sabina's artistic achievement. The album is uneven, with three, perhaps four, exceptional songs, and the production of a few of the deep cuts reverted to the 'ochentera' (*'eighty-ish'*) sound with programmed drums and bass lines; in particular, the second half of the album has not aged well.[125] Being idiosyncratic to a fault, prior to the release of his next album, *El hombre del traje gris* (*The Man in the Grey Suit*, 1988), Sabina boasted during an interview that he had written a collection of songs much darker than that of the previous multiplatinum album. He even remarked playfully that of the 400,000 people who had purchased *Hotel, dulce hotel*, only about 50,000 of them were true fans, and so the remaining 350,000 would have to *"swallow those sad, devasting stories"* from the new album.[126] *El hombre del traje gris* is his first album in which he shares the production with Varona and the brilliant multi-instrumentalist, Antonio García de Diego.[127] And though not nearly as important at the time as it was prophetic, Sabina cowrote his first lyric with novelist Benjamín Prado on the song "Cuando aprieta el frío" ("When the Cold Bites"). The album also features one of his most poignant compositions, "¿Quién me ha robado el mes de abril?" ("Who Has Stolen My Month of April?"). Although *El hombre del traje gris* does not repeat the commercial success of *Hotel, dulce hotel*, Sabina has included it among his three or four favorites albums.[128]

If Sabina's albums from the 1980s do not show a gradual increase in sales and critical acclaim, the music does demonstrate a steady improvement, because each album surpasses the previous one to the extent that Sabina solidifies his identity as the recording artist whom much of the Spanish-speaking world would come to admire so greatly in the nineties. Musically, Sabina's best 1980s songs are never as reliant on the slick synthesizers, monotonous bass lines, and programmed drum tracks as those of his younger movida contemporaries, although there is evidence of all these touches in those studio albums.[129] One observes a gathering of momentum toward the end of the decade and, once his musical collaborators Varona and García de Diego were in place by 1988, Sabina was poised for the major achievements of what could be termed his *decennium mirabile*. By the release of *Mentiras piadosas* (*White Lies*, 1990), this extraordinary rock-star-poet hybrid would be completely comfortable in his skin, confident, and unerringly make all the best creative decisions for the next ten years. Though this permutation, too, would witness at least two resets—the unexpected collaboration with Fito Páez and his choice of producer for *19 días y 500 noches* (1999)—Sabina becomes an artist in full control of his creative powers, emulating his much-admired Bob Dylan of the mid-1960s.

At the zenith of his artistry and commercial success, Sabina records his multiplatinum, critically acclaimed albums of the decade: *Mentiras piadosas*, *Física y química* (1992), *Esta boca es mía* (1994), *Yo, mí, me, contigo* (1996), and *19 días y 500 noches*. In 1998, Sabina recorded yet another studio album in collaboration with Argentinian singer-songwriter Fito Páez, *Enemigos íntimos*. While many of the songs on the album are excellent—for example, Sabina's vivid and moving paean to Madrid, "Yo me bajo en Atocha" ("I'm Getting Off at Atocha [Station]")—the duo never toured because of their highly publicized feud. After the release of the album, Sabina and Páez would not speak to each other for years.

Unlike the discography of the previous decade, each of these albums (with the exception of *Enemigos íntimos*) from the 1990s does seem to surpass the previous one in terms of its critical and commercial success. Sabina himself identifies three of these recordings as among his four best; additionally, all his personal favorites among his songs were composed during this decade.[130] *Mentiras piadosas* was notable because one of its songs, "Con la frente marchita" ("With a Weathered Brow," a line from a famous Carlos Gardel *tango*), helped open the Argentinian market for Sabina; "Y nos dieron las diez" ("And It Struck Ten O'clock on Us"), the *ranchera*-style hit single from *Física y química*, did much the same in Mexico.[131] *Física y química* also features Sabina's amusing tribute to the actresses who starred in the films of Pedro Almodóvar, "Yo quiero ser una chica Almodóvar": "Yo quiero ser una chica Almodóvar, / como Bibi, como Miguel Bosé, / pasar de todo y no pasar de moda, / bailar contigo el último cuplé" ("*I want to be an Almodóvar girl,*

/ like Bibi, like Miguel Bosé, / to experience everything and never go out of style, / to dance the last cuplé with you").[132]

With the next album, *Esta boca es mía*, Sabina achieved his first classic of uniformly brilliant songs, eclectic arrangements, and highly poetic lyrics. In fact, so good was the lyric of the title track, the first two verses were used by no less a poet than Mario Benedetti as an opening citation to his celebrated collection of poems, *El olvido está lleno de memoria* (1995).[133] Even English-language music reviewers began to take notice, with *Billboard*'s John Lannert suggesting that "with a little luck, *Esta Boca Es Mía* could also score in the United States."[134] In retrospect, we can say with certainty that Lannert was incorrect, because even in the 1990s Sabina's music was hardly promoted in this country beyond the word-of-mouth of fans. Furthermore, regardless of how brilliant his music of this period may be, Sabina's songs have never propelled people en masse to the dance floor, which is the basic criterion for successful Spanish-language music in the United States. This is, perhaps, the unavoidable trade off for those that would prioritize lyrics over melodies and rhythms (Dylan and Leonard Cohen have never inspired listeners to cut the rug, either). That Latino music crossover would occur a little later, near the turn of the millennium, and would largely involve Spanish-American artists such as Marc Anthony, Shakira, and Ricky Martin. But Lannert was correct in that Sabina's music of this period is so enjoyable and of such quality that it may have—with the appropriate promotion and touring—cornered some respectable portion of the American market north of the Río Grande.

English-language reviews of his subsequent albums were similarly enthusiastic. Reviewing *Yo, mí, me, contigo*, Paul Verna calls the album "a brilliant collection of poetic anecdotes seething with clever wordplay, biting wit, and taut arrangements."[135] Upon the release of *19 días y 500 noches*, considered by most to be his best album, Sabina is acknowledged as "the finest lyricist among Spain's legion of singer/songwriters—including the new under-30 crowd."[136] The triumphant success of *19 días y 500 noches* is especially remarkable when one considers the frenetic pace of Sabina's muse in the second half of the nineties, as well as the fact that he invited Alejo Stivel, a younger musician and former member of the band Tequila, to produce the album instead of the proven team of Varona, García de Diego, and himself. The result of Sabina's collaboration with Stivel is a highly polished production built around the cantautor's hoarse, distinctive vocals with no attempt to ameliorate them.[137] *19 días y 500 noches* also features successful collaborations with Antonio "Tony" Oliver, a cinematographer and writer, on the lyrics of several songs including "A mis cuarenta y diez" ("At my Forty and Ten"), "Como te digo una 'co' te digo la 'o'" ("As I Say 'co' to You I Say the 'o' to You"), "De purísima y oro" ("Of Sky Blue and Gold"), and "Pero qué hermosas eran" ("But How Beautiful They Were").[138]

In addition to his five studio albums and the collaboration with Fito Páez, Sabina's creative intensity was so great he also managed to record another double album of live music by the end of the nineties, *Sabina y Cía. Nos sobran los motivos* (2000), which featured the folky, harmonica-driven original, "Rosa de Lima" ("A Rose from Lima"), written for his long-time Peruvian girlfriend, Jimena Coronado.

It was during this decade of prodigious production that Sabina perfected the creative exercise of combining commercially appealing music with poetic lyrics. In this period, he gave much thought to the fundamentals of songwriting and poetic expression in order to refine his craft. Sabina believes that "[u]n buen poema no es por definición la mejor letra de canción, aunque a veces sí, y una buenísima letra de canción, sin la música, no suele ser un buen poema" ("[a] *good poem is not, by definition, the best song lyric, although at times it is, and a terrific song lyric, without the music, is not usually a good poem*").[139] With musical support from his talented collaborators Varona and García de Diego, Sabina was gradually able to liberate himself from the work of penning melodies and determining arrangements, and instead devote himself more fully to his lyrics. In the same interview with Menéndez Flores, Sabina reveals that his modus operandi has been, "siempre hacer una letra completa . . . Muchas veces con una melodía precaria y provisional, y luego les digo a los músicos que trabajen a partir de ahí" ("*always make a complete song lyric . . . Often with a precarious, provisional melody, and then I tell the musicians to work from there*").[140] The actual division of labor between the musicians is described by Joaquín Carbonell: Varona "*picks first flowers of the song*," which is to say that with his reliable pop sensibility, he provides some of the structure of verses, bridges, and choruses for the song; García de Diego wraps up the composition by determining the instruments, the arrangement, the rhythm, and the instrumental solo.[141]

On the great albums of the nineties, the musicianship under the direction of Varona and García de Diego is uniformly brilliant, making for the first time Sabina's music as visceral as it was cerebral. In particular, García de Diego's elegiac *arpeggios* and chord progressions (played on a twelve-string Portuguese guitar) in "De purísima y oro," his Spanish guitar in "Ruido" ("Noise"), and his bluesy licks in "Ganas de . . ." ("In the Mood for . . .") stand alongside the work of the most talented American or British guitarists of the same period. Apart from the contributions of Varona and García de Diego, Sabina's mature work is also enriched by the captivating voice of Olga Román, who sings harmony so beautifully on songs such as "Por el bulevar de los sueños rotos" ("Along the Boulevard of Broken Dreams"), "Esta boca es mía" ("This Mouth is Mine"), and "Y sin embargo" ("And Yet"). Sabina has observed that his studio collaboration with Varona, García de Diego, and Román has been so close and productive, they are much more of a musical group than others who routinely promote themselves as such.[142] Sabina's many collaborations with other musicians are also remarkable. On the five albums starting with *Física y química* and ending with *19 días y 500 noches*, Sabina cowrote or recorded songs with Rocío Dúrcal, Charly García, Ariel Rot, Pedro Guerra, Caco Senante, Fito Páez, Pablo Milanés, and Chavela Vargas. Such productive collaborations demonstrate that Sabina is not only generous with his talent but also appreciative of the talents of other performers.

Working more closely with others in the 1990s resulted in Sabina—who was always a tireless worker—becoming even more dedicated to the songwriting process. Sabina evolved from being a talented but haphazard composer, writing lyrics on the napkins of bars whenever the inspiration struck,[143] and into a professional singer-songwriter with an eye toward the recording studio. This change was important for several reasons, not the least of which was the manner in which it began the process of moderating his personal conduct. Though not quite Jerry Lee Lewis, the Andalusian has demonstrated the tendency of many rock-and-roll performers to aspire to outrageous excesses of drink, drugs, and sexual activity. In fact, more than many other musicians, Sabina has made such behavior the centerpiece of his songs, the result of which being that the more innocuous facet of his popular persona—that of the urban troubadour—is occasionally eclipsed by that of the unrepentant hedonist who snorts cocaine and frequents prostitutes. Sabina's candid description of his nocturnal carousing and drug use is one of the most remarkable confessions of such behavior by any celebrity, in any language, country, or era. "Yo amo el alcohol y las drogas pero detesto a los drogadictos y a los borrachos . . . Lo que [los intoxicantes] no pueden es crear la creatividad. Ahora bien, una copita, un canuntito y una rayita te ponen en un estado mucho mejor para escribir. Antes, otra gente lo hacía con absenta o con opio" (*"I love alcohol and drugs but I hate drug addicts and alcoholics . . . What [intoxicants] cannot [do] is create creativity. However, a little glass, a little joint, a little line of cocaine puts you in a much better state to write. Before, other people used to do it with absinthe or opium"*).[144] On numerous occasions, the Spanish media has accused Sabina of promoting drug use in his songs, a charge that he has denied.[145] What is rarely observed is that Sabina has also recorded songs—for example, "Princesa," "Pobre Cristina" ("Poor Christina"), and "Conductores suicidas" ("Suicide Conductors")—that describe in stark detail the dangerous consequences of drug use.

Sabina achieved fame comparatively late in life—by the mid-1990s he was already in his late forties. Early in the same decade, he also became the father of two daughters, Carmela Juliana and Rocío, with Isabel Oliart, the daughter of a prominent Madrid politician and a talented writer in her own right. Being intelligent, he was undoubtedly aware of the clichéd, pathetic appearance of a musician approaching fifty but still consumed by the excesses of a rock-and-roll animal half his age: "En muchas ocasiones me he sentido víctima del personaje por mí creado y culpable de haber colaborado en mi caricatura" (*"On many occasions I have felt a victim of my self-created persona and guilty of having collaborated on my caricature"*).[146] The increasingly literary bent of Sabina's activities in the early 2000s, especially following the minor stroke which he suffered during the night of August 23–24, 2001, coincided with the final stages of his gradual, somewhat reluctant abandonment of nocturnal ramblings.[147] There is evidence that a serious mellowing was beginning to occur in the late nineties, well before his medical emergency, when he began to spend more time at home with his Peruvian girlfriend, Jimena Coronado. Around this time the cantautor was quoted as saying, "Yo no tuve crisis de los treinta ni de los cuarenta, pero sí de los cincuenta. Cambio de vida bastante serio, que coincide con la vida con Jimena" (*"I didn't have a crisis in my thirties, nor in my forties, but I did in my fifties. Quite a serious life change, which coincides with [my] life with Jimena"*).[148] All these factors undoubtedly encouraged Sabina to slow down and, consequently, dedicate himself more earnestly to the composition of lyrics. Perhaps the result of this change is expressed in the song "Camas vacías" ("Empty Beds"), from the album *Dímelo en la calle* (2002): "ya no cierro los bares, ni hago tantos excesos, / cada vez son más tristes las canciones de amor" (*"I don't close the bars anymore, nor do I go to such excesses / the love songs are getting sadder and sadder"*).[149]

As a major recording artist, Sabina is uncommonly generous to his fans. While the length of a typical studio album is about thirty to forty minutes, his great albums of the nineties all clock in at over fifty: *Mentiras piadosas* (52:45); *Física y química* (53:07); *Esta boca es mía* (53:04); *Yo, mí, me, contigo* (54:53); the concluding album, *19 días y 500 noches*, could easily have been a double album for a more commercially self-conscious artist, since it contains nearly sixty-eight minutes of music (the Argentinian edition of the album includes two additional songs, putting its total time to well over seventy minutes). The importance Sabina places on his lyrics obligates him to take the entire process of songwriting more seriously, making him an album-oriented—rather than a single-oriented—music artist. Furthermore, there is no filler or even instrumentals on his albums. Sabina often records and performs in musical styles drawn from around the Spanish-speaking world; the variety of genres, so astutely arranged on his best albums, represents another truly remarkable achievement: *tango, rumba, norteña, ranchera*, to name only a few. He has reached even farther with occasionally surprising results, recording songs with *flamenco* rhythms ("Ruido"), New Orleans-flavored jazz ("La canción de las noches perdidas"), metal ("La del pirata cojo"), and reggae ("¿Qué estoy haciendo aquí?"). The Andalusian has even rapped ("Como te digo una 'co' te digo la 'o'") and scatted ("Dos horas después" and "Paisanaje"). The opportunity to become so creatively eclectic was well earned. After his initial successes, Sabina soared into that rarified air of the artist who could enter the recording studio and do just about anything he or she wished to do. Sabina has clearly made the most of the opportunity.

As Menéndez Flores observes, there is a certain improbability when one considers Sabina's enormous success: "Había nacido al mundo de la canción, quince años atrás, como cantautor. Sin embargo, con una habilidad que se escapa a toda lógica supo zafarse de cualquier tipo de etiquetas y logró triunfar con un cóctel de rock, pop y baladas, a pesar de ser casi una década mayor que los músicos que cultivaban esos estilos" ("*He had been born to the world of song, fifteen years earlier, as a cantautor. However, with an ability that defies logic he learned to free himself from any kind of label and managed to triumph with a cocktail of rock, pop and ballads, in spite of being almost a decade older than the musicians that were cultivating those styles*").[150] The melodies of Sabina's best songs are captivating, at times even inspired; of that there is no doubt. However, more than to anything else, his great success is a testament to the incomparable value of intelligent lyrics, especially in an age that seems to be moving away from the literary and toward illiteracy, or what Sabina has dubbed the "*globalization and standardization not of culture, but of the uncultured.*"[151]

Sabina is the first to admit that since his minor stroke, his work has become increasingly literary; he also seems less preoccupied with replicating his platinum super-productions of the nineties. He attributes this to "*becoming drunk with poets*" much more often, and the fact that since his albums are produced at a slower pace than in the 1980s and 1990s, the songs have become more "*literary.*"[152] The cantautor revealed his intentions near the end of *Sabina en carne viva*, explaining to Menéndez Flores that his future plans were going to have more to do with writing than concert performances, and that one day he would like to produce a memoir resembling a "*collage . . . a kind of Joycean monologue.*"[153] Sabina's last four studio albums—*Dímelo en la calle*, *Alivio de luto* (2005), *Vinagre y rosas* (2009), and *Lo niego todo* (2017)—have gradually demonstrated more out-sourcing of the musical composition to other talents (predominantly to Varona, García de Diego, and Leiva, a younger Spanish singer-songwriter and musician); simultaneously, fans have seen an increased lyrical collaboration with Benjamín Prado, the estimable Spanish writer, to the extent that it is difficult to ascertain authorship on many of these later songs. Taking these trends into consideration, one may view *Dímelo en la calle* as the last, truly classic Sabina album, one in which he writes all the lyrics himself (albeit the co-credit with Subcomandante Marcos on "Como un dolor de muelas"), and participates in the musical composition of eight of the fourteen songs. *Dímelo en la calle* is also the last album co-produced by the triumvirate of Sabina, Varona, and García de Diego. On the next album, *Alivio de luto*, Sabina is the sole lyricist on only six of the thirteen songs and assists with the music on only four. *Vinagre y rosas* exhibits an even greater disengagement from his craft, with the cantautor writing the lyrics of only three of the fourteen songs. Since lyrics indisputably take precedence over music for Sabina, the relinquishment of the musical side of his art—in this, the fifth decade of his career—is not entirely unexpected. But the ambiguity over which portion of the lyrics are his or Benjamín Prado's makes it next to impossible to analyze them as the Andalusian's work.

Many of those closest to Sabina have been candid about the diminished quality of the three studio albums that followed *19 días y 500 noches*. Pancho Varona, for example, stated that Sabina collaborates too much with Prado; he adds that *Alivio de luto* and *Vinagre y rosas* are excessively sad and represent a moment of *"hitting bottom"* for his friend.[154] Not surprisingly, Sabina himself acknowledges his declining musical ambitions following *19 días y 500 noches*. In a sonnet written for the weekly newspaper *Interviú*, on the occasion of his fifty-ninth birthday, he confesses, "Las musas que me colman el puchero / lucen menos en forma cada día, / ¿quién iba a suponer que llegaría / tan martes este doce de febrero?" (*"The muses that used to fill my stewpot / show themselves each day to be less in form, / who could imagine that this 12th of February / would turn out to be so Tuesday?"*).[155] But most would agree that Sabina has earned the right to work with a little less diligence at this late stage of his career. The lyrics co-written with Prado from recent albums are still quite good, though they do lack the brilliance and wit of those which he wrote by himself. If he did not take his work so seriously, he could easily record more albums of inferior quality with his collaborators, albums which would almost certainly sell extremely well. But in the wider context of the music industry and his career, Sabina has never been a sell-out. Writing in 1986, Maurilio de Miguel—Sabina's most critical biographer—recognized the artist's exceptional integrity: "Lo cierto es que sus planteamientos jamás fueron los del cantante estrella y que buscó antes el reconocimiento a su trabajo que el éxito" (*"What is certain is that his fundamentals never were those of the singer-superstar and that he sought the recognition of his work before success"*).[156]

A somewhat reluctant live performer, Sabina finally toured the United States in 2011. His series of concerts in New York City, Los Angeles, and Miami led him, in his words, to *"relive an old dream of [his] youth."*[157] The final album, *Lo niego todo*, could perhaps be seen as a collaborative album between Sabina and Spanish singer, musician, and songwriter Leiva, who not only composed (or helped to compose) the music for eight of the twelve songs, but also served as the album's producer. *Lo niego todo* was a remarkable critical and commercial success, quickly selling well in excess of 100,000 copies. With its retrospective lyrics, such as those of the evocative title track, the album also suggested something of a coda for Sabina's career. In support of the album and despite his weakened voice, Sabina toured extensively in support of *Lo niego todo*, even returning to give concerts at several U.S. venues.

To close this biographical chapter, Sabina has recently, at seventy-one years of age, done something that anyone familiar with his songs from the 1980s and 90s would never have expected him to do. In November 2019, he proposed marriage to his girlfriend of the past twenty years, Jimena Coronado. That we even know Sabina proposed would not have been possible without the unexpected revelation of Joan Manuel Serrat, who broke the news during a television interview in Argentina.[158] On June 29, 2020, Sabina and Coronado were married at a private civil ceremony in Madrid. The news of the wedding brought much joy to his fans, most of whom had endured weeks or months of self-imposed quarantine during the COVID 19 pandemic. The year 2020 did not begin auspiciously for the cantautor. Even before the virus swept through Europe, Sabina had suffered a most unfortunate seventy-first birthday when, during a performance with Serrat at Madrid's WiZink Center, he fell from the stage and had to be transported to the Ruber International Hospital. There, unexpectedly, he underwent surgery to remove an intracranial hematoma. Upon regaining consciousness after the successful procedure, the first words out of the Andalusian's mouth were a groggy request for a cigarette. When he did not receive one quickly enough, Sabina insisted, "Quiero fumar" ("*I want to smoke*"),[159] thus exemplifying the Spanish popular expression, "Genio y figura, hasta la sepultura."

There will of course come a time when Sabina will stop performing live and recording new material. And although in 1999 he sang that the tree that will become his "traje de madera" ("*wooden suit*") had not yet been planted, nor had the priest who will recite his extreme unction even become an "*altar boy*," it is probably safe to admit today that the tree is now a sapling and that the priest is probably enrolled at the seminary.[160] Like Dylan, we no longer expect Sabina to stay forever young. Nevertheless (and at the risk of discounting his recent accident), Sabina is in good health, happily married, and we can certainly expect new poems, more irreverent quotes, additional collections of his artwork, and perhaps even some new songs. Forty years ago, Sabina recorded one of his earliest masterpieces, "Pongamos que hablo de Madrid," in which he described his adopted hometown with keenly bittersweet descriptions and potent metaphors. At the end of that recording from *Malas compañías*, he expressed the wish to be buried in Andalusia, where he was born, because in Madrid "*there's no room for anyone.*"[161] But as Menéndez Flores explains, Sabina has, in his body of his work, virtually recreated the city as a geographic space; to take him out of Madrid would be tantamount to amputating a limb and stripping it of any identifying features.[162] It is undoubtedly for such reasons that the cantautor himself, in the margins of the lyric as it appears in *Con buena letra*, has written a second version of the final three verses of the song: "Cuando la muerte venga a visitarme / no me despiertes, déjame dormir, / aquí he vivido, aquí quiero quedarme . . . / pongamos que hablo de Madrid" (*"When death comes to visit me / don't wake me, let me sleep, / here I have lived, here I want to stay . . . / let's say I'm talking about Madrid"*).[163]

NOTES

1. "*I'm from the South / as an Andalusian / I have a happy, sad, and quiet soul, / I know how to cry between laughs, / and laugh between my tears.*" From the song "Yo soy del Sur" by Antonio Mata, from the second compact disc accompanying Fernando González Lucini's *De la memoria contra el olvido. Manifiesto Canción del Sur* (Madrid: Junta de Andalucía / Iberautor Promociones Culturales, SRL, 2004).

2. R. García Serrano and M. U. Pérez Ortega, "Cerámica popular de la provincia de Jaén: Úbeda," *Revista de dialectología y tradiciones populares* 30, no. 3 (1974): 399.

3. Michael Jacobs, *A Guide to Andalusia* (London: Penguin Books, 1991), 346. Sabina also alludes to this popular expression at the beginning of a remarkable poem he wrote shortly after visiting Ubeda in 2006 or 2007, "Del rosa al amarillo (doloras)," in *Esta boca es mía*, illus. Gustavo Otero (Barcelona: Ediciones B, 2010), 368–69.

4. Graham Wade, *Segovia: A Celebration of the Man and his Music* (London: Allison & Busby, 1983), 36.

5. Sabina and Menéndez Flores, *Sabina en carne viva*, 252. The *zarzuela* is a Spanish lyrical-drama—in many ways a prototype of Spanish opera—which dates from the first half of the seventeenth century. Its origins continue to be debated but, because Andalusia tends to be the epicenter of Spanish folklore, many zarzuelas are set in that region. Zarzuelas enjoyed a resurgence of popularity and were played on the radio after the Civil War. Manuel Vázquez Montalbán asserts that the people considered the zarzuela their literature and the primary example of music with "enjundia" (*"richness"*). See *Crónica sentimental de España* (Madrid: Espasa-Calpe, 1986), 49.

6. See the terrific extended interview of Sabina conducted by novelist Juan José Millás, *Conversaciones secretas*, "Episodio 1.1," Canal+ España (June 25, 2011), https://www.youtube.com/watch?v=HdrIGopF6e8 (accessed March 14, 2019).

7. Joaquín Sabina, "Joaquín Sabina. Entrevista noctámbula," Interview with Carlos Boyero, *Rolling Stone* (Spanish edition), online version (February 2000), https://www.taringa.net/+apuntes_y_monografias/entrevista-noctambula-joaquin-sabina_131ler (accessed January 30, 2020).

8. See "La muchacha que veía pasar los trenes" in Maurilio de Miguel, *Joaquín Sabina* (Madrid: Ediciones Júcar, 1986), 172–73.

9. Quoted in Javier Menéndez Flores, *Joaquín Sabina. Perdonen la tristeza (edición revisada y actualizada)* (Barcelona: Libros Cúpula, 2018), 28–29.
10. Sabina and Menéndez Flores, *Sabina en carne viva*, 253.
11. Luis Cardillo, *Los tangos de Sabina* (Buenos Aires: Editorial Olimpia, 2003), 156.
12. Sabina and Menéndez Flores, *Sabina en carne viva*, 252.
13. Menéndez Flores, *Perdonen la tristeza*, 29.
14. Interview with Joaquín Sabina, "Garagatos Joaquín Sabina | Libro | Artika," *YouTube* (March 22, 2017), https://www.youtube.com/watch?reload=9&v=R8fsLPLDVpU (accessed November 14, 2019).
15. Miguel, *Joaquín Sabina*, 19.
16. Menéndez Flores, *Perdonen la tristeza*, 29.
17. Matías Uribe, *Polvo, niebla, viento y rock: cuatro décadas de música popular en Aragón* (Zaragoza: Ibercaja, 2003), 19.
18. José F. Colmeiro writes that *coplas* "typically reinforced traditional values associated with old Spain (Catholicism, patriotism, and patriarchalism), and, as a matter of course, were anathema to Spanish anti-Franco intellectuals and resistance fighters." "Canciones con historia: Cultural Identity, Historical Memory, and Popular Songs," *Journal of Spanish Cultural Studies* 4, no. 1 (2003): 32.
19. Vázquez Montalbán, *Crónica sentimental de España*, 41.
20. This quixotic romantic adventure would later become the partial inspiration of "Eva tomando el sol" ("Eva Getting Tan"). "Chispa" also figures prominently in the song "Una de romanos" ("A Gladiator Movie") about going to the cinema on dates during the dictatorship.
21. Sabina, "Joaquín Sabina. Entrevista noctámbula," Interview with Carlos Boyero, *Rolling Stone* (Spanish edition), online version (accessed January 30, 2020).
22. In 1965, at the very height of Beatlemania, the group from Liverpool performed two concerts in Spain, one in the famous Las Ventas bullfighting plaza of Madrid (July 2) and one in the bullfighting plaza Monumental of Barcelona (July 3).
23. In a 1978 interview, Sabina states that he went to Granada when he was seventeen. Quoted in Menéndez Flores, *Perdonen la tristeza*, 59. In the 2000 *Rolling Stone* interview with Carlos Boyero, Sabina reiterates that he was seventeen when he started his university studies.
24. Sabina and Menéndez Flores, *Sabina en carne viva*, 261.
25. Miguel, *Joaquín Sabina*, 26–27.
26. Ibid., 31.
27. Sabina and Menéndez Flores, *Sabina en carne viva*, 263–64.
28. Jairo García Jaramillo, "Las huellas borradas de Pablo del Águila," in Pablo del Águila, *De soledad, amor, silencio y muerte (poesía reunida, 1964–1968)* (Madrid: Bartleby Editores, 2017), 22.
29. Pablo del Águila, *De soledad, amor, silencio y muerte (poesía reunida, 1964–1968)* (Madrid: Bartleby Editores, 2017).
30. Sabina, "Joaquín Sabina. Entrevista noctámbula," Interview with Carlos Boyero, *Rolling Stone* (Spanish edition), online version (accessed January 30, 2020).

31. Sabina and Menéndez Flores, *Sabina en carne viva*, 140.
32. Maurilio de Miguel, e-mail message to author, January 24, 2020.
33. Visit the website, *Juan de Loxa Poesía 70*, Atrioweb (n/d), http://www.juandeloxa.com/Poesia-70/ (accessed January 15, 2020).
34. González Lucini, *De la memoria contra el olvido*, 78–79.
35. Miguel, *Joaquín Sabina*, 24. For his part, Sabina has stated in at least one interview that although he knew of the cantautors who participated in the "Manifiesto Canción del Sur" movement, he did not associate with them in a significant manner. See "Joaquín Sabina entrevista en 1989," *YouTube* (February 19, 2016), https://www.youtube.com/watch?v=mFTV3E_JOjU (accessed March 31, 2020).
36. Candeira, "La importancia de llamarse Martínez," 214.
37. Miguel, *Joaquín Sabina*, 28.
38. Joaquín Sabina, "1968," in *Con buena letra* (Madrid: Temas de Hoy, 2002), 31.
39. Sabina calls them "adláteres" (*"cronies"*) of the PCE in *Sabina en carne viva*, 255.
40. According to Menéndez Flores, Sabina actually returned home to Úbeda because of Christmas vacations. *Perdonen la tristeza*, 457.
41. Sabina and Menéndez Flores, *Sabina en carne viva*, 255–56.
42. González Lucini, *Crónica cantada de los silencios rotos*, 32.
43. Ibid., 29–30.
44. Roberto Torres Blanco, "«Canción protesta»: definición de un nuevo concepto historiográfico," *Cuadernos de Historia Contemporánea* 27 (2005): 241.
45. Sabina, "Joaquín Sabina. Entrevista noctámbula," Interview with Carlos Boyero, *Rolling Stone* (Spanish edition), online version (accessed February 4, 2020).
46. Valdeón, *Sabina. Sol y sombra*, 26.
47. Miguel, *Joaquín Sabina*, 45. See also Sabina and Menéndez Flores, *Sabina en carne viva*, 53–54. With regard to the nationality of Lesley, Sabina and his biographers refer to her as "inglesa" (*English*) and "escocesa" (*Scottish*) on different occasions. For example, in a *Rolling Stone* interview from 2000, Sabina says, "Yo tenía una novia inglesa . . ." ("*I had an English girlfriend . . .*") (quoted in Menéndez Flores, *Perdonen la tristeza*, 34). But Menéndez Flores writes "novia escocesa" on two occasions in his most recent Sabina book, *Sabina. No amanece jamás*, 97, 242.
48. Catherine Boyle, "The Politics of Popular Music: On the Dynamics of New Song," in *Spanish Cultural Studies: An Introduction: The Struggle for Modernity*, eds. Helen Graham and Jo Labanyi (New York: Oxford, 1995), 292.
49. The song "Mi primo El Nano," from the album *Yo, mí, me, contigo*, is an inspired tribute to Serrat. In the lyric, Sabina sings that the people need Serrat's "*blessed music more than they need to eat*" and that he "*would like to be like [Serrat] when he was young.*" *Con buena letra*, 157.
50. Menéndez Flores, *Perdonen la tristeza*, 44.
51. Sabina and Menéndez Flores, *Sabina en carne viva*, 260.
52. Joaquín Sabina, "Me pido primer," *Alivio de luto*, Sony-BMG 8287 674202-2, compact disc, 2005.

53. Menéndez Flores reproduces a notice from a newspaper in Jaen, Sabina's home province, dated February 4, 1971, indicating that he had received a temporary twelve-month residency and had escaped to Great Britain with a false passport to escape obligatory military service. *Perdonen la tristeza*, 36.

54. Sabina and Menéndez Flores, *Sabina en carne viva*, 264.

55. Sabina says, "A ver si Marichalar me deja, porque lo tengo ahí agarrado" ("*Let me see if the stroke lets me, because it's held [up] there*"—very likely pointing to his head), *Sabina en carne viva*, 255. The word «marichalar» is a colloquialism inspired by Jaime de Marichalar, an economist from an aristocratic Spanish family who, in 1995, married the eldest daughter of King Juan Carlos and Queen Sophia (they divorced in 2010). In 2001, Marichalar suffered a stroke and largely withdrew from public life.

56. Miguel, *Joaquín Sabina*, 34.

57. Menéndez Flores, *Perdonen la tristeza*, 43.

58. Menéndez Flores, *Sabina. No amanece jamás*, 232.

59. See Menéndez Flores, *Perdonen la tristeza*, 34; and Valdeón, *Sabina. Sol y sombra*, 37–39.

60. Carbonell, *Pongamos que hablo de Joaquín*, 50–51.

61. For example, ". . . siempre digo que tengo siete años menos, que son los que viví en Londres" (". . . *I always say that I am seven years younger [than what I am], those seven years that I lived in London*") *Sabina en carne viva*, 267; and, "A los veintiún años me exilié a Londres, donde viví seis años . . ." ("*At twenty-one years I went into exile in London, where I lived for six years*"), interview with Eduardo Jiménez Torres, quoted in Menéndez Flores, *Perdonen la tristeza*, 57.

62. For example, Santiago García-Castañón writes that Sabina found himself obligated to escape to London, just at the moment he was about to finish his university degree, because of the police dragnet that was closing around him. "Hacia una poética del perdedor: Joaquín Sabina o la escritura en los márgenes de la sociedad," *MIFLC Review. Journal of the Mountain Interstate Foreign Language Conference* 10 (2001): 64.

63. Menéndez Flores, *Sabina. No amanece jamás*, 242.

64. Menéndez Flores, *Perdonen la tristeza*, 34.

65. Ibid., 33.

66. During an interview for *El Mundo*, Sabina admitted that for his participation in the incident he "*wanted to feel like a hero for a day . . . getting involved throwing Molotov cocktails like the one I threw at the Banco Bilbao.*" Quoted in Sara Navas, "Un cóctel molotov en un banco y siete años de exilio en Londres: así fueron los inicios de Joaquín Sabina," *El País*, online edition (November 9, 2019), https://elpais.com/elpais/2019/11/07/icon/1573135703_285643.html#comentarios (accessed January 31, 2020).

67. Sabina, "Güisqui sin soda," *Con buena letra*, 62.

68. Valdeón, *Sabina. Sol y sombra*, 24–25.

69. Sabina, "Entrevista noctámbula Joaquín Sabina," Interview with Carlos Boyero, *Rolling Stone* (Spanish edition), online version (accessed February 4, 2020).

70. Miguel, *Joaquín Sabina*, 44–45. See also Sabina and Menéndez Flores, *Sabina en carne viva*, 260–61. In his interview with Carlos Boyero, Sabina explains

that he told Lesley he wanted to "*see his people*" in London, which she understood as his departure. After a fierce argument, Sabina left her house and began the solitary phase of his exile. "Joaquín Sabina. Entrevista noctábula," Interview with Carlos Boyero, *Rolling Stone* (Spanish edition), online version (accessed February 4, 2020).

71. Antonio Muñoz Molina, "Joaquín Sabina," in Menéndez Flores, *Perdonen la tristeza*, 440.
72. Miguel, *Joaquín Sabina*, 49.
73. Sabina and Menéndez Flores, *Sabina en carne viva*, 270.
74. Miguel, *Joaquín Sabina*, 46; and Menéndez Flores, *Perdonen la tristeza*, 59.
75. Menéndez Flores, *Perdonen la tristeza*, 38.
76. Miguel, *Joaquín Sabina*, 53–54.
77. Sabina and Menéndez Flores, *Sabina en carne viva*, 268.
78. The song "Rap del optimista" from the 1988 album *El hombre del traje gris* sounds like a reggae in parts, but on the whole has a more conventional rhythm, like that of Latin pop.
79. Sabina and Menéndez Flores, *Sabina en carne viva*, 139.
80. Ibid., 266–67.
81. Menéndez Flores, *Perdonen la tristeza*, 43.
82. Valdeón, *Sabina. Sol y sombra*, 81.
83. Menéndez Flores, *Perdonen la tristeza*, 279–80.
84. Valdeón, *Sabina. Sol y sombra*, 137.
85. Sabina and Menéndez Flores, *Sabina en carne viva*, 111.
86. Ibid., 362.
87. Menéndez Flores, *Perdonen la tristeza*, 48–49.
88. Ramón del Valle-Inclán, *Luces de Bohemia. Esperpento*, ed. Alonso Zamora Vicente (Madrid: Espasa-Calpe, 1987), 38.
89. Sabina and Menéndez Flores, *Sabina en carne viva*, 125–26.
90. Ibid., 281.
91. "Mi primer disco, *Inventario*, ay, es un disastre" ("*My first album, 'Inventario,' ug, it's a disaster*"). Ibid., 125.
92. Valdeón, *Sabina. Sol y sombra*, 43.
93. José F. Colmeiro, "Canciones con historia: Cultural Identity, Historical Memory, and Popular Songs," *Journal of Spanish Cultural Studies* 4, no. 1 (2003): 41.
94. Torres Blanco, "«Canción protesta»," 241.
95. Sabina quoted in Menéndez Flores, *Perdonen la tristeza*, 58.
96. Maurilio de Miguel, e-mail message to author, January 24, 2020.
97. Miguel, *Joaquín Sabina*, 62–63.
98. David A. Pharies, *A Brief History of the Spanish Language*, Second edition (Chicago: University of Chicago Press, 2015), 130.
99. José Luis Gallero, *Sólo se vive una vez. Esplendor y ruina de la movida madrileña* (Madrid: Ediciones Ardora, 1991), 10.
100. Elena Gascón-Vera, "Más allá de la Movida: España en los 90," *Pespectivas sobre la cultura hispánica. XV aniversario de una colaboración interuniversitaria*, coords. John P. Gabriele and Andriena Bianchini (Córdoba: Tipografía Católica, S.C.A., 1997), 166. Sabina recounts his lone, unsuccessful performance at the

Rock-Ola, during which actor Antonio Banderas accompanied him on the chorus of "Pisa el acelerador" ("Step on the Gas") while most of the crowd sat on the floor of the venue. Valdeón, *Sabina. Sol y sombra*, 84.

101. Sabina has described the movida as an *"elitist"* and superficial expression of community among its most visible participants; he adds that he was never a part of it. What he does praise, however, is the vibrant nocturnal culture of the capital that exploded and filled the streets under the auspices of Enrique Tierno Galván's term as mayor. *Sabina en carne viva*, 90–91.

102. Quoted in Gallero, *Sólo se vive una vez*, 280.

103. Menéndez Flores, *Perdonen la tristeza*, 67.

104. Miguel, *Joaquín Sabina*, 93.

105. Fernando González Lucini, "Canciones con historia: «¡Qué demasiao! (una canción para el Jaro)» . . . Joaquín Sabina y Pulgarcito," *Cantemos como quien respira* (June 15, 2014), http://fernandolucini.blogspot.com/2014/06/canciones-con-historia-que-demasiao-una.html (accessed January 18, 2020).

106. Sabina and Menéndez Flores, *Sabina en carne viva*, 112–13.

107. Joaquín Carbonell, e-mail message to author, May 24, 2020.

108. Valdeón, *Sabina. Sol y sombra*, 56.

109. Sabina, "Joaquín Sabina. Entrevista noctámbula," Interview with Carlos Boyero, *Rolling Stone* (Spanish edition), online version (accessed February 5, 2020).

110. Valdeón, *Sabina. Sol y sombra*, 72–73.

111. Esther Mucientes, "Muere Javier Krahe a los 77 años," *El Mundo* (July 13, 2015), https://www.elmundo.es/cultura/2015/07/12/55a2329ce2704ef3278b4575.html (accessed February 9, 2020).

112. Valdeón, *Sabina. Sol y sombra*, 95.

113. This initial stanza is from Aute's warmly satirical song he composed for his friend, "Pongamos que hablo de Joaquín," the lyric of which is reproduced in its entirety in Miguel, *Joaquín Sabina*, 9.

114. Sabina, "Negra noche," *Con buena letra*, 55.

115. Perceptively, Maurilio de Miguel ponders the significance of the second verse of the chorus, "negra noche, espero tanto de ti" (*"black night, I hope for so much from you"*), which may indeed cause a listener to contemplate for what exactly Sabina's *"black night"* may be a metaphor. *Joaquín Sabina*, 130.

116. Sabina's transformation between *Malas compañías* and *Ruleta rusa* would not be without its consequences. With regard to serious, critical assessment, there is a decline in both the number and quality of references to his work starting in the mid-1980s. Following the shift from politically committed cantautor to commercially successful recording artist, Maurilio de Miguel's biography (1986) is the only serious work dedicated to Sabina until his critical and commercial successes of the next decade. Menéndez Flores seems to be aware of the relative paucity of serious attention given to Sabina's work when he writes that, in spite of the prodigious record sales, it has not *"been valued as it should be in reality."* *Sabina en carne viva*, 120. During a 2002 interview, Carlos Boyero asks Sabina directly if he is aware that many detest him, considering him a *"sell-out"* and an imposter

with "*pseudo-aggressive postures and lyrics that seek commercial success.*" Sabina responds that he cannot waste his time thinking about such things and, referencing his record sales, suggests that there must be something more at work than simply marketing. Sabina, "Joaquín Sabina. Entrevista noctámbula," Interview with Carlos Boyero, *Rolling Stone* (Spanish edition), online version (accessed February 5, 2020).

117. Sabina, "Tirso de Molina, julio 2016," Interview with Julio Valdeón, in *Sabina. Sol y sombra*, 489.

118. Valdeón, *Sabina. Sol y sombra*, 106.

119. Sabina and Menéndez Flores, *Sabina en carne viva*, 126.

120. Miguel, *Joaquín Sabina*, 165.

121. Quoted in Ibid.

122. Valdeón, *Sabina. Sol y sombra*, 162–65.

123. Sabina, "El joven aprendiz de pintor," *Con buena letra*, 65.

124. Menéndez Flores, *Perdonen la tristeza*, 135.

125. For an interesting account of *Hotel, dulce hotel*'s composition and production, see Valdeón, *Sabina. Sol y sombra*, 135–51.

126. Quoted in Menéndez Flores, *Perdonen la tristeza*, 144.

127. García de Diego is a virtuoso and his participation has greatly enhanced Sabina's music. As Carbonell points out, almost immediately on *El hombre del traje gris* one hears the sounds of electric guitars as they should sound, rather than the programmed, soulless notes heard *ad nauseum* throughout the 1980s. See *Pongamos que hablo de Joaquín*, 233–34. To appreciate the improvement García de Diego brought to Sabina's sound, compare the technically accomplished but mostly unremarkable heavy metal guitar solo of "Ring, ring, ring," from *Ruleta rusa*, to the guitar solo of "Conductores suicidas," from *Física y química*, with its fluidity, bounce, and clear tone.

128. Sabina and Menéndez Flores, *Sabina en carne viva*, 136.

129. For a description of how Sabina actively tried to resist the 'ochentera' (*eighties-ish*) sound being imposed on *Ruleta rusa* by producer Jorge Álvarez, see Valdeón, *Sabina. Sol y sombra*, 85–88.

130. Sabina and Menéndez Flores, *Sabina en carne viva*, 136. Carbonell also selects the four albums—*Física y química*, *Esta boca es mía*, *Yo, mí, me, conmigo*, and *19 días y 500 noches*—as Sabina's best. *Pongamos que hablo de Joaquín*, 480.

131. Valdeón, *Sabina. Sol y sombra*, 194.

132. Sabina, "Yo quiero ser una chica Almodóvar," *Con buena letra*, 122. A «cuplé» was a variety of cabaret dance or torch song performed in the early twentieth century, often by men in drag. The verse "el último cuplé" may also be a reference to the title of a popular Spanish movie from the fifties starring Sara Montiel.

133. Menéndez Flores, *Perdonen la tristeza*, 204.

134. John Lannert, "Joaquín Sabina's Time Has Come," *Billboard* (Week Ending July 16, 1994), 43, 4.

135. Paul Verna, "Joaquín Sabina. Yo, Mi, Me Contigo," *Billboard* (Week Ending August 24, 1996), 112.

136. Terry Berne and Howell Llewellyn, Joaquín Sabina. '19 Días Y 500 Noches'," *Billboard* (Week Ending November 20, 1999), 93.

137. To understand the history of why the production team of Sabina-Varona-García de Diego was replaced by Stivel on this lone album (and after the tremendous success of the previous three albums), see Valdeón, *Sabina. Sol y sombra*, 306–9.

138. For the best treatment of this brief collaboration, which prefigures Sabina's more routine co-crediting of lyrics on subsequent albums, see Ibid., 309–11.

139. Sabina and Menéndez Flores, *Sabina en carne viva*, 106.

140. Ibid., 109.

141. Carbonell, *Pongamos que hablo de Joaquín*, 405–6.

142. Sabina and Menéndez Flores, *Sabina en carne viva*, 91.

143. Ibid., 128. There are many other references to his early, haphazard approach to songwriting.

144. Sabina, "Joaquín Sabina. Entrevista noctámbula," Interview with Carlos Boyero, *Rolling Stone* (Spanish edition), online version (accessed February 5, 2020).

145. Maurilio de Miguel reproduces an article from Spain's largest daily newspaper, *El País*, dated June 12, 1986, in which Sabina is accused of promoting the use of cocaine. The cantautor responds in the article that *"singers do not promote anything"* and that the *"official stratum"* of society *"lacks a sense of humor."* *Joaquín Sabina*, 168.

146. Ibid., 31.

147. In 2006 Sabina admitted, "[T]e diré que ese tipo de aficiones noctámbulas, tabernarias, goliárdicas y puteras las tengo abandonadas rotunda, absoluta y radicalmente. No he perdido la afición, pero ahora estoy ahí metido en un pisito discutiendo conmigo mismo, con quien tengo muchas cosas que discutir" (*"I will tell you that those kinds of nocturnal, barhopping, hedonistic, whoremongering inclinations I have completely, absolutely and radically abandoned. I have not lost the inclination, but now I'm here in a nice little apartment discussing [things] with myself, with whom I have many things to discuss"*). Quoted in Sabina and Menéndez Flores, *Sabina en carne viva*, 167.

148. Quoted in Carbonell, *Pongamos que hablo de Joaquín*, 376.

149. Sabina, "Camas vacías," *Con buena letra*, 225.

150. Menéndez Flores, *Perdonen la tristeza*, 215.

151. Quoted in Ibid., 409.

152. Sabina and Menéndez Flores, *Sabina en carne viva*, 339.

153. Ibid., 352.

154. Quoted in Valdeón, *Sabina. Sol y sombra*, 437.

155. Joaquín Sabina, "Happy Birthday to Me. Dos sonetos," *Esta boca es mía*, illus. Gustavo Otero (Barcelona: Ediciones B, 2010), 410. February 12 is, of course, the cantautor's birthday. In the Spanish-speaking world, Tuesday ("martes") has traditionally been the most infelicitous of the days of the week. Taking its name from the Roman god of war, it is often associated with death and misfortune.

156. Miguel, *Joaquín Sabina*, 12.

157. Menéndez Flores, *Perdonen la tristeza*, 466.

158. "Joaquín Sabina le pide matrimonio a Jimena Coronado y Serrat rompe el secreto," *El Mundo*, online edition (November 7, 2019), https://www.elmundo.es/loc/famosos/2019/11/07/5dc44a0efc6c832e268b45cb.html (accessed January 9, 2020).

159. Darío Prieto, "Sabina, rodeado de las tres mujeres de su vida," *El Mundo*, online edition (February 15, 2020), https://www.elmundo.es/loc/famosos/2020/02/15/5e46c40a21efa05d358b45b7.html (accessed February 25, 2020).

160. Sabina, "A mis cuarenta y diez," *Con buena letra*, 193.

161. Ibid., 42.

162. Sabina and Menéndez Flores, *Sabina en carne viva*, 84.

163. Sabina, "Pongamos que hablo de Madrid," *Con buena letra*, 42.

Chapter 2

The Poetics of Joaquín Sabina's Lyrics

"La poesía está en todas partes, incluso en algunos versos."

—Joaquín Sabina[1]

SABINA AS POET

Sabina's derisive aphorism—*"poetry is everywhere, even in some verses"*—may certainly be applied to his song lyrics. Long before the publication of *Ciento volando de catorce* (2001), his best-selling collection of sonnets, many had already recognized his poetic ability. But in spite of such recognition, there have been few critical studies of his poetry and song lyrics. José F. Colmeiro observes that, as late as 2009, the "scholarly analytical bibliography" for Sabina (as well as for other cantautors) was still scarce, although there was a growing body of "descriptive or biographical" studies.[2] Only recently have scholars begun to address the paucity of research on Sabina's work.[3] Much of the reluctance to conduct such investigation is attributable to the previously discussed debate concerning the study of song lyrics as poetry: for many people, song lyrics are not sufficiently literary and so, as a scholarly endeavor, researching them is not as worthwhile as researching published poetry.

As a result, Sabina the rock-and-roll cantautor is difficult to categorize, being neither a poet nor an average lyricist. A kind of compromise assessment is often reached: Sabina is either a poet who happened to become a musician, or a musician who happened to become a poet. The Spanish poet Luis García Montero expresses this idea almost exactly when, in the prologue for Sabina's *Ciento volando de catorce*, he concludes, "Joaquín Sabina es cantante y poeta. Por ajustar más: no un cantante metido a poeta, sino un poeta metido a cantante" (*"Joaquín Sabina is a singer and a poet. More accurately: he isn't a singer turned poet, but a poet turned singer*").[4] García Montero is correct in his assessment. But he is also generous, for it is not often that a celebrated poet, admired by so many scholars, would pay such a compliment to an artist whose songs were once on the radio and whose music videos may still be seen on YouTube. In spite of such an endorsement, however, Sabina's vocation has discouraged the kind of rigorous study of his song lyrics that they deserve. In fact, the dichotomy as it is presented—Sabina as a poet who became a singer or vice versa—avoids the very medium of poetic expression being considered: the song lyrics of fifteen studio and three live albums.

For this writer, at least, there is no controversy: Joaquín Sabina is a poet—and a fine one at that. He just happens to be working in rock music, a mode of expression in which thoughtful lyrics (to say nothing of poetry) are uncommon. As explained in the previous chapter, Sabina's most consistent achievement throughout his career has been the composition of what writer Carl Eric Scott has called "literary pop songs," a genre in his opinion pioneered by Bob Dylan.[5] Even in Sabina's less-accomplished albums from early in his career, for example, *Inventario* (1978) and *Ruleta rusa* (1984), and in the densely poetic, collaborative efforts of the past fifteen years, *Alivio de luto* (2005) and *Vinagre y rosas* (2009), he has composed lyrics that are vastly superior to those of most other songwriters. While Sabina has usually had a hand in the music and arrangements of his songs,[6] he is almost invariably the sole author of his lyrics from the 1980s and 1990s.[7] The subordinate role that melodies and arrangements maintain vis-à-vis lyrics in his music is evident from a response by Sabina to a question regarding the virtues of a great song. Sabina replied, "Una buena letra, una buena melodía, una buena interpretación y algo más que nadie sabe lo que es, y que es lo único que importa: alma, corazón y vida, nada más" ("*A good lyric, good melody, a good interpretation, and something more that no one knows what it is, and yet it is the only important thing: soul, heart, and life, nothing more*").[8] Finding that "*heart, soul, and life*" is an elusive but necessary goal; for Sabina, the road to getting there starts with the lyric.

The very first verses of the very first track of his debut album, *Inventario*, unmistakably rework the imagery and vocabulary of Pablo Neruda's classic collection, *Veinte poemas de amor y una canción desesperada* (1924).[9] Similar allusions abound in Sabina's work. According to Guillermo Laín Corona, Sabina's repeated references to "golondrinas" (*swallows*) in his songs is a reference to Gustavo Adolfo Bécquer (1836–1870), the great Spanish Romantic poet, and therefore serve as a manner of boosting the "poeticidad" (*poeticism*) of the cantautor.[10] Among Sabina's favorite poets are Neruda, Juan Gelman, and César Vallejo.[11] García Montero notes the cantautor's readings of Francisco de Quevedo, the celebrated satirical author of the Spanish Golden Age.[12] Sabina was also a friend of the late Spanish poet and playwright, Rafael Alberti.[13] The point of mentioning these literary figures is to reinforce the assessment of Sabina as a poet, for not only is he fully immersed in poetry, he continues to be an avid student of its finest practitioners. While many rock and pop-music lyrics rely on meaningless verses of filler, he has endeavored to inject something much more substantial into his music. Sabina himself has quipped that the lyrics of most songs on the radio sound as if they were written by soccer players after a match.[14]

Although the *cantautor* himself would very likely find such exegesis of his work tedious,[15] this chapter will analyze, in a manner usually reserved for poetry, selected song lyrics written by Sabina. While discussing his use of rhetorical devices such as simile, *anaphora, antanaclasis,* and *auxesis,*[16] my central argument is that many of Sabina's best song lyrics are built around bold examples of antithesis. Although these devices have been called rhetorical, they appear quite commonly in poetry; because they are particularly conspicuous in Sabina's lyrics, they become the subject of analysis in this chapter. (Devices usually understood as poetic in nature—for example, rhyme, meter, and *synesthesia*—will be examined in the concluding chapter.)

The use of antithesis in poetry is so extensive that it is difficult to find studies devoted to it. Even Aristotle, the master of systematic definitions, mentions antithesis only in passing in his work, *On Rhetoric.*[17] Defined concisely as "the bringing together of contraries"—be they words, phrases, or ideas—antithesis in poetry has been investigated most thoroughly perhaps in the work of the Victorian poet Gerard Manley Hopkins (1844–1889), who also developed his own elaborate theories about it.[18] As will be demonstrated, antithesis is a powerful poetic device because it can elucidate relationships between situations or ideas that would otherwise not be apparent. Furthermore, the unexpected and even iconoclastic character of antithesis often nullifies the expectations of readers (or listeners) because it reverses the thematic expectations developed by other devices such as anaphora and auxesis. Anaphora, of course, is nothing uncommon in song lyrics; the very design of most songs—with stanzas, a repetitive chorus, even outros that repeat as they fade out—effectively requires anaphora. But even within the conventional structure of a song, a poet like Sabina is capable of using anaphora in innovative ways. The gradual incrementation of auxesis has been employed in everything from jokes told by stand-up comedians to melodramatic film dialogue. In a song such as "Más de cien mentiras" ("More than One Hundred Lies"), the gradual incrementation of auxesis structures nearly every stanza[19] as well as the chorus, where Sabina builds up from *"words,"* *"reasons,"* *"pupils [in which] we see ourselves"* to the *"lies that make life worth living"*: "Más de cien palabras, más de cien motivos / para no cortarse de un tajo las venas, / más de cien pupilas donde vernos vivos, / más de cien mentiras que valen la pena" (*"More than one hundred words, more than one hundred reasons / not to cut one's veins with a single slash, / more than one* hundred pupils where we see ourselves alive, / more than one hundred lies to make life worth living").[20]

Sabina's use of antithesis may be investigated more productively by classifying examples into three categories: lexical antithesis, antithesis of imagery, and antithesis demonstrating these previous categories within a parallel syntactic structure. (The sequence of these three categories itself offers an example of auxesis, since the kinds of antithesis are incrementally more challenging for a poet to establish.) The first variety, that of lexical antithesis, is perhaps the simplest for a poet or lyricist, being little more than the pairing of antonyms: young / old, hot / cold, light / dark, and so on. Random examples of lexical antithesis do little to make a poem distinctive; a series of them, however, related thematically to one another, may help to make a strong poem. With antithesis of imagery one observes a more sophisticated literary technique since the production of a mental image depends at least as much upon the poet's creative ability as it does upon the reception of the reader or listener. One may recognize an example of antithetical imagery in the title "Canción de otoño en primavera" ("Song of Autumn in Springtime"), a famous poem by Rubén Darío (1867–1916), the Nicaraguan poet to whom, in the initial verses of a sonnet listing *"his poets,"* Sabina gives credit for teaching him "la peregrina / alquimia del diamante y la madera," (*"the outlandish / alchemy of diamond and wood"*).[21] In Darío's poem, autumn, a familiar symbol or archetype[22] representing the final years of life, is juxtaposed with the prevailing spring, thus creating more than an anachronistic backdrop but also the mental image of the poem's protagonist clinging to the illusion of youth, which is made clear in the penultimate stanza of the poem.[23] Structural antithesis may be understood as a combination of the first two types—utilizing oppositional vocabulary or images—with an arrangement that makes the antithesis conspicuous when the lyric is sung or printed. In English, this is sometimes regarded as *parallelism* or *chiasmus* and in Spanish as *retruécano*, although those devices may not convey antithetical meanings.[24] Of the three kinds, structural antithesis is the most potent and its creation offers the greatest challenge to the poet.

LEXICAL ANTITHESIS

Through the arrangement of disparate words and images, Sabina conveys poetic insights that are at once vivid, moving, and often humorous. Examples of the three kinds of antithesis are present in his lyrics from the beginning of his recording career. While several of the tracks on *Inventario* features lyrics of an almost superfluously literary quality, the autobiographical "1968" features an unadorned stanza describing Sabina's establishment father in the historical context of upheaval, intellectualism, and student protest taking place throughout the world. Because of the sparse, unevocative nature of its description, the stanza presents itself as an example of lexical antithesis: "Mientras Ché cavaba su tumba en Bolivia / cantaba Massiel en Eurovisión / y mi padre llegaba puntal al trabajo / con el cuello blanco y el traje marrón" ("*While Ché [Guevara] was digging his grave in Bolivia / [Spanish pop singer] Massiel was singing on Eurovisión*[25] */ and my father was arriving punctually to work / in his white collar and brown suit*").[26] This lyric, probably written years before recording the album,[27] shows Sabina as a youthful poet who, despite the rich subject matter, was working largely in a mode of direct description and was not as accomplished at conjuring imagery. The three subjects depicted here—the legendary revolutionary, the pop-music singer, his father—are all engaged in activities expressed in the imperfect tense and followed by complements worthy of serving as examples in a grammar textbook; the verses have more similarities to correct prose than to poetry. But with the juxtaposition of Che Guevara and his father the police inspector, Sabina creates a potent lexical antithesis.

Although *Malas compañías* (1980) is officially Sabina's second album, it may well be considered his debut for its presentation of so many of the recurrent themes of his music.[28] Similarly, the arrangements are more successfully tailored to each track and—unlike *Inventario*, the previous album—there is no sweeping, pretentious orchestration behind his vocals. "Calle melancolía" ("Melancholy Street") and "Pongamos que hablo de Madrid" ("Let's Say I'm Talking about Madrid") are the earliest classics of Sabina's catalogue. The first of these, "Calle melancolía," uses vivid imagery and antithesis to establish the pervasive loneliness and desolation of the singer's metaphorical neighborhood. As Esther Pérez-Villalba explains, the urban landscape, with its cables, antennas, and chimneys "*vomiting smog,*" is further and further removed from the clear, unobstructed "*cielo,*" which in Spanish features the double meaning of "*sky*" or "*heaven.*"[29] The dreary, neutral tones of the grey streets and walls are momentarily defaced by a splash of color: "por las paredes ocres se desparrama el zumo / de una fruta de sangre crecida en el asfalto" ("*against the ocre walls there splashes the juice / from a blood fruit grown in the asphalt*").[30] Throughout the track Sabina conducts a poetic exercise between mundane things that exist and people who do not. For example, he inhabits a neighborhood located in a "*desolate landscape of antennas and cables*"; he returns home only to find "*shadows*" that "*populate*" the hallways and, at night, he embraces the "*ausencia*" ("*absence*") that a departed lover has left in his bed.[31] With the chorus, a synthesis of the sharp contrasts provided by lexical antithesis is achieved, with Sabina singing that he has wanted to move to the "barrio de alegría" ("*neighborhood of happiness*") for years, but has always missed the opportunity to leave the "*melancholy street.*"[32]

Similar to "Calle melancolía," "Pongamos que hablo de Madrid" also features antithesis of imagery to depict the lonely existence of the individual living in a great metropolis. However, in "Pongamos que hablo de Madrid" the references to the city are more specific, more tangible. In the first stanza Sabina locates Madrid as the place "donde se cruzan los caminos, / donde el mar no se puede concebir" (*"where the roads cross, / where the sea is inconceivable"*).³³ These verses invoke the geographical extremes of the capital—being at the center of the Iberian Peninsula and far from the coasts—as well as the famous "Kilómetro cero" plaque of the Puerta del Sol.³⁴ With its references to heroin, gin, oppressive heat, and death, the lyric of this Sabina classic is ultimately much darker than that of "Calle melancolía," an assessment with which the cantautor himself clearly agrees when he admits to Menéndez Flores that the song *"vomits on Madrid in every verse."*³⁵ Yet another track from *Malas compañías*, "Gulliver," references Jonathan Swift's prose satire and, in its outro, offers examples of lexical antithesis, all of which emphasize the central theme of the mediocre multitudes, incapable of understanding, accusing the gifted individual of transgressions such as: "de ser quien habla en el país de los mudos, ... de ser el sabio en el país de los necios, / de ser el malo en el país de los buenos, ... de ser el gigante en el país de los enanos" (*"of being who speaks in the land of the mutes, ... of being the wise man in the land of the fools, / of being the bad man in the land of the good, ... of being the giant in the land of the dwarves"*).³⁶

Sabina admits that he began to take the craft of songwriting more seriously with *Juez y parte* (1985), the studio album he recorded with the band Viceversa.³⁷ The album features more fully developed examples of antithesis in tracks such as "Cuando era más joven" ("When I Was Younger"), "El joven aprendiz de pintor" ("The Young Painter's Apprentice"), and "Princesa" ("Princess"). In these songs, Sabina often employs lexical antithesis to portray the innumerable contradictions that form one's identity. For example, in "Cuando era más joven," there is nothing permanent in the unfettered and at times misguided exuberance of his youth. In this richly autobiographical lyric, Sabina employs anaphora and auxesis to establish the listener's comprehension of a carefree life, only to dismantle it suddenly with the antithetical pairing of "placer" (*pleasure*) and "dolor" (*pain*): "Cuando era más joven cambiaba de nombre en cada aduana, / cambiaba de casa, cambiaba de oficio, cambiaba de amor, / mañana era nunca y nunca llegaba pasado mañana, / cuando era más joven buscaba el placer engañado al dolor" (*"When I was younger, I changed my name at every customs, / I changed homes, I changed jobs, I changed loves, / Tomorrow was never and the day after tomorrow never came,/ When I was younger, I searched for pleasure to deceive the pain"*).³⁸

Yet another song featuring lexical antithesis, as well as some of Sabina's finest poetry, is the fourth track from *Física y química* (1992), "A la orilla de la chimenea" ("At the Edge of the Fireplace"). Menéndez Flores describes the lyric of this ballad as "cargada de poderosas imágenes, extrema, confesional, apasionada ... en la que el autor lleva a cabo uno de los más conseguidos ejercicios literarios de toda su carrera" (*"charged with powerful images, extreme, confessional, passionate ... in which the author achieves one of the most accomplished literary exercises of his entire career"*).³⁹ With this song one senses an early draft of a theme to which Sabina would return more successfully on later albums: the romantic relationship, filled with insatiable desire but also the potential to fall into routine; it is the fear of this routine that finally compels him to abandon the relationship. Sabina has often said that the greatest songs always have a bit of affectation or schlock,[40] which is an insightful observation for, if an artist manages to skirt sentimentality by a hair's breadth, it often produces an emotional impact much more powerful for its proximity to the edge. In "A la orilla de la chimenea," Sabina expresses his convoluted feelings directly to the woman and, were it not for the potent antithetical images, perhaps the lyrics would cross that line between emotionally charged poetry and schmaltzy sentimentality:

Puedo ponerme cursi y decir	I could get cheesy and say
que tus labios me saben igual que los labios	that your lips taste the same as those lips
que beso en mis sueños.	that I kiss in my dreams.
puedo ponerme triste y decir	I could get sad and say
que me basta con ser tu enemigo, tu todo,	That it's enough to be your enemy, your everything,
tu esclavo, tu fiebre, tu dueño.	your slave, your fever, your master.
y si quieres también,	and if you also want,
puedo ser tu estación y tu tren,	I can be your station and your train,
tu mal y tu bien,	your bad and your good,
tu pan y tu vino,	your bread and your wine,
tu pecado, tu dios, tu asesino . . .	your sin, your god, your killer . . .
....	....
y si quieres también,	and if you also want,
puedo ser tu trapecio y tu red,	I can be your trapeze and your net,
tu adiós y tu ven,	your goodbye and your arrival,
tu manta y tu frío,	your blanket and your cold,
tu resaca, tu lunes, tu hastío . . .	your hangover, your Monday, your tedium . . .[1]

[1] Joaquín Sabina, "A la orilla de la chimenea," *Con buena letra* (Madrid: Temas de Hoy, 2002), 123.

Through his use of lexical antithesis in this especially melodic track, Sabina frames many of the extremes to which love compels us. Additionally, the sequencing of religious images in these verses offers clear examples of anaphora and the buildup of auxesis: "tu mal, tu bien, tu pan, tu vino, tu pecado, tu dios, tu asesino."[41] Considering love as an emotion hardly acknowledges its complexity or propensity to turn our lives upside down. In its stacking of antithetical pairings, this unusual love song ventures boldly into this thematic territory, with a perspicacity that is more unsettling than it is reaffirming.

ANTITHESIS OF IMAGERY

With each album, Sabina more convincingly demonstrates his poeticism in the medium of rock music. His development with regard to antithesis is especially remarkable in his albums from the late 1980s forward. In "El joven aprendiz de pintor," from *Juez y parte*, the narrator is a cantautor—undoubtedly Sabina himself—who, suddenly becoming famous, responds to the many critics who ignored his work before but now clamor for his attention. In all six stanzas of the song, Sabina juxtaposes his earlier identity as an artist struggling in anonymity with celebrated names such as Picasso, Camilo José Cela, Montserrat Caballé, and the legendary bullfighter Manolete.[42] Here in this lyric, Sabina seems to eschew lexical antithesis in favor of antithetical imagery, which requires some especially loaded semantics to establish the necessary conceptualization on the part of listeners. One manner of accomplishing this is by comparing his work to that of world-renowned artists, each one famous for their achievement in a different area of creativity: painting, literature, opera, bullfighting. By referencing these famous people in the description of his own accomplishment, Sabina accesses multiple sources of rich imagery. For example, in the stanza leading up to the legendary bullfighter Manolete,[43] Sabina sings of a "*clumsy amateur*" who used to tell the cantautor in jest that no one was better with the "banderillas" (colorful, sharpened sticks used on a bull's shoulders). But now that Sabina "*cuts bull ears*" in glory and has earned the admiration of the tradition's cognoscenti, that same clumsy amateur no longer makes jokes comparing him to Manolete.[44]

Others who shunned Sabina also get what was coming to them. While only a struggling cantautor, Sabina hardly mattered to the powerbrokers of the music business. In fact, as explained in the previous chapter, he was only discovered when the executive director of CBS España heard one of his songs performed by another cantautor busking in the street. But once Sabina became popular, the same people who had ignored him suddenly lined up with lucrative contracts for him to sign. This reversal of fortune is alluded to in the third stanza of the song, when a "*bold and determined*" manager, who previously was always in a meeting when Sabina wished to speak to him, now approaches him "*like a dog*" to request a live performance.[45] In his biography of the cantautor, Maurilio de Miguel recounts a specific instance of a producer named Ramón Mendezona, who had turned away Sabina earlier, but later requested a performance at the annual Fiesta del PCE (Partido Comunista de España) after Sabina had appeared on the television program *Esta Noche* the night before. Sabina told Mendezona facetiously, "*It's a shame. If you would have contacted me just yesterday, I would have cost you 30,000 pesetas. Today, however, it's going to cost you 200,000 if you want to take me to the party [a concert for the Communist Party of Spain]*."[46] Sabina saves his final comeuppance in "El joven aprendiz de pintor" for a music critic who, only a few years earlier, had disapproved of the cantautor's transition to a more radio-friendly sound. Because of Sabina's clever play on words, listeners know the exact historical moment between the release of two albums to which he is referring: "¿Y qué decir del crítico que indignado me acusa / de jugar demasiado a la ruleta rusa? / Si no hubiera arriesgado tal vez me acusaría / de quedarme colgado en calle melancolía . . ." ("*And what about the indignant critic who accuses me / of playing too much Russian roulette? / If I had not taken the risk maybe he would accuse me / of staying broke on melancholy street . . .*").[47]

"Princesa," also from *Juez y parte*, is one of Sabina's best-known songs.[48] The lyric takes the form of a monologue addressed to a girlfriend addicted to drugs, which are only alluded to in the lyrics. The song was based on the struggles of a real person with whom Sabina was acquainted during the height of the movida movement.[49] The mode of discourse in this song is direct, with the singer rebuking the girlfriend in much the same manner as Dylan does in "Don't Think Twice, It's All Right," "It Ain't Me, Babe," "Like a Rolling Stone," "Positively Fourth Street," and "Idiot Wind." The narrator of "Princesa" explains that he will do no more to enable her passage down the path of self-destruction; but neither can he save her. According to Sabina's friend, Joaquín Carbonell, "Princesa" is not only the best song on *Juez y parte*, but also the most fully developed selection on the album.[50] The development to which he is referring exists in the form of the before-and-after imagery, with the song's first stanza demonstrating how far one can fall through such an addiction, and how drugs can absolutely destroy relationships and lives. The antithesis here is provided by the descriptions of the "*princess*" before and after she became hopelessly addicted:

Entre la sirosis	*Between cirrhosis*
y la sobredosis	*and overdose*
andas siempre, muñeca,	*you're always going, dear,*
con tu sucia camisa	*in your filthy shirt*
y, en lugar de sonrisa,	*and, instead of a smile,*
una especie de mueca.	*some kind of a grimace.*
Cómo no imaginarte,	*How not to imagine,*
cómo no recordarte	*how not to remember you*
hace apenas dos años,	*hardly two years ago,*
cuando eras la princesa	*when you were the princess*
de la boca de fresa,	*with the strawberry mouth,*
cuando tenías aún esa	*when back then*
forma de hacerme daño.	*you still had that way of hurting me.*[1]

[1] Joaquín Sabina, "Princesa," *Con buena letra* (Madrid: Temas de Hoy 2002), 24.

The repetitive verse from the chorus and outro, "Ahora es demasiado tarde, princesa" ("*Now it's too late, princess*"), underscores the irreversibility of the destruction so poignantly depicted in the stanzas.[51] But the song is more than a frank description of a drug addict attempting to rob a pharmacy, or even of her boyfriend's concern over the inevitable overdose. Rather, "Princesa" is a harsh illustration of how even love is incapable of overcoming the shackles of drug addiction.[52] In other words, "Princesa" is a brief treatise on how substance abuse often negates that most powerful and redemptive of human emotions. Considering the cultural context in which "Princesa" was written, the song may be interpreted as a cautionary tale about the uninhibited lifestyle of the movida, making it not only one of the most remarkable examples of Spanish rock from the 1980s, but also one of Sabina's most acute observations about life in the capital during the decade.[53]

On the album *Hotel, dulce hotel* (1987), the lyrics of at least three of the nine tracks represent Sabina's finest poetic achievement to that point in his career. Although the quality of the album as a whole is inconsistent, *Hotel, dulce hotel* consolidated a national fan base for Sabina and made him a bankable artist within the music industry.[54] Sabina composed the songs for the album during a month spent on the island of El Hierro, in the Canary Islands, where he sought to escape from distractions, most of which he created for himself through his notoriously carefree lifestyle in Madrid and his appetite for sex and drugs. The result of this self-imposed exile was not only a few of the best lyrics Sabina had written, but also isolation as the central theme of the album. The very title, *Hotel, dulce hotel*—a tongue-and-cheek revision of the common expression, "*Home, sweet home*"—suggests the pleasure of being out of one's normal domain. "Así estoy yo sin ti" ("*This Is How I Am without You*"), the album's first single—and, in fact, Sabina's first love song[55]—features a myriad of images, some antithetical, some simply expressing abandonment. The song is structured as a series of potent similes, with the juxtaposed images producing both surprise and incongruity. Given this structure, the song is reminiscent of Leonard Cohen's "Bird on the Wire" (1969), although in that composition the Canadian singer-songwriter's similes, fewer in number than Sabina's, are built upon nouns: a bird, a drunk, a worm, etc. With Sabina, most verses in the song's ten stanzas begin with a carefully chosen adjective, establishing anaphora based on masculine-gendered examples of that part of speech. Loneliness is the result of isolation and the inexorable quality of time. The anaphora of the stanzas enhances the sense of loneliness because a sense of endlessness is produced:

Extraño como un pato en el Manzanares,	Weird, like a duck in the Manzanares River,
torpe como un suicida sin vocación,	clumsy like a reluctant suicide,
absurdo como belga por soleares,	absurd like a Belgian singing flamenco,
vacío como una isla sin Robinsón,	empty, like an island without Robinson,
....	....
Inútil . . .	Useless . . .
como el semen de los ahorcados . . .	like the semen of hanged men . . .
Macabro como el vientre de los misiles, . . .	Macabre, like the womb of a missile. . .
Más triste que torero	Sadder than the bullfighter
al otro lado del telón de acero.	on the other side of the Iron Curtain.
Así estoy yo, así estoy yo,	So I am, so I am
así estoy yo, sin ti.	so I am, without you.[1]

[1] Joaquín Sabina, "Así estoy yo sin ti," *Con buena letra* (Madrid: Temas de Hoy, 2002), 74.

Structurally, "Así estoy yo sin ti" features similes as bricks and anaphora as mortar. They are combined to produce yet another effect because, while establishing the singer's interminable isolation, they gradually lead the listener to the chorus where, unexpectedly, the structure is changed. The first line of the chorus begins not with a simile but a superlative, "Más" ("*More*"), and the final two lines feature the only complete sentence in the song: "Así estoy yo . . . sin ti." This is no coincidence or minor detail: wave-after-wave of such powerful similes, without drawing a conclusion until the chorus, expresses quite poetically the singer's loneliness, but also his inability to complete his thoughts following the woman's departure. In other words, the song illustrates how anaphora can lead a listener along an apparent progression and, when the repetition is disrupted, underscore with unexpected force the general sentiment or meaning of the lyric. "Así estoy yo sin ti" is a compelling example of a poetic fusion of structure and meaning.

In "Que se llama soledad" ("That Which Is Called Solitude"), Sabina employs antithesis of imagery repeatedly in the song's three lengthy stanzas as he reworks and builds upon the central theme of "Calle melancolía." Here, the antithesis is generated not only by feeling lonely in the metropolis, but also by the act of searching for a woman to relieve the loneliness, if only momentarily. In an uncommonly candid instance of a poet describing his creative process and the sought-after distraction that interrupts it, Sabina positions poetic composition and amorous conquest as antithetical poles. Adding complexity to such a contradictory state, Sabina reveals that he is most creative in his solitude, and that the poetry that comes forth from his solitude may in turn be used to win over the woman that he desires.

Algunas veces vuelo	Sometimes I fly
y otras veces	and other times
me arrastro demasiado a ras del suelo,	too often I drag myself across the floor,
algunas madrugadas me desvelo	some wee hours I stay up
y ando como un gato en celo	and I go about like a cat in heat
patrullando la ciudad	patrolling the city
en busca de una gatita	searching for a pussy cat
en esa hora maldita	at that damned hour
en que los bares a punto están de cerrar,	when the bars are just about to close,
cuando el alma necesita	when the soul needs
un cuerpo que acariciar.	a body to caress.
Algunas veces vivo	Sometimes I live
y otras veces	and at other times
la vida se me va con lo que escribo,	life escapes from me with what I write,
algunas veces busco un adjetivo	sometimes I search for an adjective
inspirado y posesivo	inspired and possessive
que te arañe el corazón,	that could scratch your heart sharply,
luego arrojo mi mensaje,	then I toss my message,
se lo lleva de equipaje	carried in a bottle,
una botella, al mar de tu incomprensión.	into the sea of your lack of understanding.
No quiero hacerte chantaje,	I don't want to blackmail you,
sólo quiero regalarte una canción.	I only want to give you the gift of a song.[1]

[1] Joaquín Sabina, "Que se llama soledad," *Con buena letra* (Madrid: Temas de Hoy, 2002), 78.

The final lines here suggest that the woman to whom Sabina is sending the song—or, perhaps more accurately, the poem—may not appreciate his gift at all. Instead, she will likely misunderstand it, assuming it to be some form of blackmail, perhaps a ruse to get her into bed. Jorge Luis Borges, identifying the act of creation as the essence of poetry itself,[56] once said that if one doesn't feel the poetic event upon reading it, "the poet has failed."[57] By suggesting such a misunderstanding on the part of the recipient, Sabina calls attention to the considerable amount of work and risk involved in writing poetry, and then sharing it. Stated another way, offering verse to a woman to make progress with her romantically may not always succeed. The chorus of "Que se llama soledad" unites the two contradictory impulses of Sabina—that of being alone to compose and that of finding a woman—when he sings that he speaks to the moon "de esa amante inoportuna / que se llama soledad" ("*of that inopportune lover / that's called solitude*"). Interestingly, given that "Soledad" may be a name for a Hispanic woman, it could be that Sabina has added yet another layer of complexity to his lyrics by veiled reference to an actual person. The concluding lines describing "*aquel verano / que no paró de nevar*" ("*that summer / [in which] it didn't stop snowing*"), provide a final example of antithesis, and perhaps a geographic clue as to whom was receiving his gift of song.[58]

As made clear in the previous chapter, the 1990s were the decade in which Sabina was at the height of his vitality, artistry, and commercial success. Several examples of antithesis from his studio albums of the decade are clearly the products of this zenith of creativity. One of his most beloved songs is his initial foray into the Mexican *ranchera* genre, "Y nos dieron las diez" ("And It Struck Ten O'clock on Us"), from the album *Física y química*. The song recounts a post-concert liaison with a woman who ran a bar somewhere in (apparently) Spanish America.[59] The following year, the narrator returns to the "*town facing the sea*" for another concert, and afterward goes to look for the woman in the same bar. But this time there is no one behind the bar, because the bar itself is now a branch of the "Banco Hispanoamericano" ("*Hispano-American Bank*"). With this unexpected change, the spontaneous, delightful social space of the bar has been replaced by a cold, sterile, seemingly impregnable outpost of capitalism. With a confusion of place reminiscent of a Julio Cortázar short story, the narrator is arrested by the local police after smashing the windows of the bank in his frustration.[60] At this point Sabina sings, "*sé que no lo soñé*" ("*I know that I didn't dream it*") and "*empecé esta canción en el cuarto donde aquella vez te quitaba la ropa*" ("*I started this song in the room where I once was taking off your clothes*").[61] In "Y nos dieron las diez," Sabina juxtaposes not only the extremes of a ludic setting (a bar late at night) and a bureaucratic financial institution (a bank), but—it would seem—conscious and oneiric states. Such possibilities of antithesis (and the resulting ambiguity) serve as the basis for analyzing the song's narrative in the following chapter.

The other early nineties album, *Esta boca es mía* (1994), shows Sabina at perhaps the pinnacle of his lyrical creativity. With a memorable phrase or metaphor at every turn, there is an ebullient, torrential virtuosity evident from the beginning to the end of the thirteen-track album. The fold-out liner notes and lyrics of the album run to eleven pages and are printed with text so small a magnifying glass may be necessary to read them. *Esta boca es mía* features abundant examples of the literary devices examined in this chapter, with Sabina showing a particular fondness for antanaclasis, the rhetorical device according to Aristotle in which a word, or inflections of its root, are repeated with a different meaning.[62] For example, in his warm tribute to Mexican singer Chavela Vargas, "Por el búlevar de los sueños rotos" ("Along the Boulevard of Broken Dreams"), Sabina sings, "*Las amarguras no son amargas / cuando las canta Chavela Vargas / y las escribe un José Alfredo*" ("*Bitterness is not bitter / when Chavela Vargas sings about it / and some José Alfredo writes about it*").[63] In the third track from the album, the beautifully mysterious "Siete crisantemos" ("Seven Chrysanthemums"), Sabina sheds some light on his aversion to monogamy: "*A las buenas costumbres* nunca me ha acostumbrado / del calor de la lumbre del hogar me aburrí" (*"I've never been accustomed to good customs / the warmth of the fire at home bored me"*).⁶⁴ And, in the hilariously autobiographical "El blues de lo que pasa en mi escalera" ("The Blues of What Happens on My Stairway"), the cantautor saves his most salacious example of antanaclasis for the story of an old acquaintance from his schooldays. As presented in the second stanza, he was the most outstanding student in his class but, in spite of all his promise, things began going wrong and he wound up becoming just another working stiff. If becoming *"defeated, bald and broke"* was not bad enough, upon making an unpleasant discovery he suffers a final indignity:

se quedó en los huesos	there was nothing left of him but bones
aquel día	that day
que pilló a su mujer en plena orgía	when he caught his woman in a full-on orgy
con el miembro del miembro (¡qué ironía!)	with the member of the member (what irony!)
más tonto del congreso.	who was the biggest fool in Congress.¹

¹ Joaquín Sabina, "El blues de lo que pasa en mi escalera," *Con buena letra* (Madrid: Temas de Hoy, 2002), 142.

While this instance of antanaclasis with "miembro" is much more puerile than poetic, it does reflect the generally ludic character of the song.⁶⁵ And while that *"biggest fool in Congress"* may have been the other classmate described in the first stanza, Sabina reveals that the cuckold was exceptionally talented: in his youth, he only had to move his lips to make poetry. Perhaps viewing his classmate's misfortune as an exemplary tale—or even a vindication for becoming a rock-and-roll cantautor—in the chorus Sabina exults that he has not changed and is, of course, still crazy about singing the blues.

STRUCTURAL ANTITHESIS

Sabina's final solo albums of the nineties, *Yo, mí, me, contigo* (1996) and *19 días y 500 noches* (1999), feature the finest examples of structural antithesis to be found in his oeuvre. The song "Contigo" ("With You"), from the first of the two albums, depicts a powerful, contradictory sentiment of profoundly loving a woman but being unable to live with her any longer, because whatever passion existed previously in the relationship has now dissipated. This is a theme that Sabina also developed, albeit less memorably, in earlier songs such as "Mentiras piadosas" ("White Lies") and "Amor se llama el juego" ("The Game is Called Love"). Yet again employing anaphora by beginning most verses of each stanza with "Yo no quiero . . ." (*"I don't want . . ."*), Sabina catalogues the trappings of domestic bliss: money socked away until the end of the month, shampoo chosen by the woman, even a swing set in the yard. As he rejects these fixtures of a conventional, long-term relationship, he still understands that love persists and concludes that there is but one way to escape from this impossible situation. Immediately before the chorus, he makes the startling proposal: "Lo que quiero, corazón cobarde, / es que mueras por mí" (*"What I want, cowardly heart, / is that you die for me"*).[66] In a flourish of antithesis that works on the levels of diction, imagery, and orthography, the chorus continues: "Y morirme contigo si te matas / y matarme contigo si te mueres, / porque el amor cuando no muere mata, / porque amores que matan nunca mueren." (*"And die with you if you kill yourself / and kill myself with you if you die, / because love when it doesn't die kills, / because the loves that kill never die"*).[67] With these four verses, the incompatibility depicted throughout the song loses its immediacy and the chorus virtually folds up and closes upon itself, leaving only two contradictory, eternal truths: death can end a love, but love can endure long after death.

The chorus of "Contigo" is, to say the least, an unexpected twist on a recurring theme of Sabina's songs. Carbonell has suggested that the cantautor was influenced by "No es que muera de amor" by Jaime Sabines, a celebrated Mexican poet, when he composed "Contigo."[68] But in spite of its unexpected appearance in a song heard on Spanish radio in the mid-1990s, Sabina has simply reworked the centuries-old *topos* of love's immortality, which perhaps was most famously utilized by Shakespeare in Act V Scene III of *Romeo and Juliet*. Regardless of influence, the structural antithesis of the chorus and outro of "Contigo" stands as one of Sabina's finest poetic achievements, a composition that Menéndez Flores calls a *"canto to eternal love as cinematographic as [it is] utopic."*[69] The song's poetry—coupled with its improbable country-western feel, courtesy of Wayne Bridge's understated pedal-steel guitar[70]—makes "Contigo" a classic of Spanish popular music.

"Y sin embargo" ("And Yet"), from the same album, depicts another excruciating contradiction within a romantic relationship. As a Sabina song—that is, music combined with a poetic lyric—its greatness is equal to or surpasses that of "Contigo." In fact, Valdeón has correctly asserted that "Contigo" and "Y sin embargo" are part of Sabina's *"inescapable"* catalogue,[71] and the cantautor himself includes the two songs as among his three or four favorites.[72] In the case of the second one, beyond the theme of the suffocating domestication of love, "Y sin embargo" also concerns infidelity. (Sabina has explained that the song is dedicated to Isabel Oliart, the mother of his two daughters.[73]) Here, Sabina recognizes that the woman whom he is addressing is the first that he has loved so intensely, and he would give his entire life for her. At the same time, however, he would cheat on her with "cualquiera" (*"any other woman"*). Nevertheless, a home without her is an "emboscada" (*"ambush"*), an "oficina" ("*office*") as barren as a closed bank, and with her return comes the profoundly Spanish "fiesta en la cocina" ("*celebration in the kitchen*").

The structure of this powerful song is unusual, eschewing the standard arrangement of stanzas (verses) alternating with a chorus and a bridge. Instead, there is an ebb and flow in the song, a subtle rise and fall of the melody, an intimacy of its discourse—as if the deeply conflicted feelings of the lyric were reflected in the music. The chorus of "Y sin embargo" is a starkly poetic expression of the extremes of the relationship:

Y me envenenan los besos que voy dando	And the kisses that I give poison me
y sin embargo, cuando	And yet, when
duermo sin ti contigo sueño	I sleep without you I dream about you
y con todas si duermes a mi lado	and about them all if you're at my side
y si te vas me voy por los tejados	and if you leave, I go along the rooftops
como un gato sin dueño,	like a stray cat,
perdido en el pañuelo de amargura	lost in the handkerchief of bitterness
que empaña, sin mancharla, tu hermosura.	that sullies, without staining, your beauty.[1]

[1] Joaquín Sabina, "Y sin embargo" *Con buena letra* (Madrid: Temas de Hoy, 2002), 164.

Sabina puts some of his most unforgettable metaphors into "Y sin embargo": this consuming love that captivates as much as it repels is a *"telephone ringing in a phone booth, / a palm tree / in a wax museum, / an exodus of dark swallows."*[74] Sabina's next to last metaphor—the "ramos de rosas con espinas" ("*bouquets of roses with thorns*")[75]—could be considered an appropriate representation of any serious romantic relationship. Musically, from beginning to end, "Y sin embargo" features some of the keenest licks and fills on electric guitar that Antonio García de Diego ever contributed to a Sabina song. In its exposition of a dying romance, "Y sin embargo" is not as (melo)dramatic as "Contigo." However, its antithetical images, contradictory impulses, and potent metaphors are woven more intricately and thoroughly into its lyric and music than they are in that other great love song from the album.

"Viridiana," another selection from the same album, departs from "Contigo" and "Y sin embargo" and moves in an entirely different direction. In this raucous ballad, Sabina recounts a passionate love affair (of sorts) with a Mexican prostitute. The setting is a Tijuana cabaret called "el México La Nuit" and, with its *mariachi*-imbued melody and arrangement, Sabina seems to pay tribute to Mexican popular culture or, more specifically, to the country's "Golden Age" of film. In this regard, the song is a spicy paean to the country's rich culture, in the style of his tribute to Mexican singer Chavela Vargas, "Por el búlevar de los sueños rotos." Viridiana introduces herself to the Spanish narrator by saying her last name is "veinticinco mil" (*"twenty-five thousand*"—pesos, the listener can only imagine, which is what she charges for her favors). In spite of ruining his relationship with his family, the narrator continues to see Viridiana because "*with her every night is 'Nochebuena'*[76] / *and the Carnival never ends.*" Very likely a fictional story due to its hyperbole, "Viridiana" offers another example of antanaclasis, a rhetorical device that could perhaps be understood as the antithesis of antithesis since there is no antonym or 180° reversal of a word's concept but, as previously explained, the same word (or its root) is repeated with a change in its meaning. Here, the narrator relates what made his relationship with the expensive prostitute seem like a bargain: "Tantas cosas me dio que no me daban, / tantas caricias casi de verdad, / que a mí se me olvidó que trabajaba / y ella no se acordó de trabajar" ("*So many things she gave me that [others] did not, / so many caresses that were almost sincere, / that it slipped my mind that she was working / and she didn't remember to work*).[77] Here, with reference to "*work,*" the narrator is so smitten that he loses sight of the fact that Viridiana only does what she is doing for money; for her part, with such a steady and hopelessly enamored client, she no longer feels compelled to work as hard. In other words, the narrator no longer takes account of the transactional aspect of their relationship, and Viridiana no longer provides her services with any enthusiasm. But it hardly makes a difference to this client.

"Tan joven y tan viejo" ("So Young and So Old"), the thirteenth and final track from *Yo, mí, me, contigo*, is a deliberately autobiographical song in the style of "El blues de lo que pasa en mi escalera," "Cuando era más joven," "A mis cuarenta y diez" ("Upon Turning Forty and Ten," from *19 días y 500 noches*), and "Me pido primer" ("Me First!" from *Alivio de luto*, 2005), among others.[78] The cantautor has always maintained that his music is unavoidably autobiographical.[79] But while "Cuando era más joven" was recorded in the previous decade and depicted the cantautor during his carefree youth, "Tan joven y tan viejo" reveals how Sabina felt in his late forties at the height of his professional success. It is a song sprung from a midlife self-assessment that—not surprisingly—also takes account of his artistic achievement. "Tan joven y tan viejo" is composed with neither the exuberance of "Cuando era más joven" nor the mordant wit of "A mis cuarenta y diez." The very title of the song, as with "Hotel, dulce hotel," "Y sin embargo," and "Vinagre y rosas" ("Vinegar and Roses"), underscores the antithesis of its lyric. Devoid of chorus, "Tan joven y tan viejo" has a simple structure of six four-verse stanzas; the words of the title are evoked only in the last verse of the song, which concludes with Sabina croaking Dylan's iconic refrain, "like a rolling stone."[80] After relating some of his childhood memories—"el álbum de cromos ... los niños que odiaban los espejos" ("*the album of collectable stickers ... the boys who used to hate mirrors*")—the second stanza offers a brilliant example of antithetical imagery, contrasting the youth with nothing to offer but his enthusiasm and the grande dame, symbolizing life, who beckons provocatively to him: "Apenas vi que un ojo me guiñaba la vida / le pedí que a su antojo pusiera de mí; / ella me dio las llaves de la ciudad prohibida, / y todo lo que tengo, que es nada, se lo di" (*"I barely saw the eye of life winking at me / I asked her to do whatever she wanted with me; / she gave me the keys to the forbidden city,/ [and] all that I had, which is nothing, I gave to her"*).[81]

Yet as poignant as that stanza may be, Sabina saves his best verses for the second half of the song when he reflects on the reactions of others to his occasionally difficult personality: "por decir lo que pienso sin pensar lo que digo / más de un beso me dieron (y más de un bofetón)" (*"for saying what I think without thinking [about] what I say / more than one kiss they gave me (and more than one slap in the face))."*[82] The use of parentheses here is unusual for Sabina, suggesting perhaps he was especially concerned with this lyric being considered as poetry, to be read, rather than merely sung. In these two verses one observes at least one example of antithesis: first, there is the lexical and structurally balanced *retruécano* of the verbs "pensar" and "decir"; and, finally, the clear antithesis of "beso" and "bofetón." At the vertices of these extremes, Sabina positions himself as an artist among others of the same age, although even in his late forties he predicts—correctly, in fact, as his next album would prove—that he still had much more to give. Here, starting with the reference to "Adiós muchachos," an especially poetic *tango* from the twenties,[83] Sabina reaffirms his strength and resilience as an artist, even drawing the inevitable comparison between himself and Bob Dylan: "Así que de momento, nada de adiós muchachos / me duermo en los entierros de mi generación, / cada noche me invento, todavía me emborracho, / tan joven y tan viejo, like a rolling stone" (*"So, for the moment, I'm not saying 'goodbye boys,' / I'm [only] sleeping at the burial of my generation, / every night I invent myself, I still get myself drunk, / so young and so old*, like a rolling stone").[84] With the self-portrait of the middle-aged cantautor in "Tan joven y tan viejo," Sabina has updated the activities of the youth he described eleven years earlier in "Cuando era más joven." While that young man dreamed of leaving his hometown on the *"dirty trains"* heading north, the electric cantautor of the mid-1990s has courted fame and fortune—and won them both. From the vantage of 1996, Sabina considers his place among contemporaries: he is successful, still manages to re-invent himself, and has much more music left in him. But the contradictions persist within the personalities of the young and old Sabina. While the adolescent looked for *"pleasure"* to mask the *"pain,"* the adult Sabina faces a contradiction impossible to resolve, for it is between resting on his laurels—which he refuses to do—and not becoming older. The deepest meaning of "Tan joven y tan viejo" is reflected in one of the many aphorisms compiled by Menéndez Flores in an appendix of his biography. In late 1994, shortly before recording *Yo, mí, me, contigo,* the cantautor said, "Hay que envejecer sin madurar" (*"One has to age without maturing"*).[85] Facing their mid-life crisis, many men would purchase a sports car, or (try to) get a mistress. Sabina, instead, decided to record his masterpiece with his next studio album as a solo artist.

That album, *19 días y 500 noches,* is Sabina's personal favorite among his fifteen studio albums.[86] Emilio de Miguel Martínez identifies it as the Andalusian's album of *"full maturity"* in which *"all his musical and thematic tendencies converge."*[87] In addition to selling more than 500,000 copies, Sabina won four major awards for *19 días y 500 noches*—including best pop song and best album—during the Premios de la Música ceremony held in 2000.[88] Anxious to return to solo work after a contentious collaboration with Argentinian musician Fito Páez, the album *Íntimos enemigos* (1998), Sabina pushed himself relentlessly to compose new material for his next album.[89] According to Menéndez Flores, Sabina "no solo escribió sus mejores letras hasta ese momento, sino que *todas* las canciones son redondas" ([*Sabina*] *"did not only write his best lyrics to that point, but all the songs [on* 19 días y 500 noches] *are perfect"*).[90] Among the album's thirteen tracks, several of them stand among the cantautor's most iconic: the eponymous, flamenco-flavored "19 días y 500 noches" ("19 Days and 500 Nights"), the clever detective story "El caso de la rubia platino" ("The Case of the Platinum Blonde"), the evocative snapshot of Spain in the late forties, "De purísima y oro" ("Of Sky Blue and Gold"), and the utopian "Noches de boda" ("Wedding Nights").

But in Sabina's entire repertoire, it is difficult to find another example of antithesis as masterfully conceived as that of "Una canción para la Magdalena" ("A Song for the Magdalene"), his moving tribute—or elegy, perhaps—to an over-the-hill prostitute. With its music composed by Cuban cantautor Pablo Milanés, it is without question Sabina's most irreverent example of antithesis for the manner in which he saturates it with biblical imagery. Making prostitutes or prostitution the subject matter of a song is, of course, not unusual for Sabina, and his list of such compositions includes "Negra noche" ("Black Night"), "Ring, ring, ring," "Por el túnel" ("Through the Tunnel"), "Barbi Superestar" ("Barbi Superstar"), and the aforementioned "Viridiana." While some may conclude that prostitutes represent an unusual or highly controversial topic for a songwriter, even a mainstream rock band such as the Police scored a hit single with "Roxanne" (1978). Sabina has simply researched and mined this particular topic much more deliberately than other songwriters.

"Una canción para la Magdalena" begins in a most unlikely manner, with the singer speaking to someone, a friend perhaps, about a locale out on a lonesome highway where a certain prostitute works. The place is an unremarkable business or store front, perhaps a gas station-garage with a tawdry bar, undoubtedly frequented by truckers. Like the clientele of service stations and restaurants along interstates, the people who frequent this particular place are seldom locals; transience, isolation, and loneliness predominate here. The prostitute is an older woman, well known and hired on numerous occasions by the singer. Recommending her services to the friend, the singer advises, "Y si la Magdalena pide un trago, / tú la invitas a cien / que yo los pago" (*"And if the Magdalene asks for a drink, / you invite her to one hundred / I'll pay for them"*).[91] In spite of the apparent austerity of the place, the singer acknowledges its potential for festivity. It is in the chorus, however, where Sabina creates one of his boldest juxtapositions. Here, he combines the five-star rating scale of hotels with the beauty of the highway *meretrix*—and then links her romantically to Jesus Christ:

Dueña de un corazón	*Owner of such a*
tan cinco estrellas	*five-star heart*
que hasta el hijo de un dios	*that even the son of a god*
una vez que la vio	*once he saw her*
se fue con ella.	*went with her.*
Y nunca le cobró	*And she never charged him*
la Magdalena.	*the Magdalene.*[1]

[1] Joaquín Sabina, "Una canción para la Magdalena," *Con buena letra* (Madrid: Temas de Hoy 2002), 190.

To set the record straight, the Mary Magdalene of the Bible was not a prostitute; however, over the course of many centuries, she has been conflated with them in popular memory. Today, if not a prostitute, her name does suggest a woman of ill repute. True to form, Sabina finds in the ludic atmosphere of the highway brothel the kind of acquaintances he has preferred since (at least) he gave the title *Malas compañías* to his second album: "en la casa de María de Magdala, / las malas compañías son las mejores" (*"in the house of Mary Magdalene, / the bad company is the best"*).[92] If this inversion of conventional taste was not sufficiently audacious, Sabina saves perhaps his best example of lexical antithesis, here in a parallel syntactic structure, for the final two verses:

Entre dos curvas redentoras[1]	*Between two redemptive curves*
la más prohibida de las frutas	*the most forbidden of fruits*
te espera hasta la aurora,	*awaits you until the dawn,*
la más señora de todas las putas,	*the finest lady among all the whores,*
la más puta de todas las señoras.	*the biggest whore among all the ladies.*[2]

[1] In Spanish, the adjective "redentora" has two possible meanings: that of a sharp curve that brings one back to the beginning, perhaps best translated in English as *"hairpin curve"*; and that of *"redemptive"* in the spiritual sense. Insightfully, Emilio de Miguel Martínez has observed that the use of this particular adjective is *"highly provocative"* and helps to *"maintain or increment the religious tenor of the piece."* Joaquín Sabina. *Concierto privado* (Madrid: Visor, 2008), 61.
[2] Ibid., 190.

A song about a hard-working prostitute who refused to charge at least one client (no matter his connections) could easily slip into the realm of cliché. But "Una canción para la Magdalena" becomes a paean to all prostitutes and, with its daring combination of the divine and the kitschy, of the sacred and the profane, it flirts with blasphemy to create a remarkably original and affecting synthesis. Sabina has stated that "Una canción para la Magdalena" expresses the high regard he holds for all prostitutes, not merely the ones he has known. Sabina's interest in prostitutes is more than merely sexual; by his own admission he both loves and respects them, and claims to have paid some twice as much as what they charged, even when he did not have sex with them.[93] When asked to respond to the people who claim that he has fostered a very negative image of women in his songs about prostitutes, the cantautor declined by saying, "creo que exprimí el limón en *Una canción para la Magdalena*. Pienso que lo que tenía que decir al respeto ya lo he dicho" (*"I believe that I exhausted the topic in 'A Song for the Magdalene.' I think that what I had to say with respect to the matter I've already said"*).[94] It could be said that for Sabina a prostitute working the lonesome highway represents the antithesis of a wife in a suffocating domestic setting; and while Sabina does hold women in high esteem, the loss of personal freedom that often accompanies marriage is something that he has tried to avoid for much of his life. In his songs and interviews, as we have seen, he has repeatedly expressed his displeasure at the prospect of a conventional marital relationship.[95]

Sabina y Cía. Nos sobran los motivos (2000), Sabina's third live album, bears witness to his considerable ability as a performer. The two-disc set features one-half of acoustic performances and the other half of electric. Taken as a whole, these live versions of Sabina classics, as well as an original song, "Rosa de Lima" ("A Rose from Lima"), and a new version of "Cerrado por derribo" ("Closed for Demolition") called "Nos sobran los motivos" ("We Have More Than Enough Reasons"), coming at the end of his triumphant decade, are almost uniformly inspired. Lelia Cobo, reviewing the album for *Billboard*, praised its "immaculate, lush sound" and wrote that lyrically "each song is a gem."[96] And yet this live recording begins with a poem, recited beautifully by Sabina and concluded with the dramatic *rasgueos* of Spanish guitar that begin the title track of the album. Perhaps sarcastically, Guillermo Laín Corona has written that "Este adiós" ("This Goodbye"), the sonnet that serves as something of a preamble for "Nos sobran los motivos," is *"one of the strophes most clearly perceptible as poetry since the Renaissance."*[97] Programmed at the very beginning of the live two-disc album, "Este adiós" is antithetical before a single word is rasped by its poet. The subject of the poem is the long-overdue dissolution of a relationship; the affair has gone on so long, so interminably and without further justification it would seem, that "*there are more than enough reasons*" to end it, which is the conclusion that becomes the chorus of the song that follows. The message here is not the "can't live with you, can't live without you" of earlier songs, but rather, bluntly, "get lost, we're through." The initial stanza of "Este adiós" features an abundance of antithetical imagery, carefully structured with the negative concept in the initial position and the positive—now an impossibility—concluding each verse: "Este adiós no maquilla un hasta luego, / este nunca no esconde un ojalá, / estas cenizas no juegan con fuego, / este ciego no mira para atrás" ("*This 'goodbye' does not conceal an 'until later,' / this 'never' does not hide a 'god willing,' / these ashes do not play with fire, / this blind man does not look back*").[98] It seems fitting to conclude this chapter about the poetics of Sabina's song lyrics with a sonnet. But Sabina's subsequent albums also feature striking examples of antithesis. The album *Dímelo en la calle* (2002), in particular, utilizes the device often, perhaps most memorably in "La canción más hermosa del mundo" ("The Most Beautiful Song in the World").[99] But in the later albums it is more of a challenge to interpret the song lyrics because it is nearly impossible to determine who the author of a particular verse may be—an observation made by others who have considered the selections on *Alivio de luto*, *Vinagre y rosas*, and *Lo niego todo* (2017).[100]

Through literary devices such as anaphora, antanaclasis, and auxesis, used in his song lyrics alongside examples of antithesis, Sabina does much more than convey images and concepts—he also directs the thought of his listeners, often leading them to unexpected conclusions. The sense of surprise or astonishment that his verses often produce is one of the main reasons Sabina is so highly regarded as a lyricist. His prodigious power to move his listeners emotionally is extraordinary in the medium of rock music, and more akin to the ability of the finest poets to similarly move their readers with their verse. As Sabina has admitted on occasion, he originally wanted to become a poet, but life steered him down the path of the cantautor. At the 2002 recital at El Escorial where he made that admission, Sabina also explained that his unforeseen career has suited him well since "*it's much more exciting to scream poetry at people from a stage.*"[101] Antithesis suits Sabina's art because, like the device itself, the sentiments conveyed in his songs often exhibit extremes that typically venture beyond the affective range of the mainstream.

NOTES

1. "Treinta aforismos de verano. Primera entrega," *Esta boca es mía. Edición completa de los versos satíricos*, Illus. Gustavo Otero (Barcelona: Ediciones B, 2010), 358.

2. See Colmeiro's "Review of Esther Pérez-Villalba's study, *How Political Singers Facilitated the Spanish Transition to Democracy, 1960–1982: The Cultural Construction of a New Identity*," *Bulletin of Spanish Studies* 86 (2009): 449–50.

3. Much of the best research on Sabina's lyrics and poetry has been published in the past five years. In particular, see the collection edited by Laín Corona, *Joaquín Sabina o fusilar al rey de los poetas*.

4. Luis García Montero, "El mundo de Joaquín Sabina," in *Joaquín Sabina, Ciento volando de catorce* (Madrid: Visor, 2001), 8.

5. Carl Eric Scott, "What Bob Dylan Means to Literature, and to Song," *Modern Age* 59, no. 2 (Spring 2017): 76.

6. In spite of the fact his song lyrics have received more acclaim, Sabina should not be underrated as a musical composer. As Argentinian producer-musician Alejo Stivel points out, Sabina excels at creating, highly original melodies, such as that of "19 días y 500 noches." Quoted in Valdeón, *Sabina. Sol y sombra*, 317.

7. Joaquín Sabina and Javier Menéndez Flores, *Sabina en carne viva. Yo también sé jugarme la boca* (Barcelona: Ediciones B, 2006), 108.

8. Carbonell, *Pongamos que hablo de Joaquín*, 188. Sabina makes a similar but more elaborate explanation during the extended interview with Menéndez Flores, *Sabina en carne viva*, 106.

9. Sabina's first stanza of verse: "Las cosas que me dices cuando callas, / los pájaros que anidan en tus manos, / el hueco de tu cuerpo entre las sábanas, / el tiempo que pasamos insultándonos" (*"The things that you say to me when you're silent, / the birds that nest in your hands, / the hollow of your body between the sheets, / the time that we spend insulting each other"*) recalls several of Neruda's poems of the collection, both in terms of the imagery—birds, hands, sheets—and general vocabulary. "Inventario," *Con buena letra* (Madrid: Temas de Hoy, 2002), 28. Compare Sabina's stanza with, for example, a few of the verses from Neruda's poem number 15: "Me gustas cuando callas porque estás como ausente, / y me oyes desde lejos, y mi voz no te toca. / Parece que los ojos se te hubieran volado / y parece que un beso te cerrara la boca." *Veinte poemas de amor y una canción desesperada*, ed. Hugo Montes (Madrid: Castalia, 1989), 103.

10. Laín Corona, "Sabina ¿no? es poeta," 81.

11. Sabina and Menéndez Flores, *Sabina en carne viva*, 140, 359.

12. García Montero, "El mundo de Joaquín Sabina," 8–9.

13. See the liner notes of the 1988 album, *El hombre del traje gris*, BMG-Ariola, 259322, 1988 (compact disc).

14. Quoted in Luis Cardillo, *Los tangos de Sabina* (Buenos Aires: Editorial Olimpia, 2003), 115.

15. "No quiero que se enfaden los que las han hecho, pero he sido absolutamente incapaz de leerme una tesis doctoral sobre mi persona" (*"I don't want the ones who have done them to get angry, but I have been absolutely incapable of reading a doctoral thesis about my persona"*). Sabina and Menéndez Flores, *Sabina en carne viva*, 122–23.

16. "Anaphora" is repetition, in which the same expression (word or words) recur at the beginning of two or more lines, clauses, or sentences. "Antanaclasis" is the repetition of a word while shifting from one of its meanings to another. "Auxesis" is an arrangement of words in ascending order of gravity. Hugh C. Holman and William Harmon, *A Handbook to Literature*, Sixth edition (New York: MacMillan, 1992), 21; and, Jean Franco, *César Vallejo: The Dialectics of Poetry and Silence*

(London: Cambridge University Press, 1976), 218. To be clear, although these devices are being identified as "rhetorical," they have been utilized in poetry on innumerable occasions and therefore are occasionally described as "poetic devices." Either term—rhetorical or poetic—may be appropriate for the present study since of course the lyrics under discussion have been sung.

17. In Book III (9: 7–9), Aristotle begins discussing some examples of *lexis* featuring opposites, and only in the next paragraph uses the term antithesis. Translator George A. Kennedy explains that Aristotle suddenly "speaks of antithesis as the sort of thing he is discussing" and adds, "[f]or his readers it was hardly a technical term, since the meaning was clear from its two roots, as in *opposition*." *On Rhetoric*, trans. George A. Kennedy (New York: Oxford University Press, 2001), 242–43.

18. See, for example, Maria R. Lichtmann's chapter, "'Thoughts Against Thoughts': Antithesis in Hopkins' Sonnets," in *The Contemplative Poetry of Gerard Manley Hopkins* (Princeton: Princeton University Press, 1989), 100–28.

19. "Stanza" will be used instead of "verse" here, in order to use the second term more productively in reference to individual lines of a song lyric.

20. Sabina, "Más de cien mentiras," *Con buena letra*, 148.

21. Joaquín Sabina, "Mis poetas. Dos sonetos," *Esta boca es mía. Edición completa de los versos satíricos*, illus. Gustavo Otero (Barcelona: Ediciones B, 2010), 382.

22. "The symbol . . . is the communicable unit, to which I give the name archetype: that is, a typical or recurring image. I mean by an archetype a symbol that connects one poem to another and thereby helps to unify and integrate our literary experience." Northrop Frye, *Anatomy of Criticism. Four Essays* (Princeton: Princeton University Press, [1957] 1990), 99.

23. "Mas a pesar del tiempo terco, / Mi sed de amor no tiene fin; / Con el cabello gris me acerco / A los rosales del jardín" ("*Yet regardless of stubborn time, / My thirst for love has no end; / With grey hair I approach / The rosebushes of the garden*"). From the bilingual edition, *Songs of Life and Hope/Cantos de vida y esperanza*, eds. and trans. Will Derusha and Alberto Acereda (Durham: Duke University Press, 2004), 136–41. Compare these verses of Darío with the following stanza, composed entirely by Sabina for the suggestively titled "Canción de primavera" from his last studio release, *Lo niego todo* (2017): "Conseguí llegar a viejo / verde mendigando amor, / ¿qué esperabas de un pendejo / como yo?" ("*I got to be a dirty / old man begging for love, / what did you expect from a dumbass like me?*"). From the album's liner notes, *Lo niego todo*, Sony Music, 889854133221, 2017 (compact disc).

24. For example, the saying "All for one and one for all" could be seen as an example of structural antithesis because there is an opposition implied by "all" versus "one." But the Spanish popular expression, "Muchas vueltas da la vida, las vueltas dan mucha vida," translated as "*Life gives many twists and turns, and many twists and turns give life*," would be properly understood as simple parallelism or a "retruécano" since "twists and turns" are not necessarily antithetical to the general understanding of "life." Retruécano, then, is the simple repetition of a phrase with a reverse meaning.

25. Massiel is a Spanish pop singer who won the Eurovision Song Contest in 1968 performing "La, la, la," a song originally by the Dúo Dinámico. Massiel

replaced cantautor Joan Manuel Serrat in the competition because the Catalonian refused to sing the song in Spanish.

26. Sabina, "1968," *Con buena letra* (Madrid: Temas de Hoy, 2002), 31. Seemingly to anticipate criticism of this early lyric, Sabina scribbled in the page margin, "¿qué queréis? tenía 18 años" (*"What do you expect? I was eighteen"*).

27. Menéndez Flores, *Perdonen la tristeza*, 50.

28. Ibid., 67.

29. Pérez-Villalba, *How Political Singers Facilitated the Spanish Transition*, 188–89.

30. Sabina, "Calle melancolía," *Con buena letra*, 38.

31. Lola Pérez Costa has compared the protagonist of this early song with don Quijote because, as he walks through the city, he compares himself to someone who travels "a lomos de una yegua sombría" (*"on the back of a dark mare"*). Cervantes' hero famously travels on what was formerly an old work horse. Also reminiscent of don Quijote, Sabina's protagonist encounters disillusioning paradoxes in the course of his travels, for example, the *"doors that deny what they hide"* and the *"shadows that populate the halls."* See "La melancolía en la obra de Joaquín Sabina," *Espéculo: Revista de estudios literarios* 26 (2004), http://webs.ucm.es/info/especulo/numero26/sabiname.html (accessed June 29, 2019).

32. Sabina, "Calle melancolía," *Con buena letra*, 38.

33. Sabina, "Pongamos que hablo de Madrid," *Con buena letra*, 42.

34. The "Kilómetro cero" (*Zero Kilometer*) plaque reads "Origen de las carreteras radiales," and thus marks the very spot from which the major national highways radiate outward to the distant regions of Spain.

35. Sabina and Menéndez Flores, *Sabina en carne viva*, 128.

36. Sabina, "Gulliver," *Con buena letra*, 41.

37. Sabina and Menéndez Flores, *Sabina en carne viva*, 127.

38. Sabina, "Cuando era más joven," *Con buena letra*, 63.

39. Menéndez Flores, *Perdonen la tristeza*, 181.

40. Valdeón, *Sabina. Sol y sombra*, 259.

41. Ibid., 123.

42. Sabina, "El joven aprendiz de pintor," *Con buena letra*, 65.

43. Born Manuel Laureano Rodríguez Sánchez in 1917, Manolete is unquestionably Spain's most legendary *torero*. He died in Linares, in August 1947, after being gored by a formidable bull named Islero; Franco then ordered three days of national mourning.

44. Ibid., 65.

45. Ibid.

46. Miguel, *Joaquín Sabina*, 108.

47. Sabina, "El joven aprendiz de pintor," *Con buena letra*, 65.

48. "Princesa" features lyrics written by Sabina and music composed by Antonio Muriel. Menéndez Flores, *Perdonen la tristeza*, 100.

49. See Valdeón, *Sabina. Sol y sombra*, 112. In his series of interviews with Menéndez Flores, the cantautor himself reveals that the *"princess"* was a beautiful young woman from Logroño who struggled with heroin addiction but, fortunately, overcame it and was living well in Germany. *Sabina en carne viva*, 321–22.

50. Carbonell, *Pongamos que hablo de Joaquín*, 164.

51. Ibid., 24.

52. See Jorge González del Pozo's stimulating essay, "La 'Princesa' de Joaquín Sabina: nostalgia a caballo entre el amor y el miedo," *Bulletin of Hispanic Studies* 87, no. 3 (2010): 353–70.

53. "Princesa" may not be the only example of Sabina expressing his reservations with the vertiginous liberalization of Spanish society following the death of Franco and the advent of the movida. The song "Una de romanos" ("A Gladiator Movie"), from the album *El hombre del traje gris* (1988), looks back nostalgically on dates as a libidinous teenager, going to the cinema and watching boring, black-and-white, Franco-era films that usually took place during the era of the Roman Empire. In a rare coda, Sabina sings, "Hoy que todos andan con vídeos porno-americanos, / para ver contigo me alquilo una de romanos" ("*These days, when everyone goes for American porn videos, / to watch [something] with you I'll rent a gladiator movie*"). *Con buena letra*, 89.

54. Sales of the album exceeded 400,000 copies, making Sabina popular not only in Spain but in Spanish America. Menéndez Flores, *Perdonen la tristeza*, 135.

55. In Sabina's explanation of the hit single's genesis, a journalist friend pointed out to him that he had never composed a love song to that point in his career. "Así estoy yo sin ti" was, consequently, his first attempt at a love song. Menéndez Flores, *Perdonen la tristeza*, 106. What is remarkable is that as moving as "Así estoy yo sin ti" is, Sabina admits that he was not inspired by the love of a particular person at the time, but that "hice una canción de amor sin tener ese amor" ("*I made a love song without having that love*"). Sabina and Menéndez Flores, *Sabina en carne viva*, 133.

56. Borges, of course, was not pioneering a new concept with this assertion. "Poetry" is derived from "poiesis" (Ancient Greek, ποιεῖν, plus the suffix -σις, -sis), which means "to make, create, produce, to compose." "poiesis, n.," *OED Online* (Oxford University Press, March 2020), (accessed April 7, 2020).

57. Jorge Luis Borges and Roberto Alifano, *Twenty-four Conversations with Borges. Including a Selection of Poems*, trans. Nicomedes Suárez Araúz, Willis Barnstone, and Noemí Escandell (Housatonic, MA: Lascaux Publishers, 1984), 37.

58. If the song is about an actual woman, it may be that she was from Argentina or Chile since Sabina sings of the "*strange*" summer in which "*it didn't stop snowing*." However, in the page margin of the lyric, Sabina scribbled, "No se llamaba Soledad" ("*She was not called Soledad*"). "Que se llama soledad," *Con buena letra*, 78.

59. Sabina revealed in an interview that the real-life setting for "Y nos dieron las diez" was not a Spanish-American coastal city, but Lanzarote, in the Spanish Canary Islands. See Valdeón, *Sabina. Sol y sombra*, 204–5.

60. Considering the vandalism depicted in this lyric and his legendary "colocación" ("*placement*") of a Molotov cocktail in a branch of the Banco de Bilbao during his days as a university student, it would be fair to say that Sabina dislikes banks.

61. Sabina, "Y nos dieron las diez," *Con buena letra*, 120.

62. Aristotle, *On Rhetoric*, 243.

63. Sabina, "Por el búlevar de los sueños rotos," *Con buena letra*, 135.

64. Ibid., 137.
65. This is not the first time Sabina has used "miembro" in a play on words. In the song "Oiga, doctor" ("Hey, Doctor"), from the album *Hogar dulce hogar*, the singer complains that in addition to his life becoming intolerable since he became happy, he also suffers from erectile dysfunction. To treat his condition, he takes his doctor's advice and obtains a membership at a gymnasium, only to discover that "cada miembro me hincharon / menos el viril" ("*each member [of my body] swelled up on me / except the viril [member]*"). Sabina, *Con buena letra*, 80.
66. Ibid., 154.
67. Ibid.
68. Carbonell, *Pongamos que hablo de Joaquín*, 192.
69. Menéndez Flores, *Perdonen la tristeza*, 221.
70. Valdeón, *Sabina. Sol y sombra*, 259–60. Wayne Bridge is a legendary pedal-steel guitarist who performed for the Flying Burrito Brothers and innumerable recording sessions.
71. Ibid., 254.
72. Sabina and Menéndez Flores, *Sabina en carne viva*, 136.
73. Carbonell, *Pongamos que hablo de Joaquín*, 228.
74. Ibid., 164.
75. Ibid.
76. "Nochebuena" is, of course, Christmas Eve. But the Spanish can also convey a literal meaning of "*good night*."
77. Sabina, "Viridiana," *Con buena letra*, 165.
78. Another more recent song, "Viudita de Clicquot" ("Little Widow of Clicquot"), from *Vinagre y rosas* (2009), is also autobiographic, although it is difficult to determine authorship since the lyric is cowritten with Benjamín Prado. With perhaps some inside knowledge that Sabina—rather than Prado—authored the vast majority of the lyric, Menéndez Flores accepts it as Sabina's work and cites a verse in his penetrating essay about the autobiographical element in the cantautor's most memorable songs. "Sabina, el gran tema de Joaquín Martínez," *Joaquín Sabina o fusilar al rey de los poetas*, ed. Guillermo Laín Corona (Madrid: Visor, 2018), 22.
79. Speaking to his interviewer, Sabina said, "Como bien has dicho, seas novelista, pintor o cantante, tu biografía está en lo que hace" ("*As you have said well, whether you be a novelist, painter or singer, your biography is in what you do*"). Sabina and Menéndez Flores, *Sabina en carne viva*, 360.
80. Sabina, "Tan joven y tan viejo," *Con buena letra*, 168.
81. Ibid.
82. Ibid.
83. This famous *tango* features music by Julio César Sanders and a lyric written by the poet César Vendani. Its first line is "Adiós, muchachos, compañeros de mi vida" ("*Goodbye, boys, my lifelong companions*"), and in the remaining verses the protagonist, who seems to be close to death from an illness, shares memories from his life. Carlos Gardel recorded the song in 1928. The basic theme of this tango, therefore, could not be more dissimilar to that of Sabina's "Tan joven y tan viejo" which—although wistful in parts—casts a defiant gaze toward the future. For an

entertaining treatment of the tango and its occasional influence on Sabina's music, see Luis Cardillo, *Los tangos de Sabina*.

84. Sabina, "Tan joven y tan viejo," *Con buena letra*, 168.
85. Sabina quoted in Menéndez Flores, *Perdonen la tristeza*, 409.
86. During an interview with Julio Valdeón, Sabina unequivocally selects *19 días y 500 noches* as his favorite among his studio albums. "Tirso de Molina, julio de 2016," in *Sabina. Sol y sombra*, 483.
87. De Miguel Martínez, *Joaquín Sabina*, 20.
88. Menéndez Flores, *Perdonen la tristeza*, 272.
89. Sabina and Menéndez Flores, *Sabina en carne viva*, 264–65.
90. Menéndez Flores, *Perdonen la tristeza*, 254–55 (italics in the original).
91. Sabina, "Una canción para la Magdalena," *Con buena letra*, 190.
92. Ibid.
93. Ibid., 167.
94. Sabina and Menéndez Flores, *Sabina en carne viva*, 166.
95. In an interview focused on the women he has loved throughout his life, the cantautor states—with no small measure of hyperbole—that what he desires most in a woman is *"total availability . . . without costs and commissions."* *Sabina en carne viva*, 305. One can only assume that whatever Sabina means by *"costs"* and *"commissions"* is emotional and not pecuniary.
96. Leila Cobo, "No Sobran los Motivos" [sic], *Billboard* 119, no. 9 (March 3, 2001): 18.
97. Laín Corona, "Sabina ¿no? es poeta," 48.
98. Lyric cited in Ibid., 48–49.
99. Much of the lyric is in a descriptive mode, cataloging meaningful places and things in Sabina's life, but the verse following the first iteration of the chorus is a highly antithetical family portrait, with a *"bastard grandfather,"* a *"single wife,"* a *"godfather"* in the foreign legion, and a *"twin brother"* invested in *"ambulatory shopping."* "La canción más hermosa del mundo," *Con buena letra*, 213.
100. See, for example, Laín Corona, "Sabina ¿no? es poeta," 64–69. For his part, Menéndez Flores dedicated a chapter of his recent book, *Sabina. No amanece jamás* (2016), to the lyrics written by Sabina in collaboration with others because, "es . . . imposible saber con certeza qué versos salieron de la cabeza de Joaquín y qué otros fueron creados por sus compinches" (*"it's . . . impossible to know with certainty what verses came from the mind of Joaquín and which other ones were created by his buddies"*), 14. The selection "Crisis," from *Vinagre y rosas*, features lyrics composed entirely by Sabina. "Crisis" also features examples of antithesis—"Crisis en el cielo, / crisis en el suelo" (*"Crisis in the heavens, / crisis in the ground"*)—although the device is not sustained throughout the song. One of the cantautor's satirical verses of the same title, published in the journal *Interviú* a year before *Vinagre y rosas* was released, appears to be an early version of the song lyric. *Esta boca es mía*, 466.
101. Quoted in Menéndez Flores, *Perdonen la tristeza*, 411.

Chapter 3

"Los cuentos que yo cuento" ("The Stories That I Tell")

"*No soy cantante, soy un contante.*"

—Joaquín Sabina[1]

SABINA AS NARRATOR

While *cantar* is the Spanish verb for "to sing," *contar* is that for "to tell," as in "to tell a story." Understanding what those words mean and then, perhaps, hearing Sabina's gravelly voice during a recent concert, one may fully appreciate his witticism.[2] During the course of Sabina's career, and especially since the album *Física y química* (1992),[3] his voice has certainly become hoarser. He has also become increasingly more like a poet and less like a songwriter, to the point of nearly abandoning the composition of music altogether, a transformation exemplified by his most recent album, *Lo niego todo* (2017).[4] In the past two decades, Sabina has evolved into much more of a writerly figure, publishing best-selling books of poetry, two hefty collections of satirical verse, an epistolary collection, a compilation of miscellaneous materials, and an assemblage of original artwork.[5]

If Sabina had not become a recording artist, he very likely would have become a poet. In his own estimation, he probably would have become a professor of literature at a provincial university, writing poems in his spare time that "*no one would have ever read.*"[6] On other occasions, Sabina has declared that his goal in life had been to become a writer. After stating that he became a successful cantautor by "*pure accident,*" Sabina confesses, "[m]i proyecto no era ser Dylan, sino Antonio Muñoz Molina" ("[m]*y project was not to be Dylan, but Antonio Muñoz Molina*" [the celebrated Spanish novelist who, like Sabina, is a native of Úbeda]).[7] There are many reasons to believe the sincerity of that confession, but perhaps the most compelling is because Sabina demonstrates considerable talent at that most fundamental skill of the novelist: telling a story. The previous chapter has shown that Sabina does not excel simply at the composition of literary song lyrics because, in most examples, listeners can expect much more than a memorable phrase or two. In fact, his best lyrics showcase an astonishing poeticism in which the entire composition of the lyric—from the first word to the last—lends itself to a unified, coherent meaning.

The narrative dimension of Sabina's songs has received significantly less attention than their poetic qualities.[8] As his biography demonstrates, Sabina has dedicated himself to becoming a poet—both through his song lyrics and in the conventional sense—more than to any other creative activity; in fact, independent of his career as a musician, Sabina has published three collections of serious poetry and two thick editions of satirical verse. In this sense, "poet" is understood as someone who is prodigiously creative in their use of words, with much imagination and expressive ability, but not necessarily a storyteller. But of course poetry can encompass narrative, and it turns out that Sabina's talent for storytelling is considerable. On a general level, the stories that he tells in his songs are oral micronarratives, invoking that richest of traditions which produced *The Iliad*, *The Odyssey*, and *Beowulf*.[9] As we will see, Sabina also structures his stories with classical techniques such as in medias res to heighten the listener's interest in plot development and characterization. In spite of these qualities, Sabina remains a poet who is underappreciated as a narrator. This is probably because he has written many more songs that do not tell a story and so, it would seem, his skill at storytelling is subordinate to his poetic ability in the conventional sense. Furthermore, since he rarely talks about narrative, his accomplishment in regard to storytelling seems to be casually achieved. The predominance of his nonnarrative poetry makes Sabina distinct from literary figures such as Edgar Allan Poe or Jorge Luis Borges, who wished to be considered first as poets but are more admired today for their short stories.[10] But on at least one occasion, Sabina has been candid about his interest in narrative, revealing that as a child his father inspired in him not only a love of words but of putting them together to tell stories.[11] The Andalusian's friend and occasional collaborator, novelist Benjamín Prado, draws attention to the elements of Sabina's storytelling ability:

> He hablado mucho de la categoría de Joaquín como poeta, pero sería injusto no mencionar que, en cierto sentido, sus canciones también esconden a un novelista en miniatura, porque en ellas es muy importante su capacidad para narrar, para contar historias que, efectivamente, tienen su argumento, su protagonista

y sus personajes secundarios, a veces su planteamiento, su nudo y su desenlace a escala.

I have spoken a great deal about Joaquín's importance as a poet, but it would be an injustice not to mention that, in some sense, his songs also conceal a novelist in miniature, for in those songs [his] capacity to narrate, to tell stories, is very important because, effectively they have a plot, a protagonist, their secondary characters, at times their depiction, their climax, and their denouement, all done to scale.[12]

In this chapter, I will analyze the lyrics of eight songs belonging to different periods of the career of this *"novelist in miniature"*: "Ciudadano cero" (1985), "Pacto entre caballeros" (1987), "¿Quién me ha robado el mes de abril?" (1988), "Medias negras" (1990), "Peor para el sol" (1992), "Y nos dieron las diez" (1992), "El caso de la rubia platino" (1999), and "¿Qué estoy haciendo aquí?" (2017).[13] While there are many approaches that could elucidate his skill as a storyteller, the analysis of these particular songs will demonstrate that Sabina uses sophisticated narrative techniques elaborated upon by such theorists as Gérard Genette, Wayne C. Booth, and Tzvetan Todorov. There have been, of course, many singers and songwriters who have demonstrated considerable skill as storytellers. A few of them are quite adept at developing character—fleshing out, as it were—the protagonists and antagonists as they sing their dialogue,[14] which represents an aspect of narrative-in-song that is mostly unremarkable in Sabina's *oeuvre*. Nevertheless, the songs being examined in this chapter show Sabina to have an exceptional talent for structuring narratives, even to the extent of working in literary genres as select as the fantastic and the detective story.

STRUCTURING NARRATIVE

At the most basic level, narratives are usually linear with a beginning, middle, and end. But the ordering of events, presentation (or omission) of details, perspective, commentary, and even involvement of the narrator in the story being told are all key considerations when we analyze a more sophisticated and intriguing narrative. And while those considerations are essential to virtually any story told well, whether its form is that of a novel or short story, other considerations such as concision, ellipsis, precision of vocabulary, and carefully crafted conclusions (often producing surprise) are of paramount importance when the texts are much shorter in length.[15] A song lyric featuring a narrative is one example of this kind of short text, and many of the same considerations for composing short stories and micronarratives also apply to narratives embedded in song. For example, a standard pop or rock song represents a medium of aural expression normally listened to, from beginning to end, in a matter of a few minutes; the brevity of the medium heightens the intensity of the narrative's final effect since the typical listener is less likely to be distracted by something else and thereby disrupt his or her full immersion in the story.[16] For his immense vocabulary and literary acumen, Sabina is especially well suited for these shorter narrative exercises. One of his earliest examples, "Ciudadano cero" ("Citizen Zero"), is among his personal favorites; it also his first attempt at writing the lyric for a «novela negra»—a "*noir*" or "crime novel"—and putting it to music.[17]

"Ciudadano cero" tells a story in which Sabina himself makes no appearance and the subject matter has nothing whatsoever to do with him.[18] Sabina included the song on *Juez y parte* (1985), the only studio album he recorded with the band Viceversa. During the production of the album, he wished to improve upon the pop/rock sound he had debuted on the previous album, *Ruleta rusa* (1984), this time with more talented musicians and a style of production that sounded less a product of its time. "Ciudadano cero" recounts the fictional story of a Spanish mass murderer who, after renting a room in a hostel, opens fire on people in the streets below with deadly results. The song is unusual in Sabina's catalog because of the violent subject matter, as well as for what may be interpreted as an attempt at social commentary. The song's focus on an act of violence perpetrated by a perversely motivated individual is reminiscent of "Family Snapshot," a song by the British singer-songwriter Peter Gabriel, released only a few years before *Juez y parte*.[19] "Ciudadano cero" also recalls the Bruce Springsteen composition, "Nebraska," from the eponymous album of 1982, which references an eight-day crime spree perpetrated by American mass murderer Charles Starkweather in 1958.[20] "Nebraska" is sung from the point of view of the killer and Sabina has indicated that he is not only familiar with the Springsteen album but also admires it.[21] Just like Springsteen's first-person narrator, the killer in Sabina's song shows no empathy; he is a human cipher, just as one would assume a "citizen zero" to be.

The lyric of "Ciudadano cero" features two distinct perspectives, presented in succession but shuffled chronologically, both centered on the violent act at the heart of the song. After those perspectives are presented, the track concludes with the direct speech of the perpetrator. In order to analyze the narrative structure of "Ciudadano cero" more productively, it will be helpful to use some terminology from Gérard Genette's influential work, *Narrative Discourse* (1980). The term "story" refers to what we may say actually happens sequentially, the raw material of Sabina's song from the moment the murderer rents the room in the hostel to the conclusion in which he is taken away by the police. A story, as it were, could never be fully presented because it would take hours—even days or months—and, as Genette points out, it may very well be "low in dramatic intensity or fullness of incident."[22] For this reason one of the skills of the narrator is to condense and jumble the order of the story, as well as determine the perspectives that recount it, to make it more engaging for readers and listeners. Therefore, of much greater significance is the manner in which the story is presented to listeners through the more economical and selectively composed text (in this case, a song lyric). Distinct from "story," then, Genette refers to this text alternately as "narrative" or "narrative-as-discourse."[23] (Others have preferred the term "diegesis," which is adapted from film studies.) Within the narrative itself, though, there may also be component narrative discourses, often representing diverse perspectives that distance readers and listeners from a more complete understanding of the story.

The first instance of narrative-as-discourse in "Ciudadano cero" is that of a distraught hostel manager who had rented the room to the killer without suspecting the mayhem to come. This is an unusual perspective with which to begin the song because the hostel manager's perspective is informed after the fact. Sabina has begun the story of "Ciudadano cero" after it has effectively ended. Also, the discourse provided by the manager indicates quite clearly that he is being interviewed by a police inspector and attempting to avoid being held responsible in any way for the horrific crime: "Está usted perdiendo / su tiempo conmigo, / señor comisario . . . Yo no les pregunto / nunca a mis clientes / datos personales, / me pagan y punto . . ." (*"You are wasting your time with me, Mr. Inspector . . . I never ask my clients for personal information, they pay me and that's it . . ."*). At this juncture, however, listeners do not fully comprehend what happened; instead, the only indication of the immense tragedy is when the manager says, portentously, *"no one imagined that he would hide a firearm inside the closet."*[24] Chronologically, therefore, the testimony of the hostel manager must be understood as occurring after the mass shooting.

After the first instance of the chorus, the perspective of an omniscient narrator is introduced. This narrative-as-discourse, working backward in time from the hostel manager's interview with the police, describes the events of the morning leading up to the massacre and its immediate aftermath. This kind of discourse would be identified by Genette as "heterodiegetic" because the narrator is outside of the action of the story; the initial verses of the song, offering the perspective of the manager, would therefore be "homodiegetic" because he is present as a participant in the story he tells.[25] The narrator describes the assassin loading his gun, but also putting on a jacket because he was concerned about his appearance in the inevitable photos. With each successive description provided by the heterodiegetic narrator, however, listeners soon realize that although the descriptions are coolly apathetic, they are not objective. In one of Sabina's most disturbing metaphors, the crime scene is described as "una ensalada / de sangre aliñada / con cristales rotos" (*"a bloody salad seasoned with glass shards"*). Still reporting the aftermath of the massacre, the next verses build gradually, in an irreverent example of auxesis, to the most tragic of the consequences: "Dejó un gato cojo / y un volkswagon tuerto / de un tiro en un faro. / No tuvo mal ojo: dicisiete muertos / en treinta disparos" (*"He left a cat lame / and a Volkswagon with one eye / from a shot in a headlight. / He wasn't a bad shot: seventeen dead / with thirty shots"*).[26]

Notwithstanding the final iteration of the chorus, "Ciudadano cero" concludes with nothing more than the words of the killer himself, which are presented to listeners in the form of direct speech. It cannot be considered narrative in a meaningful way because the killer merely reveals the perverse motive for his action. When he is finally apprehended and put in the back of the police van, he reveals that his motivation for the mass shooting was a morbid attempt at fame and notoriety: "Ahora –decía– / sabrá España entera / mis dos apellidos" (*"Now," he was saying, / "all Spain will know / my two last names"*).[27] In the entire song there is no direct depiction of the massacre itself because Sabina has only related what happened *afterward* through two participants *within* the story, and what happened immediately *before and after* through an insensitive narrator *outside* of the story. The closest thing listeners get to such a description of the violent act at the center of the song is the aforementioned "*bloody salad.*" Even more disturbingly, nothing is offered as the motive other than a desire for instant celebrity, an admission that comes directly from the mouth of the mass murderer. With such a variety of discourse, one would assume that a more complete picture of the crime and the events leading up to it would be provided. Instead, we have a combination of narratives that recalls the diegesis of the Akira Kurosawa film *Rashomon* (1950). The chorus of "Ciudadano cero" underscores the dubious motive and pervasive ambiguity with which the track concludes: "Ciudadano cero / ¿qué razón oscura te hizo salir del agujero? / Siempre sin paraguas, siempre a merced del aguacero. / Todo había acabado cuando llegaron los maderos" (*"Citizen zero / what dark motive made you emerge from your hole? / Always without an umbrella, always at the mercy of the downpouring rain. / Everything had ended when the cops arrived"*).[28]

In "Ciudadano cero" Sabina obscures essential details of the story behind the narrative-as-discourse and provides no more than a raw synthesis of perspectives and direct speech. In this way, listeners are not provided an explanation commensurate with the scale of the tragedy, and so they must use their imaginations. By ending the song with ambiguity rather than answers, Sabina has made the mass shooting even more horrifying to contemplate. With the presentation of peripheral details of a crime, filtered through distinct perspectives, Sabina has also established the hallmarks of the detective story, a genre he would revisit (and perfect) fourteen years later with "El caso de la rubia platino" ("The Case of the Platinum Blonde"), a song to be discussed shortly.

As previously explained, Sabina's habit of staying out all night and carousing, as well as his other legendary bohemian propensities, were particularly intense during the height of Madrid's *movida* cultural movement of the mid-1980s. During that period, Sabina often stayed out past sunrise, occasionally snorting cocaine and consorting with prostitutes. Subsequently, when the experiences from his nocturnal pursuits became the subject matter of his songs, it was never the result of random slumming or investigative "research" to fuel his creativity. Rather, Sabina participated regularly and willingly in the milieu he describes. During the 1980s he was, more than at any other phase of his recording career, *"the principal theme"* and *"absolute protagonist"* of his very best songs.[29] One such song is "Pacto entre caballeros" ("A Pact Between Gentlemen"), the third single from *Hotel, dulce hotel* (1987). "Pacto entre caballeros" captures the frenetic action of Madrid at night during the 1980s, but in a specific context that is even more controversial, even disturbing. At the very beginning of the track, without any forewarning provided by the title, Sabina puts the listener in the midst of an attempted mugging of which he is the victim: "No pasaba de los veinte / el mayor de los tres chicos / que vinieron a atracarme el mes pasado" (*"He wasn't older than twenty / the oldest of the three boys, / that came around to mug me last month"*).[30]

By beginning the song in this fashion, Sabina uses the literary technique of in medias res, in which the story opens in the middle of the action and then the narrator supplies information, through flashbacks and other devices for exposition, all of which leads up to the beginning of the action. Genette has called in medias res "one of the traditional resources of literary narration" and here Sabina employs it to great effect.[31] The fact that the song begins with the depiction of a mugging in progress—an act of violence in which the narrator could be harmed or even killed—increases from the very outset the listener's interest in the story that Sabina is recounting. In the fifth stanza of the lyric, the narrator admits that it could have been any night, even Tuesday the Thirteenth, the equivalent of Friday the Thirteenth in many Spanish-speaking countries. The three delinquents want money for drugs, a motive made obvious by their demand, "Subvenciónanos un pico" (*"Subsidize a shot [of heroin] for us"*).[32] It is also apparent to the narrator that the three are actually high on heroin: "los tres iban hasta el culo de caballo" (*"the three [of them] were stoned out of their minds on heroin"*).[33] Fortunately, one of the youths suddenly recognizes the cantautor, saying, "oye, colega, te pareces al Sabina, ese que canta" (*"Hey, buddy, you look like Sabina, that [guy] who sings"*).[34] This recognition represents a major development in the narrative of "Pacto entre caballeros" because the listener is no longer imagining an unknown, impersonal narrator but Sabina himself, who is recounting the story of what befell him late one night on the streets of Madrid. Without returning the money and items they have taken from him, the three assailants unexpectedly take Sabina out on a prolonged night on the town, drinking, smoking marihuana, snorting cocaine, and even enjoying a quick liaison with three females.

But the threat of danger lurks behind all the revelry. The track features a fast tempo and heavy riffs played by loud, distorted electric guitars. Sabina himself described the music of the track as almost heavy metal or punk.[35] The dark imagery of the situation—this unexpected night out with three strangers who were initially his assailants—is underscored when Sabina remarks that in the photo they take of themselves in a three-minute photo booth "parecemos la cuadrilla de la muerte" (*"we looked like the four horsemen of the Apocalypse"*). After the three youths steal a car, they drop Sabina off at his house and, with a wink, return his wallet, Omega watch, gold chain, and all his money. As they speed off into the night, they tell Sabina, "enróllate y haznos una copla guapa / de las tuyas" (*"Get busy and write one of your beautiful verses about us"*).[36] After the earlier revelation that the homodiegetic narrator of the song is Sabina himself, listeners now learn something even more unexpected: the request by the three young men is, in fact, the genesis of the song itself, for the *"pact between gentlemen"* is one between Sabina and the criminals: "Yo, que siempre cumplo un pacto . . . les tenía que escribir esta canción" (*"I, who always keeps up my end of a deal . . . had to write this song for them"*). In the two concluding verses of "Pacto entre caballeros," Sabina provides the denouement of his unexpectedly engaging narrative: he explains that sometime later a photo appeared in the newspaper featuring the "careto" (*"mug"*) of the tallest of the would-be assailants, who had been apprehended by the police as he tried to escape after burglarizing a millionaire's summer house.[37] With that, the outro of the song provides one of the most famous refrains from the cantautor's entire catalog: "¡Mucha mucha policía!" (*"Many, many police!"*).

Wayne C. Booth, in his description of the varieties of first-person narrators, emphasized the singularity of the *narrator-agent* because his or her participation produces a measurable effect on the course of the story.[38] In the case of "Pacto entre caballeros," the narrative itself is the product of the cantautor's participation in the night's revelry and licentious behavior. Without Sabina's involvement—his role as narrator-agent, to use Booth's terminology—the song lyric describing the night's events would not exist. Conversely, as the narrator-agent is an accomplice (or, perhaps, an accessory after the fact) to the crimes committed during the night, the three young criminals are also accomplices in the act of creating the narrative featured in the song. With the suggestive title of the song, Sabina has not only misled listeners about its subject matter but, more importantly, has elevated the criminals to the status of *"gentlemen"* as a result of their collegial treatment of him.[39] Upon the song's release in late 1987, some critics censured Sabina for what appears to be a glorification of criminal activity in the song; to this charge, the cantautor has not directly responded.[40] In another interview from the same period, however, Sabina declared that he views his narrative craft as that of an impartial, real-life photographer and made no apologies for what he depicts: "No hago apologia ni de la delincuencia ni de las drogas en mis canciones, yo solo hago crónicas. Soy como un fotógrafo, pero no de estudio, sino de los que se llevan la cámara a la calle" ("*I do not apologize for the delinquency or the drugs in my songs, I only do chronicles. I'm like a photographer, but not the kind in a studio, but rather the ones that take their camera out on the street*").[41]

A number of listeners have questioned the veracity of Sabina's story, potentially changing his status of an autobiographical narrator to that of an unreliable one.[42] Pancho Varona, Sabina's longtime musical collaborator and friend, has explained that only the first part of the song—Sabina being approached by muggers but permitted to escape upon being recognized—was true.[43] Menéndez Flores writes that the story told in "Pacto entre caballeros" is actually an amalgam of two separate anecdotes: the aforementioned one recounted by Varona and another incident in which Sabina had his jacket stolen in Elígeme, a concert venue of which he was co-owner, but had it returned discreetly and almost immediately when the thief realized to whom it belonged.[44] Like any accomplished storyteller who blends fact and fiction—a technique formerly understood as *poetic license*—Sabina abruptly dismisses concerns about the veracity of "Pacto entre caballeros" by pointing to the irrelevancy of such questions. For example, in *Sabina en carne viva*, he responds to the question of veracity by emphasizing the porous boundary between biography and fiction: "¿qué importancia tiene si lo que cuentas en una canción te ha pasado o te lo has inventado? Siempre he dicho que mis canciones están hechas con poca imaginación y exceso de autobiografía" ("*What's so important if what one recounts in a song has happened or if it has been invented? I've always said that my songs are made with only a little imagination but an excess of autobiography*").[45] In the initial edition of his song lyrics, *Con buena letra*, the singer is blunter, writing in the upper page margin, "Sí, me pasó, pero . . . ¿qué importa?" ("*Yes, it happened to me, but . . . who cares?*").[46] This minor controversy—whether the incidents really happened—seems to be a case where the narrative is so well structured and executed that, for many, it could not possibly have been a true story, since real life obeys no structures designed to heighten interest. This is an observation made by Borges when, upon being asked if fiction has to be "less unlikely than life," responded by saying, "Reality is not always probable, or likely. But if you're writing a story, you have to make it as plausible as you can, because otherwise the reader's imagination will reject it."[47] Perhaps this discussion would eventually confront Coleridge's famous dictum on the "willing suspension of disbelief for the moment," although that would take us even further away from the subject under investigation. The crux of the matter is that it is ultimately irrelevant whether the story told in this song actually occurred. The narrative-as-discourse in "Pacto entre caballeros" is so well-constructed and provocative that—although it has turned more than a few listeners into disbelievers—it has thoroughly entertained many more.

"Medias negras" ("Black Stockings") is one of Sabina's most energetic and amusing classics. It was recorded during the transitional period of the late 1980s when, following the breakthrough success of *Hotel, dulce hotel*, Sabina found himself composing songs that were perhaps a bit gloomy and inaccessible to his new fanbase, to the point of witnessing his sales decline with the release of 1988's *El hombre del traje gris*.[48] "Medias negras" remains the only selection from the album *Mentiras piadosas* (1990) that Sabina continues to perform in concert.[49] The song, which features an appealing Latino-pop rhythm vaguely reminiscent of Paul Simon's "Me and Julio Down by the Schoolyard," recounts a casual tryst with an unknown woman he meets on the streets of a large city, most likely Madrid.[50] "Medias negras" is memorable for its humor, especially in the aftermath of the liaison that had originally seemed so felicitous to the narrator-agent.

The pop or rock song recounting a romantic liaison with a surprise ending has a long and distinguished history. For example, the story of "Medias negras" recalls that of the Kinks' classic, "Lola" (1970), because of the unexpected revelation leading up to (or, in Sabina's case, following) what the narrator thinks is a satisfying sexual conquest. To the extent that the singer wakes up alone the next day, "Medias negras" also recalls John Lennon's unusually literary description of an unconsummated extramarital affair in "Norwegian Wood" (1965). Chuck Berry's "Memphis, Tennessee" (1959) and Led Zeppelin's "Fool in the Rain" (1979) are two more classic examples. Sabina's earliest attempt is "Tratado de impaciencia" ("Treatise on Impatience") from *Inventario* (1978). In that song—the only one from the album that the cantautor continues to perform without any shame[51]—the first five stanzas describe a date that did not happen because the female failed to show up. This is particularly regrettable for the singer because, as he explains in a flourish of alliteration, the liaison promised the incendiary passion of a *"bonfire"* with *"piel, sudor, saliva y sombra"* (*"skin, sweat, saliva, and shadow"*).[52] However, in the very last verse of the lyric, the singer reveals that he, too, failed to show up.[53] The romantic conquest song with a surprise denouement is a rich thematic vein that Sabina has mined successfully at other points in his career for, apart from "Tratado de impaciencia" and "Medias negras," one could also point to "Peor para el sol," "Y nos dieron las diez," "Viridiana," and "Pero qué hermosas eran," which offers listeners three surprise endings.[54]

The diegesis of "Medias negras" moves quickly, especially in the second through fifth stanzas, due to the clever dialogue which, like that of "Pacto entre caballeros," is laced with *cheli* slang.[55] A work of art—in this case, a narrative in a song—may be judged in part by how effectively its various components work together to convey a greater significance or deeper meaning. Each word or image that (re)structures reality, be it a mere symbol or a metaphor, is essential to the composition of the work. In the finest literary works, and especially in short stories and poems, there are no superfluous elements and each word serves the greater artistic purpose.[56] "Medias negras" is a strong example of a well-constructed narrative because its fast-paced dialogue and vivid metaphors lead listeners to a denouement which, in a manner very similar to that of "Pacto entre caballeros," serves as the genesis of the song itself. Also similar to "Pacto entre caballeros," we see Sabina serving as a narrator-agent who not only participates in the action depicted, but also makes a direct reference to the act of composition shortly before the song concludes.

The first verse of "Medias negras," "La vi en un paso cebra" (*"I saw her in a zebra-striped crosswalk"*) is, effectively, an example of metaphoric foreshadowing; it provides the listener a glimpse of what is to come, although he or she may only come to realize it later. Beginning the lyric with the feminine direct object pronoun "La"—which in Spanish could mean *"It"* or *"Her"*—with no referent until the narrator begins describing what the woman was wearing in the third and fourth verses, serves to deemphasize her person and instead draw attention to the crosswalk that, in any large city, one ventures across at their own risk in spite of the signals. The "paso cebra" becomes, therefore, a metaphor for the peril in which the narrator-agent unwittingly puts himself. Almost immediately, though, he (re)focuses attention on the black stockings and other parts of the woman's *ensemble*, all of which effectively draw listeners away from the initial, subtle warning. In its entirety, the first stanza presents an ambiguous subject in an urban setting, but slowly brings that subject into focus with a final magnification of details, one of which was previously introduced by the song's title: "La vi en un paso cebra / toreando con el bolso a un autobús, / llevaba medias negras, / bufanda a cuatros, minifalda azul" (*"I saw her in a zebra-striped crosswalk / bullfighting a bus with her purse, / she was wearing black stockings, a checkered scarf, a blue miniskirt"*).

The unnamed woman, who perhaps saw the narrator-agent admiring her as she crossed the street, suddenly approaches and asks him for a light; then, to dispel concerns about her intentions (to some extent), says, "—tranqui, que me lo monto de legal—, / salí ayer del talego, / qué guay si me invitaras a cenar" (*"Relax, I'm on the up and up, / I got out of the slammer yesterday, / how nice if you invited me to dinner"*).[57] The dialogue unfolds as the narrator-agent tries to seduce the woman. With the rain falling, he asks from under his umbrella, *"Where are we going, blondie?"* Not missing a beat, she responds with the provocative *"Wherever you take me,"* which in Spanish is a more clever and flirtatious response due to the use of the subjunctive mood: "a donde tú me lleves." Raising the ante on her suggestion, the narrator-agent takes her to his austere apartment which, he assures her, will have everything they need: a mattress, a stove, and each other.

At the apartment, the narrator-agent prepares supper for the two of them—warmed-up soup, a sausage, some bread, red wine—a meal which is at once romantic and picaresque. With the second glass of wine, she strips out of her wet clothes and the narrator-agent can only succumb to her charms. At the same time, however, Sabina provides yet another example of foreshadowing that this casual engagement is going to turn out badly for him. "Y yo que nunca tuve / más religión que un cuerpo de mujer, / del cuello de una nube / aquella madrugada me colgué" (*"And me who never worshipped / anything other than a woman's body, / by the neck from a cloud /* [in] *the wee hours of that night / I hung myself"*).[58]

In the morning, the protagonist wakes up to find that the woman has disappeared. Just as her body was the focus of his attention—to the point of becoming an object of religious fetishism—the physical disappearance of her body is especially impactful: "Estaba solo cuando / al día siguiente el sol me desveló, / me desperté abrazando / la ausencia de su cuerpo en mi colchón." (*"I was alone when / the following day the sun disrupted my sleep, / and I awoke embracing the absence of her body on my mattress"*).[59] But this woman is quite unlike the one that had flown away on Lennon in "Norwegian Wood." Sabina's lover turns out to be a thief, for on the way out of his apartment, she stole his wallet and computer while he slept. Once more walking that fine line between sincere sentimentality and sappiness, Sabina sings that the worst thing that was stolen was his *"heart"* and, although he was deceived, it was not altogether bad. Sabina marvels at her transformation from the night before to what she turned out to be in the morning: "De noche piel de hada, / a plena luz del día Cruella de Ville [sic],[60] / maldita madrugada / y yo que me creía Steve McQueen" (*"At night skin as smooth as a fairy's / in the full light of day, Cruella de Vil, / damned morning, / and here I thought I was Steve McQueen"*). Following the disappointment expressed by that candid admission, Sabina suddenly addresses his listeners directly, breaking the fourth wall as it were, to request a favor: "Si en algún paso cebra / la encuentras, dile que le he escrito un blues; / llevaba medias negras, / bufanda a cuadros, minifalda azul" (*"If you find her / in some zebra-striped crosswalk, tell her that I've written a blues for her; / she was wearing black stockings, / a checkered scarf, a blue miniskirt"*).[61]

While "Medias negras" features one of his most linear narratives, Sabina has also utilized a song structure composed of three vignettes, each depicting different settings and characters.[62] These short, impressionistic sketches establish scene rather than sequences of related actions or other hallmarks of plot development. In this regard, the vignette is easily adapted to song lyrics and is, perhaps, more closely related to poetry than to narrative genres such as the short story, micronarratives, or even flash fiction. Like a medieval triptych connected by iron hinges, the only relationship between the individuals featured in these slice-of-life depictions is the general theme of the song, often conveyed by means of the chorus.[63] The vignette is a particularly interesting manner of creative expression because combinations of them often reveal unexpected dynamics between characters and their situations that would not be as conspicuous with the more standard approach of a unifying narrative. A series of vignettes, presented without any assertions about their relationship, is a form of expression without direct statement, thus making this structure distantly related to the techniques of ironic mode.[64] Additionally, by including three such sketches in a single lyric, Sabina is able to magnify the particular concept he wishes to express through the device of *auxesis* which, as discussed in the previous chapter, is an incremental increase or intensification of a sense or meaning the artist wishes to impart. In the specific songs to be examined, the sadness or sense of tragedy is heightened in each successive vignette.

A few of the most memorable examples of Sabina's three-vignette compositions include "El blues de lo que pasa en mi escalera" ("The Blues of What Happens on my Stairway"), the aforementioned "Pero qué hermosas eran," and, most recently, "¿Qué estoy haciendo aquí?" ("What Am I Doing Here?") and "Churumbelas" ("Little Girls") from his last studio album, *Lo niego todo*. But Sabina's best-known example is, indisputably, "¿Quién me ha robado el mes de abril?" ("Who Has Stolen My Month of April?") from *El hombre del traje gris*.[65] This particular song is imbued with such poignancy that Juan de Loxa, a man of profound poetic spirit, admitted that it had "*gone around in [his] head*" during many nights of insomnia and disappointment.[66] In this song, Sabina first depicts a homeless man living on the street, then a pregnant high school student, and finally his own (fictional) mother. Valdeón has described this particular narrative-as-discourse as, "*Three stories, three illustrations, so that a succession of unforgettable losers pass.*"[67] Rather than "*losers*," though, it may be more appropriate to see these characters as victims since all three have had their hope—their "*month of April*"—taken from them. While the vignette of the homeless man is quite sad, it is not nearly as moving as the two that follow. Listeners can commiserate with the high school student—the "chica de BUP"[68]—as her world falls apart and she tries to focus on something as remote from her life as a Latin lesson. Sabina describes tears of "desamor" running down the lined paper of her notebook as the song transitions to the chorus: "¿Quién me ha robado el mes de abril?

/ ¿Cómo pudo sucederme a mí?" ("*Who has stolen my month of April? / How could this have happened to me?*"). Perhaps Sabina's most sympathetic portrait of someone unlucky in love is that of the third vignette, the sketch of the wife betrayed by her husband for a hairstylist "*twenty years younger.*" When the "*husband of my mother*" and his much younger girlfriend take photos of themselves laughing in Paris, the singer describes his matriarch sitting "derrotada en el sillón, / se marchita viendo Falcon Crest / mi vieja . . ." ("*vanquished in the armchair / she withers away watching 'Falcon Crest' / my dear old mother . . .*").[69]

In "¿Qué estoy haciendo aquí?,"[70] the cantautor's most recent example of this tripartite structure, the first vignette presents a young, single woman named Marisa who puts in long hours at a tedious job; at night she tries to find excitement, and maybe love, at a singles bar called the Florida. But Sabina tells us that all she will find there are "desatinos del corazón" ("*mistakes of the heart*"). In the second vignette, we meet a Midas-like young banker named Jimmy who tries to flee the country with a bag full of loot in the back seat of his Bentley and the police in hot pursuit. With some of the cantautor's signature ambiguity, at the end of his vignette Jimmy apparently loads a pistol, aims, but misses whomever or whatever the target may have been (perhaps, upon being cornered by the police, he too tried his hand at Russian roulette). The last vignette presents Encarna and Charly, a married couple who abuse alcohol and each other. Sabina depicts their marriage as one in which there is no longer any reciprocity, a situation representing the absolute nadir of the domesticated relationship he has always spurned: "se miran uno al otro y no ven nada, / se gritan porque ya no hay más que hablar" ("*they look at one another and see nothing, / they scream at each other because there's nothing left to say*"). The sketch of this couple ends with Encarna in the police station, nursing her right eye with an apparent bruise the color of watermelon.[71]

In "¿Qué estoy haciendo aquí?" the listener is given the depictions of two individuals and a married couple who wonder why they are in such a "*dead end*" ("callejón sin salida"), and so the shared affliction is as metaphoric as that of the unhappy people we observe in "¿Quién me ha robado el mes de abril?" In spite of the different themes that, respectively, unify the vignettes of each of the two songs, the characters in "¿Qué estoy haciendo aquí? do in fact share some similarities with those of the earlier example. Marisa is another young woman who, like the "chica del BUP," looks for love but cannot find it. Encarna and Charly represent the dissolution of a marriage, just as the mother of the earlier song watches a melodramatic American soap opera, withering away while her husband enjoys himself in Paris with his much younger girlfriend. With his luxury automobile and fortune from global stock markets, Jimmy seems to be the antithesis of the homeless man from the earlier song, but he still illustrates the adage that great wealth does not always bring happiness.[72] Although it would be next-to-impossible to know if Sabina intended to draw parallels between these two similarly structured songs written almost thirty years apart, it is interesting to note that they are the only two from Sabina's entire output of fifteen studio albums (as a solo artist) that feature questions as their titles.

"Peor para el sol" ("All the Worse for the Sun"), from the album *Física y química*, is centered on a story of a sexual dalliance similar to that of "Medias negras," but this time the lyric also touches upon the topic of marital infidelity. Somewhat surprisingly, here it is the woman (and not Sabina) who is participating in the extramarital affair. "Peor para el sol" is the last example being examined for the way in which Sabina employs the traditional techniques and resources of a narrator because, of perhaps all his songs, it is the most cleverly conceived and realized narrative. Others express a similarly high opinion. Emilio de Miguel Martínez, a professor of Spanish Medieval literature, has called "Peor para el sol" a *"literary work executed with complete technical success."*[73] Columnist and critic Santiago González compared the lyric of "Peor para el sol" with the narratives of famous short story writers and *bolero* lyricists.[74]

The story of "Peor para el sol" unfolds over the course of a day—a complete twenty-four-hour cycle—making its story longer than that of either "Pacto entre caballeros" or "Medias negras." Sabina, again in his role of narrator-agent,[75] meets a married woman in a bar and spends a wild night of romance with her; the next evening he returns to the bar to wait for her, uncertain of her return. As with "Medias negras," the song begins with a fast-paced conversation leading to a liaison with an unknown woman, this time at her apartment which is located conveniently near the bar. "Peor para el sol" seems to be the sister song of "Que se llama soledad," not only because of the similar melody but because the setting of both is probably Buenos Aires. The highly metaphoric chorus underscores the theme of marital infidelity:

Peor para el sol	All the worse for the sun
que se mete a las siete en la cuna	that at seven o'clock crawls into the crib
del mar a roncar,	of the sea to snore away,
mientras un servidor	while yours truly
le levanta la falda a la luna.	lifts the skirt of the moon.[1]

[1] Joaquín Sabina, "Peor para el sol," *Con buena letra* (Madrid: Temas de Hoy, 2002), 130.

What is especially remarkable in the story of "Peor para el sol" is not so much that Sabina begins the story in medias res as he did in "Pacto entre caballeros," but that its first verse is an example of an uncontextualized dialogue—in this case a direct question—which confronts listeners after only a few seconds of lead-up instrumentation: "¿Qué adelantas sabiendo mi nombre? / Cada noche tengo uno distinto" ("*What do you gain by knowing my name? / Every night I have a different one*").[76] The unknown speaker continues, explaining that (s)he "*obeys the voice of instinct*" and is looking for "*a discreet lover*," before finally posing another question, "*Don't you want to try?*"[77] The antiphonal[78] is unusual in Sabina, to say nothing of the manner in which he assumes—as listeners eventually discover—the voice of the woman that he meets in the bar. Certainly, any fan hearing the beginning would naturally assume that Sabina was uttering these initial words, given his well-earned reputation as a womanizer.[79] But it is the woman's words that begin the song. Furthermore, by starting the narrative in this fashion—with the brazen invitation, completely uncontextualized—Sabina is heightening the engagement of listeners even more than what would occur with a standard, situational example of in medias res.

At the same time, Sabina manages to establish characterization without the listeners being certain of who is speaking. As Emilio de Miguel Martínez points out, if the woman begins the song by asking what there is to gain by learning her name, there must have been (at least) one earlier question, which is shrewdly omitted by Sabina in order to draw listeners further into the story. The listener of "Peor para el sol" is thus introduced into a provocative conversation, in an unknown setting, sometime after the *tête-à-tête* had started. In spite of his love of words, Sabina shows that he "no abusa innecesariamente de su empleo y, a base de amputar excrecencias, es capaz de conseguir . . . pequeñas y vibrantes escenas teatrales" (*"does not unnecessarily abuse their use and, by amputating outgrowths, is capable of achieving . . . small and vibrant theatrical scenes"*).[80] As is the case with good theatre, subtle details lead to larger concepts in "Peor para el sol." The dialogue, for example, shows the woman to be an uninhibited free-spirit like Sabina. The lewd self-indulgence of their solitary night of romance is conveyed with the "*fashion show of lingerie*" she performs for him, as well as with the line of cocaine they cut on the glass of a framed wedding photo in her apartment.[81] The early confession of the woman—that she goes out at night, obeying her instincts and hoping to find a lover—sounds quite similar to Sabina's in "Que se llama soledad," when he admits to "*patrolling*" the city during the wee hours of the night like a "*cat in heat.*"[82]

Sabina reveals in an interesting way how deeply affected he was by the woman, by expressing that most unlikely of misfortunes that can befall a poet: a loss for words. After explaining to the woman that he does not want a long-term relationship—telling her, in fact, that he was lured to her apartment by her hips rather than her heart—Sabina proffers one of his most deprecating examples of metafictional discourse. Breaking off his conversation with the woman, he suddenly asks his listeners directly, "Y después . . . ¿para qué más detalles?, / ya sabéis: copas, risas, excesos" ("*And afterward . . . what's the point of more details?, / all of you already know: drinks, laughter, excesses*").[83] With that admission, Sabina seems to be weary of his own hedonistic persona. Then, finding the task of describing her and their night together impossible, he poses yet another question to his listeners, "¿cómo van a caber tantos besos / en una canción?" ("*How are so many kisses going to fit / in a song?*").[84] For the denouement of the story, Sabina returns to the bar where he met the woman the night before and, in spite of her stern promise that she would never see him again, listeners are left wondering if she does, in fact, reappear. In the final verses of the song, Sabina reveals that as he sits at the bar he hears the words, "*I was dying, my dear, to see you again*," but cannot determine if it was her "*ardent voice*" in his ear or if he merely dreamed it.[85] Considered in its entirety, "Peor para el sol," is similar to a complete rotation of the celestial bodies depicted in the chorus: the story returns to where it began. At the beginning of the song, listeners are thrust unexpectedly into the middle of a conversation; at its conclusion they find themselves sitting at the same barstool but confronting a different kind of ambiguity.

THE FANTASTIC

Although no one would consider "Peor para el sol" an example of a fantastic narrative, a pervasive ambiguity that concludes a narrative is indeed one of the defining characteristics of the literary genre. Though many theorists have done their best to explain it in their own words, the most rigorously deduced definition of the fantastic still belongs to Tzvetan Todorov who, writing in 1970, stated that the following assertion by a first-person narrator was at the very core of the genre: "'*I nearly reached the point of believing*': that is the formula which sums up the spirit of the fantastic. Either total faith or total incredulity would lead us beyond the fantastic: it is hesitation which sustains its life."[86] To establish this hesitation on the part of readers, the writer of the fantastic story must leave the denouement not only impossible to unravel, but more like a Gordian knot that becomes tighter with each attempt to untie it. This highly unusual denouement is produced by balancing the possibility of one explanation of what happened against another: the *uncanny* explanation, which means an unlikely event (or series of events) not opposed to the laws of nature; and the *marvelous* explanation, when the supernatural intercedes to determine the outcome of the story.[87] The classic effect of fantastic literature is an impenetrable ambiguity, which is established because the reader cannot determine if an uncanny event occurred or if some agency beyond the laws of the natural universe, such as a ghost or a divine intervention, decisively changed the course of the story's development. Because it is difficult in narrative discourse to establish the conditions to produce this effect, and because once it is produced the narrative is obliged to conclude ("The book closed, the ambiguity persists"[88]), short stories are the most suitable medium for the fantastic. Naturally, such a constraint also makes the micronarratives of songs highly appropriate for the genre. Although there are many other new and stimulating considerations in the current discussion of fantastic literature—for example, the requirement that the story generate fear[89]—it is Todorov's basic formulation that will be referenced here, not merely for its applicability but because, as David Roas explains, the fifty-year-old text has generated the most theoretical and critical interest in the fantastic.[90]

That Sabina has dabbled in this most rarified of literary genres may itself be fantastic to contemplate. But there exists biographical evidence for such a possibility. While discussing how he came to love literature at an early age, the cantautor said that in his home his father kept a copy of the collected works of Emilio Carrere (1881–1947).[91] This Madrid-born author wrote numerous short stories and novellas in an array of genres including Gothic, horror, and the fantastic. Mohamed Ben Slama, in his recent monograph on the author, says that Carrere cultivated the fantastic short story in the *"pure"* style of E. T. A. Hoffmann and Edgar Allen Poe, but with a Spanish character very much his own.[92] As the earlier analyses of Sabina's songs indicate, there are at least two structural considerations that facilitate the admittedly remote possibility of a fantastic reading of some of his work: first, the relatively short duration of a song necessarily leads to the omission of details, which of course would facilitate an ambiguous conclusion. Second, there is the incontestable fact that in Sabina's best lyrics, he is both narrator and protagonist. Along these lines and independent of any fantastic reading of his work, Sonia Beatriz Barbero and Cecilia Malik de Tchara have quite insightfully observed that Sabina's many songs in which he figures as a protagonist and poet—what they term his "autoficción metapoética" (*"metapoetic self-fiction"*)—frequently produce uncertainty or ambiguity.[93] Whomever the author may be, the second consideration of first-person narration makes just about any given story a much more fertile environment for the fantastic effect to be produced. This is because as readers, "we wonder if what we believe we perceive is not in fact a product of the imagination."[94] Such conjecture strengthens the uncanny interpretation of key events, which is generally more difficult for a storyteller to establish than the supernatural interpretation that is at odds with it.[95] When our perception is filtered through another consciousness, a layer of subjectivity is imposed upon every narrative detail. Normally we do not experience such a perspective with an omniscient third-person narrator, and so we generally accept the actions and details conveyed in that mode as entirely credible.

"Y nos dieron las diez" ("And It Struck Ten O'clock on Us") was inspired by Sabina's memories of innumerable concerts given throughout Spain and Spanish America.[96] According to Menéndez Flores, it is not only the number that the cantautor usually performs to close his concerts; it is very likely the most celebrated song of his entire catalog.[97] Because of its brassy, *ranchera* arrangement, Sabina has speculated with no small amount of pride that within twenty years popular musicians will be performing the song as part of their standard repertoire.[98] During concerts, the cantautor often performs the song during encores; it is, in fact, the selection that closes the acoustic side of the live album, *Sabina y Cía. Nos sobran los motivos* (2000). "Y nos dieron las diez" is also the sister song of Enrique Urquijo's "Ojos de gata" ("Cat Eyes"), recorded in 1991 with his band, Los Secretos. As the story goes, Sabina wrote the partial lyric for the song on a napkin one night in a bar, and then shared it with Urquijo, with each of them later completing their own versions.[99] Urquijo's lyric is about a singer who, after a concert, drinks too much and offends a woman he meets working a bar; the concluding verses, interpreted with Urquijo's soulful vocals, generate unexpected sympathy: "¿Pero cómo explicar / que me vuelvo vulgar / al bajarme de cada escenario?" (*"But how do I explain / that I get vulgar / when I come down from a stage?"*).[100] Identical to the version by Los Secretos, Sabina's begins with a presentation of setting, "*It was a town facing the sea, one night, after the concert*"; however, its *vals* rhythm, plucked on guitar, makes his version more reminiscent of the Mexican *corrido* genre it seems to have been modeled upon.[101]

Urquijo's lyric is identical to that of Sabina until the bartender asks him to sing a song for her, in return for which she will give him free drinks. In Sabina's lyric, she only offers to serve him a single rum and Coke. "Y nos dieron los diez" then moves into completely different territory from that of "Ojos de gata," because the protagonist and the bartender manage to find themselves alone in the bar and begin to flirt with each other. (Unlike Urquijo, Sabina apparently knows how to manage his drinking.[102]) After closing the bar, they walk to his hostel, kissing passionately at every lamppost because, as Sabina explains, "Yo quería dormir contigo y tú no querías dormir sola" (*"I wanted to sleep with you and you didn't want to sleep alone"*).[103] After a night of lovemaking—"y desnudos al anochecer nos encontró la luna" (*"and the moon found us naked at nightfall"*)—the narrator relates that they said goodbye to each other, as well as "ojalá que volvamos a vernos" (*"Let's hope that we see each other again"*).[104] At this juncture, the narrative-as-discourse fast-forwards one year to the following summer when, fortuitously, the narrator-agent finds himself giving another concert in the same seaside town.

But he is about to suffer a cruel disappointment. After the concert, he has no success whatsoever searching for the bartender, and the locals cannot provide so much as *"half a word"* about her. Sabina exclaims, "parecía como si / me quisiera gastar el destino una broma macabra" (*"it seemed as if / destiny wanted to play a macabre joke on me"*).¹⁰⁵ It is as if she never existed. His last hope is lost entirely when he visits (what he believes to be) the bar of the previous summer: "No había nadie detrás / de la barra del otro verano / y en lugar de tu bar / me encontré una sucursal del Banco Hispanoamericano" (*"There was no one behind / the bar of the past summer / and in the place of your bar / I found a branch of the Hispanic-American Bank"*).¹⁰⁶

This development—that last summer's locale of bacchanalia and courtship has been replaced by a sterile bank—is worse than a buzz kill. And neither is it a random detail: even the casual observer, once familiar with Sabina's biography, would have to admit that he has never been an *aficionado* of banks. Sabina has been especially repulsed by people who conflate the sincerity of human emotions with the pecuniary. Duly noted in his early single, "Güisqui sin soda" ("Whisky No Soda"), is the declaration that Sabina sold his soul to *"Beelzebub"* for love, not for money.¹⁰⁷ And in "El blues de lo que pasa en mi escalera," he reserves his most caustic, spittle-soaked brush strokes for the portrait of a curvaceous gold-digger who receives a seven-figure settlement upon divorcing her husband for a *"less boring"* man, accomplishing this social climb as "la seductora / bruja que escondía / bajo la falda una calculadora" (*"the seductress / witch who used to hide / a calculator under her skirt"*).¹⁰⁸ It has also been suggested that the presence of the bank may also be topical, alluding to neoliberal economic policies in Spanish America during the late 1980s that led to *"the blind dictatorship of progress and the mania of banks evicting bars."*¹⁰⁹ In any case, his reaction is violent and he throws rocks at the bank, smashing its windows (apparently there was no Molotov cocktail at hand). As the local police put him in handcuffs, the protagonist utters five words that, at this point of the narrative, would have given Todorov himself pause for thought: "sé que no lo soñé" (*"I know I didn't dream it"*).¹¹⁰ At the police station, the narrator-agent completes the perfunctory report claiming that he only had three drinks. Upon his release, he returns alone to the hostel and the song concludes in much the same metafictional manner as "Pacto entre caballeros" and "Medias negras," with the cantautor citing the experience as the inspiration for what listeners have heard: "y empecé esta canción / en el cuarto donde aquella vez te quitaba la ropa" (*"and I started this song / in the room where once I was undressing you"*).¹¹¹

Admittedly, there is at best only a minimal amount of ambiguity at the conclusion of "Y nos dieron las diez," which makes it difficult to interpret the song as a fantastic text on its own merits. This is because in the first half—that is, in the first two and a half stanzas—there is not enough metonymic groundwork laid to lead listeners to a fantastically ambiguous conclusion.

Considered in and of itself, the song is simply not designed to produce what Todorov identified as the "first condition of the fantastic": *"the reader's hesitation."*[112] This is because by the end of the song, the most likely explanation of what happened is that the subject of the narrator-agent's desire, the bartender, simply went away and disappeared during the year that elapsed between concerts. People disappear all the time. Since the question of what happens in the narrative-as-discourse may be answered with some assurance, on the basis of the song lyric itself the fantastic reading is difficult to sustain. In regard to the narrator-agent's specific inability to locate the bar, there may be two "uncanny" explanations for the confusion. First, it may be that the previous summer's liaison was in fact a dream; at one time or another, we all have experienced the peculiar sense of déjà vu and, being a traveling musician, the narrator-agent probably enjoyed many similar liaisons with comely bartenders.[113] The second uncanny explanation could be that the protagonist was too intoxicated after (the alleged) three rum and Cokes to find the bar and so, mistakenly, he took a wrong turn and stumbled into a bank.

A larger problem with a fantastic reading is that the "marvelous" explanation, with its requisite (perception of a) supernatural intrusion, is hardly even suggested in "Y nos dieron las diez." This is of paramount importance for, as Roas explains, the presence of a supernatural phenomenon is the one indispensable element of fantastic literature[114] and, beyond the wish of "ojalá" (understood in its literal sense to the extreme, *"God willing"*) in the twenty-ninth verse, the narrative-as-discourse of "Y nos dieron las diez" does not give listeners so much as a minor example. Clearly, the requisite dilemma of interpretation, producing that "hesitation" on the part of the listener, cannot be convincingly established when imposing a fantastic reading on the micronarrative of "Y nos dieron las diez." Furthermore, one does not note fear or any other feeling of discomfort, such as uneasiness or trepidation, in the reaction of the narrator-agent (and, therefore, neither do listeners experience such emotions), which are standard reactions to the emergence of the fantastic. In fact, the narrative is entertaining, even comical in its denouement.[115]

But there are some extratextual considerations that, quite unexpectedly, revive a fantastic interpretation of "Y nos dieron las diez." The total creative output of a few artists, no matter the medium in which they work, occasionally demonstrates a striking consistency that gives even the neophyte an immediate sense that a specific work was the result of their endeavor. One manner of achieving this is a recurrence of themes and/or signature aesthetic touches throughout the corpus of their work. It could be something obvious and simple, such as a Hitchcock cameo, or something that takes a little more effort to observe and then piece together, such as the brilliant colors or resilient female protagonists in Almodóvar's films. An aesthetic touch by Sabina that may be observed consistently over the course of his forty-year recording career is an imaginative cross-referencing between songs and albums. By repeatedly recalling past songs, albums, and incidents in his material, Sabina has enhanced the remarkable continuity of his work and left a definitive stamp on his compositions that identify them as his.[116]

In the 1996 album, *Yo, mí, me, contigo*, there are two songs that allude to "Y nos dieron las diez," which is the initial track of the *Física y química* album released four years earlier. The first allusion, from the song "Es mentira" ("It's a Lie"), could potentially have some bearing on a fantastic reading of "Y nos dieron las diez." Partially in Italian, listeners hear the verse "non e vero que nos dieran las diez" (*"it's not true that it struck ten on us"*),[117] which could be an innocent denial of a random hour or, perhaps, a confession that the story told in the earlier song is a fabrication. For anyone familiar with Spanish culture, ten o'clock is an unlikely hour to cite in the context of nocturnal activities; for that reason, it is quite improbable that this hour would be mentioned randomly on two occasions, isolated in meaning from one another, in two different songs over a four-year period. Of this particular verse, Menéndez Flores has written that Sabina refers to the earlier classic to deny that what happened ever occurred.[118] This confession that *"it's not true that it struck ten on us"* would reflect what Sabina has posited as his general approach to art: "¿Qué es el arte? Una hermosa mentira. . . . yo no suporto la mentira en el comportamiento de la gente, pero en la literatura es lo único que quiero" (*"What is art? A beautiful lie. . . . I don't put up with lies in the behavior of people, but in literature it's the only thing I want"*).[119] This is, after all, a recording artist who has an album titled *Mentiras piadosas*, a song of the same title, and another song called "Más de cien mentiras," which makes the argument that there exist at least one hundred lies that make our lives worth living.

If, on the basis of this verse in "Es mentira," the incidents of the earlier song are simply a lie, it would align the song's narrative-as-discourse more closely to a fantastic reading. This is because the extratextual statement from "Es mentira" strengthens the sense of doubt underlying the "sé que no lo soñé" statement by the narrator-agent of the earlier song. Nevertheless, if "Es mentira" is to be believed (!), there remains the problem of "Y nos dieron las diez" lacking the element of the supernatural. But with the cantautor's rejection of the veracity of the story, we have the next best thing because the influence of the author upon the story he or she is narrating is as profound as that of the supernatural within the confines of fictional narrative. By referring to the earlier song in "Es mentira" and recanting its veracity, Sabina is turning the dual worlds of the narrator and the narrated inside-out, in a manner similar to (but not nearly as dramatic as) the famous Julio Cortázar micronarrative, "Continuidad de los parques" ("The Continuity of Parks," 1964).[120] The boundary between the story of the text—in this case, a song lyric—and the world inhabited by cantautors and their listeners is thus blurred. Genette describes a "shifting" that can occur with the "sacred frontier" between "the world in which one tells, [and] the world of which one tells." The French structuralist then cites Borges who, discussing the "uneasiness" produced when those two worlds are inverted, had written, "Such inversions suggest that if the characters in a story can be readers or spectators, then we, their readers or spectators, can be fictitious."[121] In terms of the emotions that this may inspire in listeners, this "uneasiness" is probably closer to Todorov's "hesitation," since doubt has been cast on the story they had once believed.

The second allusion from *Yo, mí, me, contigo* is provided by "Aves de paso" ("Passing Birds"), an especially melodic track that offers an unusual combination of loving nostalgia and mild misogyny.[122] According to Menéndez Flores, the song is a poetic dedication to a few of the women that have "*quenched the thirst*" of the cantautor—and afterward vanished forever.[123] Sabina is discreet, presumably mentioning only a single, recognizable name of someone in his life ("Jimena"), and so "Aves de paso" does not risk becoming an *exposé*. The song is also a tour de force of Antonio García de Diego's musicianship for, according to the album's liner notes, he plays four instruments: percussion, harmonica, electric guitar, and keyboards. But it is his work on that last instrument—those lively yet sentimental chords—that make "Aves de paso" such a moving tribute to a few of the women with whom Sabina enjoyed a brief romance. Shortly after alluding to "la intrépida cholula argentina"[124] who inspired the song "Peor para el sol," Sabina acknowledges "la reina de los bares del puerto / que una noche después de un concierto / me abrió su almacén de besos con sal" ("*the queen of the bars of the port / who one night after a concert / opened her storeroom of salty kisses*")[125] A much more obvious reference to "Y nos dieron las diez," than the cryptic, partially Italian verse of "Es mentira," these verses also counterbalance the disbelief in what happened in that seaside town after a concert.

With our faith in the story somewhat restored, we may recall that in "Que se llama soledad," "Medias negras," "Peor para el sol," and "Y nos dieron las diez," Sabina gives us narratives that takes the listener from the most intimate relationship with the opposite sex to an isolation or (even) solitary confinement where, significantly, his musical inspiration occurs. There is clearly a thread that unites these four songs, but may any of it be believed? As Menéndez Flores informs Sabina near the beginning of their book-length interview, "Disculpa la duda, . . . pero es que cuesta mucho creer lo que cuentas, Joaquín" ("*Excuse the doubt, . . . but it takes a great deal to believe [the stories that] you tell, Joaquín*").[126] Sabina has said that his aesthetic has always been one of deception ("impostura"),[127] and in the case of "Y nos dieron las diez" there are indeed more questions raised than answered.

SABINA AS "HUELEBRAGUETAS"

The detective story is related to the fantastic in that both genres inspire an unusually intense curiosity in the reader. Such curiosity may be understood as what Booth calls the reader's "desire for causal completion," which stands as "one of the strongest of interests available to the author" wishing to engage his or her readers.[128] In other words, both genres pique the reader's interest in what ultimately occurs. What distinguishes the two genres, however, is that the heightened desire for causal completion is provoked at the front end of the detective story (such desire is, in fact, the story's *raison d'être*) and cleverly manipulated until the final resolution. But in the case of the fantastic tale, the desire for causal completion is provoked more gradually and strategically, and then left unresolved, usually quite suddenly and at the conclusion. In this sense, then, examples of the two genres typically conclude in contradictory manners: the detective story ends when readers find out what happened; the fantastic story ends only when there is absolutely no possibility of such disclosure. Todorov also noted important similarities within his genre-based approach to understanding the fantastic. He viewed the detective story as a deliberate stroll down the path of the "uncanny" explanation, whereas the fantastic meanders between the "uncanny" and the "marvelous," resisting any attempt to prioritize one interpretation over the other:

> The murder mystery, in which we try to discover the identity of the criminal, is constructed in the following manner: on one hand there are several easy solutions, initially tempting but turning out, one after another, to be false; on the other, there is an entirely improbable solution disclosed only at the end and turning out to be the correct one . . . we note that the fantastic narrative, too, involves two solutions, one probable and supernatural, the other improbable and rational. It suffices, therefore, that in the detective story this second solution be so inaccessible as to "defy reason" for us to accept the existence of the supernatural rather than to rest with the absence of any explanation at all.[129]

Although "El caso de la rubia platino" is not a pure detective story in the mold of, say, a Sherlock Holmes mystery, it clearly is an example of the closely related crime story known in Spanish as the "novela negra."[130] The song is exceptional in Sabina's catalog not only because of the genre it represents, but because it is entirely fictive, even featuring the first-person narration of someone other than the cantautor. The origins of the song are interesting. Luis Cardillo, in his amusing book *Los tangos de Sabina* (2003), recounts an anecdote dating from perhaps the eighties or early nineties, in which Sabina and longtime friend and fellow cantautor from his La Mandrágora days, Javier Krahe, isolated themselves in a Franciscan convent in the outskirts of Madrid in order to produce a script about a failed detective. The setting would have been that most famous area of operations for a private detective, New York City, and he would have kept an office in the Empire State Building. However, the script was never completed and the two resumed their musical careers.[131] Since this purported script has never been published, it is impossible to determine if it was a direct inspiration for the song. As explained earlier in this chapter, "Ciudadano cero" was Sabina's first attempt at a novela negra in song. The development from that early composition to "El caso de la rubia platino" is likely what the cantautor was thinking about when, in his 2016 interview with Julio Valdeón, he discussed the difficulty of managing the intricacies of a detective story within the medium of song. Sabina initially approached the composition of "El caso de la rubia platino" as if answering a challenge, asking himself, "¿por qué no hay canciones en español que cuenten una novela negra?" (*"why aren't there any songs in Spanish that tell a noir story?"*).[132] Sabina revealed to his interviewer that even though the lyric for "El caso de la rubia platino" began as an *"experiment in style,"* he became very enthused during the creative process.[133] In his own words, it proved *"intricately difficult"* to rhyme the verses and yet recount a crime story.[134] Sabina has said—somewhat apologetically—that this second attempt at a novela negra (this time put to music composed with Alejo Stivel and guitarist Quique Berro) is one of his favorite songs among the hundreds he has recorded.[135]

"El caso de la rubia platino" is a monologue confession of an unnamed private eye (a "huelebraguetas," in Spanish slang), thus making the song a lengthy and sustained example of narrative-as-discourse. Providing listeners yet another instance of his mastery of vernaculars, Sabina creates an almost parodic characterization of the shrewd, "hardboiled" private eye, sprinkling jargon such as "cantaba regular" (*"she sounded like any woman"*), "diez de los grandes" (*"ten bills of a thousand euros each"*), as well as the metonymic, "las faldas son una lotería" (*"you take your chances with skirts* [i.e., *women*]") at regular intervals throughout the lyric. It would seem as if Philip Marlowe had become fluent in Spanish and transported to Marseille. Like most protagonists of crime fiction, our narrator-agent has a complicated past. Notably, he was once a police officer, but also spent *"three years and a day"* in prison.

Similar to songs previously discussed in this chapter, "El caso de la rubia platino" begins in medias res, with the detective explaining that he had been advanced a large sum of money and casino tokens to accept the case of *"the platinum blonde,"* which he did because he was between jobs.[136] The second stanza provides more essential background. Working without a license, the detective admits that he is often mixed up in extortion and, quite prophetically, in *"trouble with skirts."* Like any good ex-police officer, he is retained by a "pez gordo" ("*big shot*") who knows how to watch his back.[137] Before he meets the femme fatale alluded to in the title, the detective quips, "Ninguna zorra vale ese dinero" ("*No whore is worth that much money*"), which presents listeners with two possible interpretations: either the detective believes that she charges too much for her services, or that the amount of money he is being paid for taking the case is extravagant (although he is happy to accept it).

In each of the first eight stanzas of the song, the narrator provides only fragments of information, which must be assembled by listeners in order to understand what there is of a story. Much of the time, what happens may be inferred. The detective's admission that he begins falling for the vamp and vacillating about carrying through on his job was only to be expected in a noir such as this one. In a bistro, and in the company of the platinum blonde, Sabina has the narrator-agent drinking copious amounts of port wine and casually remarking, "Puede que me estuviera enamorando" ("*It could be I was falling in love*"). Working in the rich and evocative context of crime fiction, Sabina takes advantage of the opportunities to convey essential information even if it is omitted. For example, the detective has probably been hired to turn the platinum blonde over to the "pez gordo," who will no doubt have her killed. For her part, the femme fatale will work more aggressively to charm the detective, for she too must know the motive of his appearance, and her life depends on her ability to flip his allegiance. The narrator-agent hints at his growing dilemma, the burden of his obligation, and the quickly evolving situation when, using the rhetorical device of *antanaclasis*, he says, "y la rubia platino era morena / y el caso era un gran caso" ("*and the platinum blonde was a brunette / and the case was a great crime*").[138] The detective succumbs momentarily to the femme fatale. Perhaps because he does not have the money to take her to a hotel, the detective takes her to his father's house, where the old man prepares a room with two beds for his son and his voluptuous acquaintance. The detective remarks sardonically that his father was "fingiendo que la dama era una dama / y su hijo un caballero" ("*pretending that the madam was a lady / and his son was a gentleman*").[139]

The downfall of the archetypal gumshoe comes as the result of the reemergence of his past.[140] The abnormal scrutiny that a noir detective devotes to the subject of one of his cases often causes him to avoid self-examination or the recollection of what has gone before. Sabina's detective, however, experiences brief instances of lucidity, for example when he remarks that the "*bells of the past were ringing in challenge*" upon closer inspection of the case he accepted. But on the whole—and although the astute listener will understand what is to come—the narrator-agent in the initial eight stanzas seems oblivious of the danger that awaits him. Sabina's characterization of the detective occurs within the sphere of gambling—not merely in the literal sense with the many references to casinos and blackjack—but in the greater symbolism of Dame Fortune making a loser out of the player who too willingly takes risks in life. Metaphorically or literally—and even after observing that the kisses of "*bad girls . . . reek of failure*"—the narrator-agent declares that "el croupier me echaba cartas buenas" ("*the dealer was giving me good cards*") at the precise moment when his relationship with the platinum blonde turns from professional to personal.[141] In a remarkable combination of double entendre and the laconic dialogue of a man who has seen it all, the detective, as he begins falling for his victim, tells her, "«los que pusieron precio a tu cabeza / —le dije exagerando su belleza—, / se habían quedado cortos»" ("«*those that put a price on your head / —I said to her exaggerating her beauty—, / have come up short*»").[142] The observation is intended to inform the woman that her services as a high-class prostitute are underpriced but not that there is a bounty on her; on the other hand, the narrator-agent who has accepted this bounty is falling in love with her at the same time he pretends to be impervious to her charms. Simone Cattaneo observes that these words spring quite credibly from a gangster's mouth,[143] but more significant is the fact that the detective-narrator made the compliment in order to reassure his victim, intending to set her up, while at the same time unaware that he is being drawn into her subtle deception.

Todorov asserted that the detective story "plays constantly on the false testimony of the characters."[144] Of course, readers do not know that the testimony is false upon being presented with it. What is more important is that, were it not for such (false) testimony, the curiosity of readers would not be sufficiently stimulated since they would not be led toward possible accounts of the crime at the center of the story. In "El caso de la rubia platino" there is only one character providing testimony and, although it is not necessarily false, listeners gradually develop a more complete understanding of his predicament than he does. This consideration is what distinguishes Sabina's novela negra from the classic detective story, because at no point is there a need to identify a murderer. Instead, the listener's desire for Booth's "causal completion" hinges on what may eventually unfold. It is obvious that things will turn out badly for the detective, whether he kills the woman he was hired to kill, or the mogul that hired him to do it. In the pivotal ninth stanza of the lyric, the murder is revealed to be that of the femme fatale, making it clear that the detective followed through on his part of the arrangement. Recalling numerous short stories and micronarratives in which the narrative-as-discourse turns out to be a first-person confession,[145] listeners discover that the lyric of "El caso de la rubia platino" to that point is, in fact, the narrator's sworn testimony before a judge:

Ni siquiera, señores del jurado,	*I don't even, members of the jury,*
padezco, como alega mi abogado,	*suffer from, as my attorney alleges,*
locura transitoria.	*temporary insanity.*
Disparé al corazón que yo quería,	*I shot the heart that I loved,*
con premeditación, alevosía	*With premeditation, malice aforethought*
y más pena que gloria.	*and in an ingloriously half-hearted way.*[1]

[1] Joaquín Sabina, "El caso de la rubia platino," *Con buena letra* (Madrid: Temas de Hoy, 2002), 195.

In this stanza, listeners are subjected to a minor example of narratological cheating (or perhaps selective memory) in which the very individual who could disclose the entire solution is understood to have withheld the most crucial details for most of the narrative. Genette concludes that "the most classical detective story, although generally focalized through the investigating detective, most often hides from us a part of the discoveries and inductions until the final revelation."[146] And while it is not as explicit an example of breaking the fourth wall as that of "Peor para el sol," when the soon-to-be-sentenced detective addresses the court, listeners of "El caso de la rubia platino" may be considered to be the members of the jury. This unexpected involvement of listeners is a creative masterstroke by Sabina, because to this point in the song they have been obliged to piece together the fragmentary details of the detective's account, weighing evidence and hearing his testimony, which represent activities observed during a trial. By the ninth stanza of "El caso de la rubia platino," listeners realize that they have been unwittingly hearing a case in a court of law. In the final three, chorus-like stanzas of "El caso de la rubia platino," Miguel Martínez envisions the detective alone, ruminating on his motives—those *"ten bills of a thousand euros each"*—very likely in a prison yard.[147] As has been established, "El caso de la rubia platino" is not an intriguing "whodunnit," but a vivid, engaging recreation of the hardboiled detective working in his standard milieu, with all the expected devices and conventions, and disclosing at the very end a denouement all too familiar to fans of the genre: the hunter has become the hunted. A conclusion such as the one imagined by Miguel Martínez reaffirms the strength of this particular narrative-in-song by Sabina because, effectively, it has passed through three distinct phases: the initial one where listeners think they are listening to the details of an active case; the second where it turns out to be testimony before a jury (composed of the same listeners); and the third, featuring the deranged, obsessional meanderings of a con in a prison yard.

Given his role as narrator-agent in so many of his best lyrics, one might conclude that the autobiographical element is the common denominator of the songs featuring narratives discussed in this chapter. However, as we have seen in the first and last examples—"Ciudadano cero" and "El caso de la rubia platino"—Sabina also has the ability to create a completely fictional story, which in these cases is modeled on the novela negra genre. Sabina has also shown himself to be adept at using a triple-vignette structure, which brings together seemingly unrelated characters and yet provides their impressionistic snapshots a thematic unity. While it is true that Sabina's life and subject matter are often one and the same—especially in his most memorable songs—in all the songs analyzed here listeners are treated to skillfully designed narratives that heighten interest in what is being recounted. Images, dialogues, details, and words are presented economically, and at times strategically, to generate a greater emotional response on the part of listeners. Paraphrasing part of a letter the writer Jean-Louis Curtis wrote to Jean-Paul Sartre in 1950, Booth noted that readers draw together "whatever the novelist presents, scene, gesture, dramatized comment, omniscient judgment, into a single synthesis."[148] In all these compositions—but particularly in "Y nos dieron las diez" and "El caso de la rubia platino"—Sabina excels in his role of *"novelist in miniature,"* creating one brilliant synthesis after another for those who listen carefully to the songs or read their lyrics.

NOTES

1. Listed among ninety-nine other memorable quotations in Javier Menéndez Flores' *Joaquín Sabina. Perdonen la tristeza (edición revisada y actualizada)* (Barcelona: Libros Cúpula, 2018), 408.

2. "[E]scribo canciones con muy mala voz y con muy buena letra" (*"I write songs with a very bad voice and with very good lyrics"*). Sabina, quoted in Sabina and Menéndez Flores, *Sabina en carne viva. Yo también sé jugarme la boca* (Barcelona: Ediciones B, 2006), 289.

3. In the liner notes of the album, Sabina thanks Antonio Cuesta for caring for his *"abused vocal cords."*

4. Of the twelve tracks on the album, Sabina collaborated on the music of one song, and composed the music entirely for only one other ("Churumbelas"). In terms of the lyrics, Sabina penned only four songs by himself and the remainder in collaboration with Benjamín Prado.

5. *Ciento volando de catorce* (Madrid: Visor, 2001); *Esta boca es mía* (Barcelona: Ediciones B, 2005); *Esta boca sigue siendo mía* (Barcelona: Ediciones B, 2007); *A vuelta de correo. Sabina epistolar* (Madrid: Visor, 2007); *El grito en el suelo. Poemas publicados en el diario Público* (Madrid: Visor, 2013); *Muy Personal* (Barcelona: Planeta, 2013); *Garagatos* (Barcelona: Artika, 2016).

6. Menéndez Flores, *Perdonen la tristeza*, 44.

7. Ibid.

8. The most outstanding recent scholarship on Sabina's ability as a narrator is Emilio de Miguel Martínez's "Sabina canta historias (técnicas y recursos de un narrador)," in *Joaquín Sabina o fusilar al rey de los poetas*, ed. Guillermo Laín Corona (Madrid: Visor, 2018), 89–159.

9. I insist on the validity of this mildly outrageous assertion because Sabina, like the singers of those great oral narratives, employs syntactical devices such as hyperbaton to complete rhymes, and also maintains a relatively standard meter. Sabina's use of hyperbaton, rhyme, and meter will be discussed more thoroughly in the concluding chapter.

10. When asked if Poe's short stories were the best expression of his creative genius, Borges responded, "I believe that we find in them most of his successful work, more than in any other genre he practiced, more than in his poetry and literary criticism. His detective stories earned him a place in literature." Jorge Luis Borges and Roberto Alifano, *Twenty-four Conversations with Borges. Including a Selection of Poems*, trans. Nicomedes Suárez Araúz, Willis Barnstone, et al. (Housatonic, MA: Lascaux Publishers, 1984), 44.

11. Menéndez Flores, *Perdonen la tristeza*, 29.

12. Prado, "Cómo olvidar una canción," 19.

13. According to the album's liner notes and Menéndez Flores, the lyrics of "¿Qué estoy haciendo aquí?" were cowritten by Sabina and Benjamín Prado. *Perdonen la tristeza*, 386.

14. Bob Dylan has shown considerable ability for conveying a character's personality when he adopts his or her voice in a song. Listen, for example, to the different voices in such songs as "Seven Curses," "Tangled Up in Blue," and "Hurricane" (lyric cowritten with Jacques Levy). An even greater talent at characterization in song was that of Sandy Denny, the lead singer of Fairport Convention for three classic albums. Some outstanding examples of her storytelling ability are longer narratives such as "Matty Groves," "Tam Lin," and the Dylan composition "Percy's Song."

15. Fernando Valls, "Sobre el microrrelato: otra filosofía de la composición," in *Mundos Mínimos. El microrrelato en la literatura española contemporánea*, ed. Teresa Gómez Trueba (Gijón: Llibros del Pexe/Cátedra Miguel Delibes, 2007), 119.

16. The writerly tactic of using short texts to maintain a reader's attention was most famously postulated in 1846 by Edgar Allen Poe: "If any literary work is too long to be read at one sitting, we must be content to dispense with the immensely important effect derivable from unity of impression—for, if two sittings be required, the affairs of the world interfere, and everything like totality is at once destroyed." "The Philosophy of Composition," *The Poetry Foundation* (n/d 2020), https://www.poetryfoundation.org/articles/69390/the-philosophy-of-composition (accessed May 30, 2020).

17. See Sabina's handwritten margin notes for "Ciudadano cero," *Con buena letra* (Madrid: Temas de Hoy, 2002), 64. Sabina writes that it was his first lyric intended as a "novela (cine) negra," which underscores the highly visual attributes of the song.

18. Menéndez Flores observes insightfully that from the very first albums, Sabina's *"intense biography"* has provided *"material of enormous value for constructing his songs." Sabina. No amanece jamás* (Barcelona: Blume Editorial, 2016), 84. It may be said that when a song of Sabina's does not feature him as protagonist, or his implicit point of view, it is the exception rather than the norm.

19. From the album *Peter Gabriel* (aka, *Melt*), Geffen Records, DIDX 001873 2035-2, 1980 (compact disc).

20. Bruce Springsteen, *Nebraska*, Columbia, CK 38358, 1982 (compact disc).
21. Joaquín Sabina, "Tirso de Molina, julio de 2016," Interview with Julio Valdeón, *Sabina. Sol y sombra* (Valencia: Efe Eme, 2017), 490.
22. Gérard Genette, *Narrative Discourse. An Essay in Method*, trans. Jane E. Irwin (Ithaca: Cornell University Press, 1980), 27.
23. Ibid.
24. Joaquín Sabina, "Ciudadano cero," *Con buena letra* (Madrid: Temas de Hoy, 2002), 64.
25. Genette, *Narrative Discourse*, 244–45.
26. Sabina, "Ciudadano cero," *Con buena letra*, 64.
27. Ibid. The shooter's admission is reminiscent of the dying words of "El Jaro," the notorious Spanish delinquent, from Sabina's earlier song, "Qué demasiao," who observed darkly after being shot, *"they're going to put me on television for this." Con buena letra*, 39.
28. Sabina, "Ciudadano cero," *Con buena letra*, 64.
29. See Javier Menéndez Flores, "Sabina, el gran tema de Joaquín Martínez," in *Joaquín Sabina o fusilar al rey de los poetas*, ed. Guillermo Laín Corona (Madrid: Visor, 2018), 14.
30. Sabina, "Pacto entre caballeros," *Con buena letra*, 76–77.
31. Genette, *Narrative Discourse*, 36.
32. See the following definition of "pico": "Inyección de heroína u otra droga en la vena" ("*Injection of heroin or other drug in the vein*"). Víctor León, *Diccionario de argot español y lenguaje popular. Nueva edición ampliada* (Madrid: Alianza Editorial, 1998), 136.
33. Sabina, Pacto entre caballeros," *Con buena letra*, 76.
34. Ibid.
35. Sabina and Menéndez Flores, *Sabina en carne viva*, 135.
36. Sabina, "Pacto entre caballeros," *Con buena letra*, 77.
37. Ibid.
38. Wayne C. Booth, *The Rhetoric of Fiction*, 2nd edition (Chicago: University of Chicago Press, 1983), 153–54.
39. "Pacto entre caballeros" is not the only song by Sabina to feature delinquents and criminals as protagonists. Among the many examples of such subject matter, *Malas compañías* features an ode to a young car thief, "¡Qué demasiao!", *El hombre del traje gris* includes "¡Al ladrón, al ladrón!," about an old pickpocket, and *Mentiras piadosas* has "Con un par," about a notorious thief named Dionisio Rodríguez.
40. Menéndez Flores, *Perdonen la tristeza*, 134.
41. Quoted in Ibid., 98.
42. "For lack of better terms, I have called a narrator *reliable* when he speaks for or acts in accordance with the norms of the work . . ., *unreliable* when he does not. . . . Nor is unreliability ordinarily a matter of lying . . . It is most often a matter of what James calls *inconscience*; the narrator is mistaken, or he believes himself to have qualities which the author denies him." Booth, *The Rhetoric of Fiction*, 158–59.
43. "Pancho Varona explica cómo surgió la canción «Pacto entre caballeros» de Joaquín Sabina," *ABC Cultura*, Digital edition (January 11, 2019), https://www.abc

.es/cultura/musica/abci-pancho-varona-explica-como-surgio-cancion-pacto-entre-caballeros-joaquin-sabina-201901101212_noticia.html (accessed July 21, 2019).

44. Sabina and Menéndez Flores, *Sabina en carne viva*, 135.
45. Ibid.
46. Sabina, "Pacto entre caballeros," *Con buena letra*, 77.
47. Jorge Luis Borges, *Borges on Writing*, eds. Daniel Halpern, Frank MacShane, et al. (Hopewell, NJ: The Ecco Press, [1973] 1994), 45.
48. This transitional period ends in 1992 with the album *Física y química*, which was then followed by the three albums considered by many to be his finest: *Esta boca es mía* (1994), *Yo, mí, me, contigo* (1996), and the multiplatinum *19 días y 500 noches* (1999).
49. Menéndez Flores, *Perdonen la tristeza*, 162.
50. On the live album, *Sabina y Cía. Nos sobran los motivos* (2000), Sabina begins the song by singing "En Linares-Baeza," a reference to the train station a few miles to the west of Ubeda, his hometown. The melody of "Medias negras" is recycled by Sabina for the song "El Café de Nicandor" from the 2002 album *Dímelo en la calle*.
51. Sabina quoted in Valdeón, *Sabina. Sol y sombra*, 44.
52. See Simone Cattaneo's interesting discussion of this song in the first part of his article, "A mitad de camino entre la canción y el cuento. Pongamos que hablo de Joaquín Sabina," *Narrativas de la posmodernidad del cuento al microrrelato*, ed. Salvador Montesa Peydró (Málaga: AEDILE, 2009), 421–26.
53. Sabina, "Tratado de impaciencia," *Con buena letra*, 29.
54. Cowritten by Antonio Oliver, the lyric of "Pero qué hermosas eran," recounts the passionate relationships with three different women, each one of whom provides Sabina an unwelcome surprise.
55. "Medias negras" is only one of many songs that feature Sabina's flair for authentic street slang, especially that which was prevalent during the movida movement of the mid-1980s.
56. See the beginning of Miriam W. Rice, "Metaphorical Foreshadowing in La Regenta," *Hispanófila* 71 (1981): 41–42.
57. Sabina, "Medias negras," *Con buena letra*, 114.
58. Ibid.
59. This verse recalls one of the concluding images of loneliness in "Calle Melancolía": "me abrazo a la ausencia que dejas en mi cama" ("*I embrace the absence that you leave in my bed*"), *Con buena letra*, 38.
60. The Disney villainess Cruella de Vil, from the animated film *One Hundred and One Dalmatians* (1961), is not only hideous, she also wants puppies in order to make a fur coat out of their hides.
61. Sabina, "Medias negras," *Con buena letra*, 114.
62. The vignette is defined as "a sketch or brief narrative characterized by precision and delicacy." Holman and Harmon, *A Handbook to Literature*, Sixth edition (New York: MacMillan, 1992), 496.
63. An early example of a pop song composed of impressionistic vignettes united by a chorus is the Beatles' "Eleanor Rigby" (1966), although it features but two characters in virtually the same setting. The great, glam-rock example, Lou Reed's "Walk

on the Wild Side" (1972), is a song that Sabina undoubtedly knows and admires. "Walk on the Wild Side" offers portraits of five different characters—Holly, Candy, Little Joe, Sugar Plum Fairy, and Jackie—as they come to New York City. Sabina has expressed enthusiasm for Reed and his music on numerous occasions, and even dedicated a verse to the American singer-songwriter in the first of two sonnets, "Mis juglares. Dos sonetos," in *Esta boca es mía. Edición completa de los versos satíricos*, illus. Gustavo Otero (Barcelona: Ediciones B, 2010), 386.

64. Northrup Frye, *Anatomy of Criticism. Four Essays* (New York: Princeton: Princeton University Press, [1957] 1990), 60–61.

65. According to Menéndez Flores, "¿Quién me ha robado el mes de abril?" is the only song from *El hombre del traje gris* that Sabina continues to perform in concert. *Perdonen la tristeza*, 147.

66. Quoted in González Lucini, *De la memoria contra el olvido*, 14.

67. Valdeón, *Sabina. Sol y sombra*, 169.

68. An abbreviation for *Bachillerato Unificado Polivalente*, a three-year program of general studies that was instituted in the 1970s for high school-age students.

69. Sabina, "¿Quién me ha robado el mes de abril?," *Con buena letra*, 88.

70. Cowritten with Benjamín Prado, "¿Qué estoy haciendo aquí?" is Sabina's first authentic reggae. As further evidence of his complete immersion in the genre, in the outro Sabina begins singing "No Woman, No Cry," perhaps paying homage to the great Bob Marley.

71. Lyrics from the liner notes of the album, *Lo niego todo*, Sony Music, 889854133221, 2017 (compact disc).

72. This represents a recurring minor theme in Sabina's songs. For example, his sympathetic portrait of heiress Christina Onassis, "Pobre Cristina" from *Mentiras piadosas* (1990), begins with the stunning, "Era tan pobre / que no tenía más que dinero" ("*She was so poor, / she didn't have anything but money*"). Sabina also invokes the theme in "Más de cien mentiras" from *Esta boca es mía* (1994): "Tenemos . . . pobres exquisitos, ricos miserables" ("*We have . . . exquisite poor people, miserable rich people*"). *Con buena letra*, 103, 149.

73. Emilio de Miguel Martínez, "Sabina canta historias (técnicas y recursos de un narrador en canciones)," in *Joaquín Sabina o fusilar al rey de los poetas*, ed. Guillermo Laín Corona (Madrid: Visor, 2018), 106.

74. Quoted in Valdeón, *Sabina. Sol y sombra*, 216.

75. Sabina is without question the protagonist or narrator-agent of the song, for as Pancho Varona explains the woman was an Argentinian named Andrea. Between Sabina and Varona, she was simply known as "Peor para el sol" and thus immortalized by the song. Valdeón, *Sabina. Sol y sombra*, 217–18. In the collection of lyrics, *Con buena letra*, Sabina also jots "se llamaba Andrea" in the page margin of "Peor para el sol," 130.

76. Ibid.

77. Ibid.

78. "Antiphon" originally referred to a manner of singing psalms in which the choirs alternated verses. In literature, however, it may be used to describe the successive changes of speakers in a dialogue.

79. Sabina's friend, Aragonese cantautor Joaquín Carbonell, writes extensively of the seductive charm the Andalusian holds for the opposite sex. With a dose of comic understatement, Carbonell explains, "Joaquín no es distinto, tan sólo ha podido poner en práctica sus fantasías eróticas: acostarse con una mujer (al menos) distinta cada noche. Y hay que reconocer que la profesión de cantante ayuda mucho, muchísimo" ("*Joaquín is not different, he has only been able to realize his erotic fantasies: to go to bed each night with (at least one) different woman. And one should recognize that being a singer helps much, very much*"). *Pongamos que hablo de Joaquín. Una mirada personal sobre Joaquín Sabina* (Barcelona: Ediciones B, 2011), 38.

80. Miguel Martínez, "Sabina canta historias," 103.

81. Sabina, "Peor para el sol," *Con buena letra*, 130.

82. Sabina, "Que se llama soledad," *Con buena letra*, 78.

83. Sabina, "Peor para el sol," *Con buena letra*, 130.

84. Ibid.

85. ". . . no sé / si soñé o era suya la ardiente / voz que me iba diciendo al oído / «me morías de ganas, querido, / de verte otra vez»." Sabina, "Peor para el sol," *Con buena letra*, 130.

86. Tzvetan Todorov, *The Fantastic: A Structural Approach to a Literary Genre*, trans. Richard Howard (Ithaca: Cornell University Press), 31 (italics in the original).

87. Ibid., 41.

88. Ibid., 43.

89. See, for example, David Roas, "Hacia una teoría del miedo y lo fantástico," *Semiosis, Tercera época* 2, no. 3 (January–June 2006): 95–117. For his part, Todorov wrote that fear is not a necessary condition for the fantastic to occur. *The Fantastic*, 35.

90. David Roas, "La amenaza de lo fantástico," in *Teorías de lo fantástico*, ed. David Roas (Madrid: Arco/Libros, 2001), 42–43.

91. Sabina and Menéndez Flores, *Sabina en carne viva*, 289.

92. Mohamed Ben Slama, *El arte de asustar. Las caras del miedo en los relatos de Emilio Carrere* (Almería: Círculo Rojo, 2018), 238.

93. Sonia Beatriz Barbero and Cecilia Malik de Tchara, "La autoficción metapoética de Joaquín Sabina: El lugar desde el que se dice 'poeta'," *RECIAL: Revista del Centro de Investigaciones de la Facultad de Filosofía y Humanidades, Áreas Letras* 6, no. 7 (2015), https://dialnet.unirioja.es/ejemplar/406764 (accessed March 12, 2020).

94. Todorov, *The Fantastic*, 36.

95. This is because the supernatural element in fiction is understood to be exceptional, and therefore more likely to be accepted by a reader because it is clearly advertised for what it is. But the inclusion of highly improbable or wildly coincidental situations in a fictional setting compromises much more easily a reader's willingness to believe what is depicted, because he or she doubts that such situations occur normally within their conception of reality (see Borges' observation cited earlier in note 47).

96. Menéndez Flores, *Perdonen la tristeza*, 176.

97. Ibid.

98. Sabina and Menéndez Flores, *Sabina en carne viva*, 136.

99. See Valdeón, *Sabina. Sol y sombra*, 202–5.
100. Enrique Urquijo, "Ojos de gata," *Los Secretos. Grandes éxitos*, GEMA-BIEM, 0630 17065 2, 1996 (compact disc).
101. The classic *corrido* usually begins with a presentation of time and place, setting the scene for the historical event it popularly depicts. For the most thorough definition of the corrido, see the introduction of Vicente T. Mendoza's classic study, *El corrido mexicano* (Mexico, D.F.: Fondo de Cultura Económica, [1954] 1993), vii–xliv.
102. See the anecdotes about Sabina's remarkable ability to hold his drink in the section, "Conservado en alcohol," in Carbonell, *Pongamos que hablo de Joaquín*, 372–73.
103. Sabina, "Y nos dieron las diez," *Con buena letra*, 120.
104. Ibid.
105. Ibid.
106. Ibid.
107. Sabina, "Güisqui sin soda," *Con buena letra*, 62.
108. Sabina, "El blues de lo que pasa en mi escalera," *Con buena letra*, 142–43.
109. Valdeón, *Sabina. Sol y sombra*, 203.
110. Sabina, "Y nos dieron las diez," *Con buena letra*, 120.
111. Ibid.
112. Todorov, *The Fantastic*, 31 (italics in the original). We may replace "reader" with "listener" here without altering the substance of the statement.
113. When discussing the inspiration for "Y nos dieron las diez," during an interview with the magazine *Cambio 16*, Sabina exhibits a remarkably hazy recollection. He is unable to confirm if it actually happened to him or to a musician in his band: "Como me ha pasado, si no a mí, a alguno de mis músicos alguna vez" (*"As it has happened to me, if not to me, to one of my musicians one time"*). Quoted in Menéndez Flores, *Perdonen la tristeza*, 176.
114. Roas, "La amenaza de lo fantástico," 7–8. Roas also affirms that "cuando lo sobrenatural no entra en conflicto con el que suceden los hechos (la «realidad»), no se produce lo fantástico" (*"when the supernatural does not enter in conflict with the occurrence of facts («reality»), the fantastic is not produced"*), 9–10.
115. Roberta Previtera, however, has suggested a connection between the fantastic and humor in a recent article about the micronarratives of Ana María Shua, observing that both genres *"question the order of the world."* See "Entre la risa y el escalofrío: la metaficción de los microrrelatos de Ana María Shua," *BRUMAL. Revista de la investigación sobre lo fantástico* 6, no. 1 (Spring 2018): 102.
116. The deliberate manner in which Sabina's last album, *Lo niego todo*, references his earlier songs is quite conspicuous. For example, the title track (and its music video) is thoroughly autobiographic, referencing songs ("me ha robado el mes de abril"), albums "ángel con alas negras," and even recent events, such as the four million euros Sabina was ordered to pay the Spanish Treasury Department in 2014 ("El tiburón de hacienda, / confiscador de bienes"). With its extended, plangent notes, the guitar solo of "Lo niego todo" recalls that of his breakthrough single of 1987, "Así estoy yo sin ti." Even more remarkable is the song "Lágrimas de mármol" ("Tears of Marble"), the lyric of which is one of four on the album composed entirely by

Sabina. In this defiant song, he alludes to recent tragedies—his stroke, the death of a dear friend (possibly a reference to cantautor Javier Krahe, who passed away in July 2015)—and looks bravely to whatever the future may hold for him. The lyric mixes the irreverent with the solemn: "Dejé de hacerle selfis a mi ombligo / cuando el ictus lanzó su globo sonda, / me duele más la muerte de un amigo / que la que a mí me ronda" ("*I stopped taking selfies of my navel / when the stroke launched its observation balloon, / the death of a friend pains me more / than that which is stalking me*"). But the general theme of "Lágrimas de mármol" is one of affirmation, giving this splendid late composition by Sabina the unmistakable echo of the Sinatra standard, "My Way." From the liner notes of *Lo niego todo*, Sony Music, 889854133221, 2017 (compact disc).

117. Sabina, "Es mentira," *Con buena letra*, 156.
118. Menéndez Flores, *Sabina. No amanece jamás*, 55.
119. Sabina and Menéndez Flores, *Sabina en carne viva*, 23, 32.
120. Sabina is familiar with Cortázar's work, including what the Argentinian wrote apart from his celebrated short stories and novels. See the cantautor's reference to Cortázar in *Sabina en carne viva*, 98.
121. Genette, *Narrative Discourse*, 236. The specific text of Borges cited by Genette is "Partial Enchantments of the Quijote," *Other Inquisitions, 1937–1952*, trans. Ruth L. C. Simms (Austin: University of Texas Press, 1964), 46.
122. The lyric of "Aves de paso" shows perhaps the influence of a poem by José Hierro (1922–2002), "Destino alegre" ("Happy Destiny," 1947). See Valdeón, *Sabina. Sol y sombra*, 264.
123. Menéndez Flores, *Perdonen la tristeza*, 223.
124. A verse that may be translated as "*the intrepid Argentinian starfucker.*"
125. Sabina, "Aves de paso," *Con buena letra*, 159.
126. Sabina and Menéndez Flores, *Sabina en carne viva*, 27.
127. Ibid., 33.
128. Booth, *The Rhetoric of Fiction*, 126.
129. Todorov, *The Fantastic*, 49.
130. The term "novela negra" is often used interchangeably with «novela policíaca», both of which may be translated to "*noir novel,*" "*roman noir,*" "*crime novel,*" or simply "*crime fiction.*" The best-known American writers in this vein are undoubtedly Raymond Chandler, Dashiell Hammett, and James Ellroy. The best-known Spanish author is Manuel Vázquez Montalbán.
131. Cardillo, *Los tangos de Sabina*, 161–62.
132. Sabina, "Tirso de Molina, julio de 2016," Interview with Julio Valdeón, 490.
133. Valdeón, *Sabina. Sol y sombra*, 490.
134. Simone Cattaneo notes that some may object to a crime story realized in the form of rhymed verse, but goes on to applaud Sabina's bold "*hybridization of genres.*" Cattaneo also underscores the utility of rhyme for sustaining the melody of song. "A mitad de camino entre la canción y el cuento," 429.
135. Sabina and Menéndez Flores, *Sabina en carne viva*, 136.
136. Sabina, "El caso de la rubia platino," *Con buena letra*, 194.
137. Ibid.

138. Ibid.
139. Ibid.
140. The best cinematographic example of this principle is Jacques Tourneur's *noir* classic, *Out of the Past* (1947), which stars Robert Mitchum, Jane Greer, and a youthful Kirk Douglas. Valdeón notes the similarities between the plot of "El caso de la rubia platino" with that of the Tourneur film. *Sabina. Sol y sombra*, 324.
141. Sabina, "El caso de la rubia platino," *Con buena letra*, 194.
142. Ibid.
143. Cattaneo, "A mitad de camino entre la canción y el cuento," 428.
144. Todorov, *The Fantastic*, 83.
145. Some notable examples include Poe's "The Tell-Tale Heart" (1843), Borges' "El jardín de senderos que se bifurcan" (1941), and Enrique Anderson Imbert's "El crimen perfecto" (1994).
146. Genette, *Narrative Discourse*, 196–97.
147. Miguel Martínez, *Joaquín Sabina*, 83.
148. Booth, *The Rhetoric of Fiction*, 53.

Conclusion

The Poetry of Joaquín Sabina and Bob Dylan

"Las letras de Sabina, comparadas una a una con las de Dylan, son superiores."

—Paco Lucena, former manager
of Joaquín Sabina[1]

AN ANXIETY OF INFLUENCE?

While Lucena's statement certainly represents the minority opinion, comparisons between Joaquín Sabina and Bob Dylan[2] are a *locus communis* in the critical appraisal of the Spaniard and his music.[3] For the many interstices between their careers, the prestige they enjoy being considered the sole authors of their work (even when they are not),[4] and the standard of excellence they maintain with their lyrics, such comparisons are easily drawn. To be clear from the outset, there is little reason to believe that Dylan knows who Sabina is, or if he even listens to Spanish-language music recorded in the past forty years. Although they are relatively close in age and, in the past thirty years or so, their respective tours would have presumably brought them into proximity with one another,[5] Dylan and Sabina have never personally met.[6] Sabina praises Dylan's music effusively, often mentioning the considerable influence the Minnesotan exerted on his early development.[7] Like many other musicians, Sabina has an almost spiritual reverence for Dylan's landmark single, "Like a Rolling Stone," calling it his *"Bible."*[8] Elsewhere, in a sonnet dedicated to the *"troubadours"* who have exercised the greatest influence on his work, Sabina credits Dylan with teaching him *"capricious insolence,"* a quality he deems necessary for the artist who wishes to remain fresh and outside the mainstream.⁹ Demonstrating his fondness for the paradoxical, Sabina has also said that while Dylan's guitar, harmonica, and voice are *"lousy"* ("el culo"), he remains *"the best"* singer-songwriter.¹⁰

Perhaps because of Sabina's admiration of Dylan, there exist many articles and critiques written by authors who, explicitly or inexplicitly, express the opinion that the Spaniard's best music would not have been possible without the American's earlier example. At times this opinion appears to be a truism among the mostly Spanish critics who are familiar with the work of the two artists. Presumably, the anxiety of influence Sabina must have felt as he composed his songs has been powerful. To quote literary scholar Harold Bloom, it would seem that the Spaniard has "misread" the Minnesota bard in order to "clear imaginative space" for himself, although some would claim he has not been entirely successful and that many of his songs are still derivative of Dylan's.¹¹

The purpose of this chapter is not merely to discuss the many parallels between these two artists, but to examine in detail where their bodies of work diverge from one another. Although their creative production is correctly understood as their respective accomplishments in music, lyrical composition, arrangement, performance, and interpretation (to say nothing of other considerations), the present examination will focus on their lyrics. It is far too easy to assert that one body of work influenced the other, and since Dylan's recording career began in 1962 and Sabina's sixteen years later, to declare the preeminence of the former does not require much thought. What presents more of a challenge—and would prove considerably more rewarding—is to try to gauge the extent of that widely accepted influence. In this chapter it will be discovered that, as a poet working in the medium of rock music, Sabina often uses literary techniques in his songs that Dylan does not employ as successfully in his. By first examining some points of comparison—attention to rhyme, hyperbaton, verbal irony, simile, and so on—some of the major similarities that figure into the general assessments of the artists will be elucidated. Then, by focusing on the important differences seen in representative work—attention to meter, synesthesia, subject matter, literary influences, and finally a brief "case study" comparing two thematically related songs by Sabina and Dylan—the conclusion will be drawn that after the requisite recognition of Dylan's primacy, Sabina, through his poetic lyrics, has established a rich imaginative space for himself that is well beyond the sphere of the American's influence. In other words, the extent of Dylan's impact on Sabina has been exaggerated. For this author, the question is less about Bloom's "poetic misreading or misprision"¹² than it is the careful consideration of the individual merits found in the work of these legendary songwriters.

Before comparing and contrasting their work, it would be helpful to elaborate on the prevailing estimations of Dylan and Sabina. In regard to the American's influence and accomplishment, one need not look far to find many, well-deserved encomiums. In his 1988 speech inducting Dylan into the Rock and Roll Hall of Fame, fellow musician Bruce Springsteen spoke of his musical influence on every act from the Beatles to the Electric Prunes, asserting that Dylan "freed your mind" in the same manner that Elvis "freed your body."[13] One may also consider Harvard professor Richard F. Thomas' judgment that Dylan is the "supreme artist of the English language" in his time.[14] Of course there is the matter of Dylan's Nobel Prize in Literature, which he received in 2016. Sabina, too, has received his share of accolades. In a marvelously conceived tribute to the cantautor, Spanish journalist Ángel Antonio Herrera calls Sabina *"the Dylan for those of us who don't know English."*[15] Author and *sabinista* extraordinaire Javier Menéndez Flores calls the cantautor *"our Leonard Cohen of the night . . . our well-read Johnny Rotten, . . . our golden rascal on the altars."*[16] Julio Valdeón writes that Sabina's songs are the *"sentimental, intellectual, and poetic chronicle of Spain"*—and perhaps of other Spanish-speaking countries, at the very least Argentina.[17]

In spite of their acclaim, when Dylan and Sabina are discussed together, the former is usually viewed as the creative originator and the second as an ersatz, Spanish-language version of the American singer-songwriter, a bit like the output if someone were to paste the concluding paragraph of Joyce's "The Dead" (1914) into an online translator set for Spanish. But both artists developed independently in their respective countries and eras: just as the United States produced many singer-songwriters during the 1960s, with Dylan quickly distancing himself from the pack, Sabina's professional trajectory in Spain demonstrates a similar progress, albeit happening later.[18] Sabina did not discover Dylan's music until about 1971, when his girlfriend at the time put the album *John Wesley Harding* (1967) on the turntable for him.[19] The standard, relational description of the two musicians is exemplified in a recent article by Luis García Gil, "Joaquín Sabina: tras las huellas de Dylan" ("*Joaquín Sabina: in the footsteps of Dylan*").[20] While observing artistic differences between the two—differences acknowledged by Sabina himself on more than one occasion—García Gil draws bold comparisons between Dylan's songs and those of Sabina. Much of the evidence for Dylan's influence may be traced to statements the Spaniard made during interviews. For example, "Talkin' New York" is the inspiration for "Pongamos que hablo de Madrid";[21] "I Shall Be Released" for "Arenas movedizas" ("Quicksand");[22] "To Ramona" for "Peces de ciudad" ("City Fish");[23] and, perhaps most obviously, "Knockin' On Heaven's Door" for "¿Quién me ha robado el mes de abril?"[24] Sabina also admits that his autobiographical classic, "Cuando era más joven," was inspired in part by Dylan's youthful interest in train-hopping,[25] which in turn was probably inspired by reading Woody Guthrie's

Bound for Glory (1943) and Beat literature such as Jack Kerouac's *On the Road* (1957).[26]

But other examples of Dylan's influence from García Gil's article are tenuous at best. For instance, although they feature identical tempos, the melody of "Rainy Day Women #12 & 35" is much simpler than that of "Pastillas para no soñar" ("Pills Not to Dream"). Furthermore, the songs are in different keys (F and A, respectively), the arrangements could hardly be more dissimilar, and, while the lyric of the American's song features cleverly rhymed free association, the Spaniard's lyric is a witty endorsement of a hedonistic lifestyle. Another specious example from the article is that of "¿Quién es Caín, quién es Abel?" ("Who is Cain, who is Abel"), a song that Sabina dedicated to fellow cantautor Luis Eduardo Aute and included in the recompilation box set, *Punto . . . y seguido* (2006). In García Gil's view, Sabina imagines Aute singing *"watercolors of Dalí"* and painting *"Dylanesque novels,"*[27] and on the basis of those verses offers this minor song as another instance of the American's influence. But Sabina in fact mentions several other artists in "¿Quién es Caín, quién es Abel?", including cantautors Silvio Rodríguez, Pablo Milanés, and Joan Manuel Serrat. Most importantly, the melody of the song is not adapted from a Dylan tune, but from one Aute himself composed and performed for his friend Sabina on the live album, *Joaquín Sabina y Viceversa: En directo* (1986), "Pongamos que hablo de Joaquín" ("Let's Say I'm Talking about Joaquín"). If examples such as these represent the standard by which creative debt is to be discerned, one might as well declare that "Positively 4th Street" was the inspiration for "El joven aprendiz de pintor,"[28] since it has been suggested that Dylan's song—so full of indignation—was directed at certain individuals (such as *Sing Out!* editor Irwin Silber) of the folk scene that had its epicenter somewhere around West Fourth Street in Lower Manhattan; in the mid-1960s, a few of these individuals excoriated the Minnesotan for going electric.[29] This finger-pointing style of songwriting, exhibited by Dylan fairly frequently in the mid-1960s, has been the source of other alleged instances of artistic debt on Sabina's part.[30]

It is also worth considering that even if there are a half-dozen or so songs that Sabina modeled consciously on the work of rock music's greatest songwriter, the Spaniard has still composed a total of approximately four hundred songs during his career.[31] Sabina's *oeuvre* also shows the influence of many songwriters besides Dylan. During his exile in London, he began listening to other English-language artists, including the Rolling Stones, Leonard Cohen, and J. J. Cale. Sabina has said that the songs by others he most admires are far from being the most literary, and in fact he prefers songs by Mexican singer-songwriter José Alfredo Jiménez (1926–1973) to those of Dylan.[32] Jiménez was an innate songwriter who did not know how to play guitar; his lyrics are written with a common, everyday vocabulary and yet still manage to express deeply poetic sentiments. Sabina's admiration for the Mexican's work is evidenced by the final song from his *19 días y 500 noches* (1999) album, "Noches de boda" ("Wedding Nights"), the charming duet with Chavela Vargas. Perhaps demonstrating Bloomian anxiety of influence, "Noches de boda" features virtually the same melody as "Que te vaya bonito" ("May Things Go Beautifully for You"), one of the classics of Jiménez's repertoire.[33] That this melody was probably lifted from the Mexican song shows no impropriety, nor does it diminish Sabina's accomplishment, because all the best songwriters sample the work of their favorite predecessors and make it new again. Don José Alfredo himself may have heard the melody from an earlier song. There is a compelling argument that songwriting—perhaps more than any other form of artistic expression including poetry—exemplifies most clearly that celebrated verse of the Bible, "there is nothing new under the sun."[34] But even accepting the broader tradition of reworking the songs of earlier performers,[35] Sabina is not nearly as indebted to Dylan as some would like to believe. The subtext of García Gil's article[36]—that many of Sabina's greatest songs would not exist without Dylan's antecedent—is incorrect for many reasons.

Being the most venerable of the two artists, it is indisputable that Dylan exercises some sway over the Spaniard; Dylan has also served as a major influence for countless other musicians the world over. In his classic history of rock-and-roll, *Awopbopaloobop alopbamboom*, Nik Cohn wrote that Dylan's music of the early 1960s represented a "heavy breakthrough and all kinds of people moved in behind it," including the Beatles and the Rolling Stones, and that there were suddenly "hits with songs that would have been inconceivable before."[37] Ever since those words were written in 1968, attributing a semidivine status to Dylan and appraising his lyrics as sacred texts has been the norm among many fans, fellow musicians, and most critics. So, while there is nothing wrong with looking at Dylan as the master composer of literary rock songs and acknowledging the modest influence evidenced in a few of Sabina's songs, it is neither an original nor productive critical direction to take. Not to move beyond such a stock observation is to neglect providing Dylan's immense catalog the kind of serious study it deserves.[38] Instead, it does little more than add to the kind of hagiography he has always found tedious.[39] Worse, however, is that the stereotyped casting of the American as the sun and the Spaniard as the illuminated moon commits a serious injustice to the originality of Sabina's work, including but not limited to its particularly Spanish character and the many literary techniques that he, in fact, employs in a manner superior to that of Dylan.

While Sabina has written about four hundred songs over the course of his career, Dylan has more than five hundred to his credit.[40] And while Sabina has recorded fifteen studio albums as a solo recording artist, Dylan has recorded thirty-four albums, with yet another, *Rough and Rowdy Ways*, recently released on June 19, 2020.[41] Needless to say, Dylan's magnificent run of groundbreaking albums in the 1960s is (and likely will always be) unparalleled. Furthermore, his returns to form in the mid-1970s and late 1990s/early 2000s represent late flowerings of artistry that Sabina managed to accomplish but once, in 2017, with his last album, *Lo niego todo*. But in spite of Dylan being the more prolific recording artist, the gap in terms of overall quality between he and Sabina is not as wide as one would suppose. In the Spaniard's case, with the exception of the debut *Inventario* (1978), his albums range in quality from better-than-average to outstanding, with his four- or five-album run of the nineties comparable with Dylan's legendary mid-1960s production. In fact, one might justifiably say that the nineties were to Sabina what the 1960s were to Dylan. Even the Spaniard's most recent efforts—the somber albums *Alivio de luto* (2005) and *Vinagre y rosas* (2009)—feature several strong tracks and improve with repeated listening. His most recent album, the highly collaborative *Lo niego todo*, is nothing short of an artistic triumph and undoubtedly Sabina's best album since *19 días y 500 noches*. If *Lo niego todo* were to be the Andalusian's final studio recording, it would provide a perfectly fitting coda to his long career.

As suggested earlier, Dylan's catalog also includes a considerable amount of chaff to go along with its unsurpassed yield of wheat, a case that one does not perceive as clearly with Sabina's fourteen studio albums after *Inventario*. Of Dylan's thirty-five studio albums, some have been reviewed quite negatively by a consensus of critics on both sides of the Atlantic. And although such evaluations are ultimately a matter of taste, the albums that have consistently received the most unfavorable reviews include *Self Portrait* (1970), *Saved* (1980), *Knocked Out Loaded* (1986), *Down in the Groove* (1988), and *Under the Red Sky* (1990). One of the most respected of American critics, Greil Marcus, stated that all Dylan's albums from *Street-Legal* (1978) to *Good As I Been to You* (1992) could be "written off" because he was "a singer who for a long time had nothing to sing about."[42] Another prominent rock critic, Lester Bangs, articulated a concern that must have been on the minds of diehard fans who weathered Dylan's slumps of the 1970s and 1980s. In his review of *Street-Legal* entitled "Love or Confusion?," Bangs wrote, "if in the sixties we really were ready to accept absolutely any drivel that dropped out of his mouth—a mercury mouth in the missionary times, say—then if he had released it in 1966 he just might have been able to get away with *Street-Legal*."[43] What Bangs is suggesting here is that since Dylan has shown himself to be such a great artist, truly in a league all his own, the critical estimation of unsatisfying new work tends to fall into one of two camps: that of "love" (listeners give Dylan the benefit of the doubt when he has an artistic misfire because of his incomparable body of work), and that of "confusion" (listeners do not know how to respond to what they are hearing, reserve judgment, and then anxiously await his next release). In his preface to Marcus' famously harsh review of *Self Portrait*, Benjamin Hedin sums up what he calls "the Dylan myth," which manifests itself vis-à-vis those occasional moments when it seems he enters the recording studio with little inspiration or ambition. The release of *Self Portrait*—one of Dylan's weakest efforts spread over two discs—was made all the worse because it appeared at the end of his most inspired decade of work. Hedin writes, "the myth provides license for Dylan to release any kind of material, good or bad, that he likes, and it prevents fans from taking an honest approach to new works."[44]

For at least two reasons this has never been the case with Sabina, and no such myth is associated with him. First, he has never achieved the stratospheric heights of critical acclaim that Dylan soared to at the beginning of his career, and so the reception of his work by fans is not shaped by unrealistically high expectations. In other words, the Spaniard's trajectory shows a gradual—even improbable[45]—attainment of greatness. As he himself once said, making a clever analogy to professional soccer, "Me gustaba estar en segunda división jugando al ascenso" ("*I liked to be in the second tier playing for a promotion [to the first]*").[46] For Dylan, his career has often exemplified a case of loneliness at the top. Secondly, Sabina has never thought of himself as an artist as seriously as Dylan has. After explaining his familiarity with the American's writings and recordings, Sabina reflected, "la opinión que Dylan tiene sobre sí mismo es infinitamente más elevada que la que yo tengo sobre mí, y su ironía está presente de un modo impresionante en sus canciones pero no así en su vida ni en sus escritos. Él creyó que era Dios desde siempre" ("*the opinion that Dylan has about himself is infinitely more elevated than that which I have about myself, and his irony is evident in an impressive way in his songs but not in his life or in his writings. He believed that he was God from the beginning*").[47] To be sure, this is no criticism of Dylan, because Sabina would probably agree that the American deserved to think about himself in such an exalted manner. But to exemplify the more modest opinion that Sabina has of himself and his accomplishments, Sabina once told an interviewer, "Todas las mañanas me arrodillo, me doy cabezazos contra el suelo y doy gracias por haberme permitido estafar a la gente durante tantos años" ("*Every morning I fall to my knees, I bow my head to the ground, and give thanks for having been permitted to fool people for so many years*").[48] Valdeón remarks that Sabina is the least narcissistic recording artist he has ever interviewed, even when the topic of discussion happens to be their own work.[49]

These broad-stroke portraits of Dylan and Sabina are intended to provide a base for the more detailed comparison and contrast of their song lyrics.

Consideration of their respective attention to rhyme and meter, for example, is a more substantive approach to take in regard to their music than considering their complex personalities, or even the critical reception of their combined fifty studio albums, because opinions may change; however, the songs of the two artists are always going to be available, sounding exactly the same as they did the day they were recorded. While Sabina and Dylan may be identified as cantautors or singer-songwriters with illustrious careers, there is infinitely more to these artists and their bodies of work when one moves beyond the standard generalizations to consider specifics.

HARMONY

Of the many similarities between Sabina and Dylan, perhaps the most obvious one is that they have been criticized—in most instances, unfairly—for their vocal abilities. Neither Dylan nor Sabina has a conventionally melodious voice, but both are distinctive vocalists with excellent phrasing. In their younger days, before countless live performances and innumerable packs of cigarettes, their voices sounded less weathered and more sonorous. Of the two, Dylan's nasally voice is the more versatile, being able to whine, snarl, whisper, rock, or even adopt the country idiom well enough to sing "I'll Be Your Baby Tonight" and share the mic with Johnny Cash or Emmylou Harris. Sabina exhibits better "singing diction" than Dylan, but much of that is due to the Spanish language's clarity and consistency of articulation, especially with regard to vocalic sounds. The hoarse, at times croaking vocals of their most recent albums must present an obstacle for many younger listeners if they happen to be discovering Dylan and Sabina's music. But if the two artists had been better singers, they may have been more inclined to cover material written by others, thus interfering with what is undoubtedly their greatest talent: the composition of original songs.

After their vocal abilities, perhaps the next most obvious similarity would be the abrupt stylistic change each of them made relatively early in their careers. Sabina's transition from cantautor to electrified rock performer in the early 1980s is not unlike the one Dylan completed more suddenly, on July 25, 1965, by taking out a Sunburst Fender Stratocaster, plugging it into an amp, and roaring into "Maggie's Farm" at the Newport Folk Festival. Elijah Wald has argued that switching from an acoustic to an electric guitar in concert—which hardly seems controversial today, even as fewer and fewer recording artists actually know how to play instruments—was the transcendent cultural moment of the entire decade, an act that demarcated two competing ideals: "the democratic, communitarian ideal of a society of equals working together for the common good and the romantic, libertarian ideal of the free individual, unburdened by the constraints of rules or custom."[50] When Sabina made his transition with the *Malas compañías* (1980) and *Ruleta rusa* (1984) albums, it was not nearly as momentous as what Dylan had done in 1965. During his interview with Valdeón, Sabina himself remarked upon this comparison with Dylan, saying that his turn to a more modern sound was not nearly as historic and, unlike Dylan, he was never called "Judas" for making the change.[51] However, the decision to adopt a more progressive, electrified sound on his albums was undoubtedly a greater commercial risk for the Spaniard, because he had not yet become a respected, nationally recognized performer as the American had by 1965. Furthermore, Sabina was one of the older recording artists to attempt such a change—and during the height of the youthful movida movement. Dylan's transition from acoustic to electric may have even exercised some influence on Sabina because his best live album, *Sabina y Cía. Nos sobran los motivos* (2000), is a two-disc recording that features one half "*acoustic*" and the other "*electric*." It could also be that Sabina was inspired to record the half acoustic/half electric live album by *Bringing It All Back Home* (1965), Dylan's album featuring the same division with its eleven songs and released a few months before his Newport performance.

The comparisons between Dylan and Sabina also extend into the extra-musical.[52] While Dylan and Sabina put so much work into the composition of their music, many of their album covers appear to be hastily prepared afterthoughts.[53] This is surprising because both Sabina and Dylan are talented painters with distinctive, highly developed styles. Both have worn similar styles of clothing and, in Sabina's case, his garb from La Mandrágora days closely resembles that worn by Dylan during his Rolling Thunder Review phase of the mid-to-late 1970s.[54] The two also share much of the same taste in music, even to the point of some unexpected choices such as the songs of Amy Winehouse.[55] In spite of their enormous success and stature in their respective national markets, both Sabina and Dylan are frequent collaborators with other musicians, inviting contributions from them on their albums and, at times, participating as guests on their projects.

In an influential 1967 essay, music critic Ellen Willis wrote that Dylan "relies too much on rhyme."[56] Shortly afterward, Robert Christgau went further, claiming that Dylan has an "obsession with rhyme (which he has lately begun to parody)."[57] It could also be said that Sabina has an "obsession" with rhyme. As revealed during a recent interview, "Gulliver," a deep cut from *Malas compañías*, is the Spaniard's only song that does not feature it.[58] Perhaps the best explanation of why the two artists seem to be so fixated on rhyme is that, according to Richard Goldstein, Dylan is a creator whose roots have been nourished not only by the popular music tradition that produced Woody Guthrie, Robert Johnson, Big Joe Williams, "Ramblin" Jack Elliott, et al., but also by poetic traditions.[59] In other words, just as Dylan has one foot in American popular music, he has his other firmly planted in the kind of formal poetry found in literary anthologies. Demonstrating the supremacy of the lyrical in his music, Dylan has said that he begins with words when he composes a song, which is also the same approach to songwriting that the Spaniard uses.[60] Sabina is as much of a "creator" as Dylan, but his main influences reach back to the cantautors of the 1960s who more consciously emulated poetry with their lyrics. Often associated with those cantautors is Paco Ibáñez, a legendary musician and committed political activist who does not write his own lyrics but sings the verse of famous Spanish-language poets; in spite of his many years of activism, Ibáñez is less of a classic cantautor and more of a singular musician and promoter of literary traditions. This serves as evidence that the musical context in which Sabina first developed is distinct from that of the many brilliant but less formally trained musicians to whom the young Dylan listened. Added to his broader foundation in poetry is the fact that Sabina studied Spanish philology for nearly four years, a period in which he read the work of poets who typically rhymed their verse and obeyed meter. For his part, Dylan spent a little more than a semester at the University of Minnesota, where he rarely attended class but instead broadened his musical education with friends, listening to records and performing in coffee houses around Dinkytown, a popular college neighborhood of Minneapolis.[61]

Rhyme is deeply related to the melody of a song, often serving to enhance it. In English, the basic device of rhyme is achieved by duplicating the same vocalic sound with distinct consonantal sounds preceding them, which together form a syllable usually at the end of at least two lines of verse. The coupled vocalic sounds also must be stressed, which means that a pair of words such as "bliss" and "reckless" do not produce a rhyme. Additionally, with a *true rhyme* "[t]he correspondence of sound is based on the *vowels and succeeding consonants* of the accented syllables, which must . . . be preceded by different consonants,"[62] as, for example, in "house" and "mouse," or "style" and "mile." If the two terminal syllables feature the same succeeding consonantal sound but different, stressed vocalic sounds, it is known as *near* or *oblique rhyme*, as in "poured" and "bird."[63] If the stressed vocalic sounds are identical but the final consonantal sound is different, it is called *assonance*, as observed with "bite" and "hike."[64] In Spanish the definitions of these terms may be the same, as one observes with the true rhyme "vivir" / "elegir," or slightly different than in English, usually with the addition of a terminal unstressed vowel ("rojo" / "despojo"), or an unstressed terminal vowel and consonant ("pintados" / "soldados").[65] Near rhyme in Spanish is often exemplified with pairs featuring a diphthong, such as "enfadó" and "perdió." Assonance, which is especially common in Spanish because its inventory of vocalic sounds is smaller than that of English, is exemplified by "noche" and "golpe." Beyond these technical definitions, the practice of rhyme is somewhat different between the two languages. In Spanish the rules for stressed syllables are more standard, with words dividing into syllables more predictably, and there are fewer suprasegmental considerations to complicate accentual meter. While these distinctions may make it appear that it is easier to form rhymes in Spanish, this is not necessarily the case because a greater variety of consonantal and vocalic sound combinations exist in English, to say nothing of the fact that there are more words in the English lexicon than there are in the Spanish.[66] The practical result is that there are many words "made-to-order" for rhyme in Spanish, but there is a greater selection of sounds and words to choose from in English. These different forms of rhyme and their application help lyrics to be more easily committed to memory, not only for singers who must be able to recall the words of dozens (if not hundreds) of songs during performances, but also for their listeners.

Being avid readers, Dylan and Sabina are songwriters with prodigious vocabularies.[67] So, rather than rhyme limiting their expression only to words that may be paired, the device imposes a structure on their vast inventories that compels them to greater creative expression. Such structure suits these two poets in another way because, as Christopher Ricks explains, rhyme provides for a multilayered complexity in poems or song lyrics: "Rhyme is itself one of the forms that metaphor may take, since rhyme is a perception of agreement or disagreement, of similitude or dissimilitude."[68] Thus, the presentation of harmonious subject matter might be accompanied by examples of true rhyme; discord or anxiety may be conveyed with examples of oblique rhyme or assonance. Understood in this manner, rhyme is incredibly important in literary song lyrics because it can serve as a nexus between the melody and a song's subject matter to the extent that it is expressed through words.

If not quite an obsession, their proclivity for rhyme is an outstanding quality of both Dylan and Sabina. If they were simply average lyricists with little interest in the device, they would not exhibit the surprising true rhymes, near rhymes, assonances, and bold rhyme schemes so often featured in their songs. Sabina is very conscious of the quality of his lyrics and strives "hacer rimas divertidas que nos saquen del camino trillado" ("*to make exciting rhymes that might take us out of the clichéd path*").[69] According to cantautor Joaquín Carbonell, Sabina will not tolerate incorrectly metered or poorly rhymed verse.[70] Sabina admires well composed lyrics and, for example, has expressed his admiration for the lyric of "Construção" ("Construction," 1971), by the Brazilian singer-songwriter Chico Buarque, because the rhyme is based on "proparoxytone" words (which carry their stress on the antepenultimate syllable).[71] In *Sabina en carne viva*, the cantautor shows little regard for much of the work of Charles Bukowski—and even less for that of Jim Morrison—two popular American figures who usually composed in free verse.[72] Dylan, too, appreciates the occasional challenge of rhyme. The lyric of "Mozambique," for example, began as a game in which the musician and Jacques Levy tried to discover how many words they could rhyme with "ique."[73]

Sabina has provided an example of his unusual preoccupation with rhyme by going back and perfecting a technical detail in "Así estoy yo sin ti" ("This is How I Am Without You"), one of his most iconic songs. In the original version of 1987, the first stanza is: "Extraño como un pato en el Manzanares / torpe como un suicida sin vocación, / absurdo como un belga por soleares, / vacío como una isla sin Robinsón."[74] At some point, however, the cantautor must have realized that the name of Daniel Defoe's castaway is not an "oxytone"—that is, it does not carry its stress on the ultimate syllable—but is, rather, a proparoxytone. In fact, when he originally composed the song, Sabina must have been trying to create a rhyme similar to the one in the chorus of "Caballo de cartón" ("Cardboard Rocking Horse"): "Cuando la ciudad pinte sus labios de neón / subirás en mi caballo de cartón."[75] Consequently, Sabina returned to the song lyric and replaced the problematic "Robinsón" with "camarón" ("*shrimp*"), thus creating a near rhyme with "vocación." The result of this late edit is that the cantautor replaced a much more evocative simile (a deserted island without its famous inhabitant) for a trite, almost nonsensical one (an island without shrimp), simply to correct the matter of an unstressed syllable that perhaps many of his fans would not have noticed in any case. In the lyric of the song as it appears in *Con buena letra*, Sabina underlined "Robinsón" and scrawled "sin camarón" next to the verse.[76] In live performances of the song, Sabina now sings "camarón."[77]

One of Sabina's most dazzling displays of his virtuosity with rhyme is "Seis tequilas" ("Six Tequilas"), the song that concludes the album *Alivio de luto* (2005).[78] In this lyric, the cantautor alternates between eight-line, four-line, and three-line stanzas. The three-line stanzas are especially noteworthy because Sabina seems to have selected difficult words—oxytones that carry their stress on the last syllable—to form (for the most part) true rhymes for the initial two verses of each. The concluding verses of each three-line stanza, however, all rhyme, terminating with "tonto," "pronto," "quebranto," and "canto" ("*fool*," "*quickly*," "*grief*," and "*song*"), thereby providing an additional aural unity to go along with the melody and theme of the song.[79] The intricacy of this particular lyric demonstrates the increasingly literary bent of Sabina's late career, which he and others close to him have observed on several occasions.[80]

Dylan, too, is a virtuoso of rhyme.[81] Like his Spanish counterpart, his word combinations are endlessly fascinating, and he often spices up terminal-verse rhyme schemes with internal rhymes and alliteration. "Shelter from the Storm," one of the best-known cuts from *Blood on the Tracks* (1975), is a fine example of Dylan's virtuosity. The eight four-line stanzas of the song are of the same *aabb* rhyme scheme, with the *aa* verses featuring true rhymes and the remaining *bb* either true rhymes or assonances due to the challenge presented by the pairing with "storm." Thus, the first stanza ends with "form" / "storm" (true rhyme); the second and third, "warm" / "storm" (true rhyme); and the remaining five stanzas end with examples of assonance: "corn" / "storm," "thorns" / "storm," "morn" / "storm," "horn" / "storm," and "forlorn" / "storm."[82] In Dylan's entire catalog, there may be no example of internal rhyme more memorable than the first and second lines of the four, nine-line stanzas of "Like a Rolling Stone," with "time," "fine," "dime," and "prime;" "around," "frowns," and "clowns"; and finally, "steeple," "people," "drinkin'," and "thinkin'."[83] Combined with Mike Bloomfield's chiming *crescendos* on electric guitar and Dylan's inspired phrasing, the internal rhymes—all punctuated with the same vocal pitch—help give the song its easy flow, its bounce, its remarkable quality of feeling as if it were four minutes long when it actually clocks in at a little more than six.

Sabina's fondness for internal rhyme and alliteration are appreciable in what may be his most mysterious song, "Siete crisantemos" ("Seven Chrysanthemums"), from the album *Esta boca es mía* (1994). In the seventh stanza, Sabina offers some strong examples of internal rhyme, as well as alliteration of vocalic sounds: "Me enamoro de todo, me conformo con nada: / un aroma, un abrazo, un pedazo de pan / y lo que buenamente me den por la balada / de la vida privada de fulano de tal" (*"I fall in love with everything, I am happy with very little: / an aroma, an embrace, a piece of bread / and whatever they hand out to me for the ballad / about the private life of Mr. So-and-so"*).[84] The first two verses exhibit the same kind of internal aural connections as those heard in Dylan's classic: the first features seven instances of "o," but in the next one that sound yields to a preponderance of "a." The linking in "Siete crisantemos" continues with the internal rhyme of "abrazo" and "pedazo," and then carries over to "balada" and "vida privada" in the concluding verses. In these verses Sabina employs once again the device of *auxesis*, or incrementation, sequencing random things that he would welcome if they came his way, everything from a pleasing aroma to what he might be paid for writing another candidly autobiographic song.

As we have seen, Sabina masterfully uses the repetition of anaphora to build expectations in listeners before abruptly changing course. Again, anaphora is hardly uncommon in song lyrics; similarly designed stanzas, choruses, and even fading outros often employ the device. Combined with strong instances of rhyme, anaphora and its reversal can lead to an unusually dynamic effect. Dylan has provided outstanding instances of anaphoric verse throughout his career, especially during his early folk period, for example on "A Hard Rain's A-Gonna Fall," and during his late 1970s conversion to evangelical Christianity, on songs such as "Gotta

Serve Somebody," "Do Right to Me Baby (Do Unto Others)," and "In the Garden." An early example of Dylan's use of anaphora to set up a reversal of expectations is found in "The Lonesome Death of Hattie Carroll" when, in the fourth stanza depicting the court of law and the presiding judge, the singer strings together several verses beginning "And that . . ." to gradually build a sense of the unimpeachable integrity of law, only to conclude with the disillusioning anticlimax, "And handed out strongly, for penalty and repentance / William Zanzinger with a six-month sentence,"[85] which is his punishment for murdering Hattie Carroll with a blow from his cane. Dylan's most conventionally structured and melodic track from *Blonde on Blonde* (1966), "Just Like a Woman," is an especially remarkable achievement because of its unusual combination of internal (true) rhymes, as well as what might be identified as an inverted anaphora that leads the listener to the upshot of the chorus. Dylan rhymes each word following "you" in each line of the four-line chorus—"fake," "make love," "ache," and "break"—and repeats "just like a woman" at or near the end of each line. But Dylan breaks the pattern with the concluding verse "just like a little girl,"[86] thus putting a final poetic flourish on a song that, for some listeners, presents a controversial view of women.[87]

Dylan and Sabina demonstrate such proficiency at rhyme not only because of their extensive vocabularies, but because they often shuffle the expected word order of their verses to accommodate a pairing, which is a technique used by the oral poets of antiquity. Known as *hyperbaton*,[88] such a rearrangement of syntax—often to facilitate rhyme or meter—is a distinguishing trait of the truly talented lyricist, because it represents a means by which he or she attempts to fit selected vocabulary into the lyrical structure. In other words, hyperbaton demonstrates a greater degree of engagement with a song's subject matter, and its use often evinces a broad theme that the poet is attempting to express within the constraints imposed by rhyme and meter. In lyrics where hyperbaton is not attempted, any words prove functional so long as they complete the rhyme. The result of this kind of effort is often the lyrical drivel to which listeners are perhaps expected to dance. Understood in this manner, evidence of hyperbaton is really the first and most discernible trait of the talented lyricist because it demonstrates a conscious attempt to convey a more sophisticated meaning by bending the conventional rules of word order. As an example of a better-than-average lyricist using hyperbaton almost imperceptibly, in the Beatles' single "Nowhere Man" (1965), John Lennon reorders the expected syntax of "Doesn't know where he's going (to)" to "Doesn't have a point of view / Knows not where he's going to."[89] Lennon's example not only produces a true rhyme but also complements the song's melody and avoids what would be an unintentional anaphora with "Doesn't." Such concerns on the part of skilled lyricists could be understood more generally as versification, but to build on Sabina and Dylan's extensive use of rhyme, the more specific term of hyperbaton is preferable.

An example of Sabina's willingness to shuffle the syntax of a verse comes from his early classic, "Calle melancolía." Comparing himself to a creeping plant, trying in vain to reach the sunlight spilling in through a window, Sabina introduces a key verb, "soy," at the end of the second verse, thus completing the rhyme in the fourth verse, but only through his use of *enjambment*, the technique in which "the sense and grammatical construction" of the first verse continues on to the next[90]: "Trepo por tu recuerdo como una enredadera / que no encuentra ventanas donde agarrarse, soy / esa absurda epidemia que sufren las aceras, / si quieres encontrarme, ya sabes dónde estoy" (*"I climb over your memory, like a creeping vine / that doesn't find windows where it could attach itself, I am / that absurd epidemic that sidewalks suffer, / if you wish to find me, you know where I am*).[91] The pairing of "soy" (*"I am,"* in terms of identity) and "estoy" (*"I am,"* in a locative sense) underscores the song's theme of the individual lost and isolated in the bleak urban environment.

Dylan, too, transposes what would be the expected syntax of a verse in order to complete a rhyme or maintain the integrity of the rhyme scheme. For example, singing of his youthful activism in "My Back Pages," Dylan ends the fifth verse of the initial stanza with the more poetic "said I" (rather than "I said"), which leads to an example of enjambment with the next verse, "Proud 'neath heated brow." Dylan makes this minor switch not to complete a rhyme but rather to avoid an unintended assonance with "said" and the third line that ends with "flaming roads." The only rhyming verses in the eight-line stanzas of the song are the even-numbered, with the sixth ending with the sound "ow" to prefigure the famous refrain, "Ah, but I was so much older then / I'm younger than that now."[92] Dylan performs a similar feat of rhyme and enjambment, this time with a daring true rhyme combination of "outside" and "I'd," in *Blonde on Blonde*'s deep cut "Fourth Time Around," a song that Richard F. Thomas believes is the American's attempt to one-up the Lennon classic, "Norwegian Wood." In "Fourth Time Around," Dylan completes the rhyme with an offhanded fluency, "She threw me outside / I stood in the dirt where ev'ryone walked." Then, following that indignity, he ends with a discovery: "And after finding I'd / Forgotten my shirt."[93]

After having composed so many ingenious song lyrics, Dylan and Sabina have earned the right to indulge in a *ripio* now and then, a bit of doggerel verse, in order to complete a rhyme. Menéndez Flores is correct to point out that in some early to mid-career songs, Sabina pairs words that form awkward rhymes, or should not be chosen to form rhymes at all.[94] In the song "Y nos dieron las diez" ("And It Struck Ten O'clock on Us"), after describing the first (and only) liaison with the comely bartender he meets, Sabina fast-forwards the narrative-as-discourse[95] to the following summer, when he happens to perform another concert in the same seaside town. To condense the events of the year and complete the near rhyme with "vernos" and "invierno," Sabina gives listeners a verse that is humorous for its flat, colorless functionality: "El verano acabó, / el otoño duró lo que tarda en llegar el invierno" (*"The summer ended, / the autumn lasted for as long as it took winter to arrive"*).[96] But the American songwriter is no stranger to precision or profundity being sacrificed for the demands of rhyme, either, as one may clearly observe in the precarious pairing of "Honolulu" (pronounced, "Hah-na-LU-lah") and "Ashtabula" in "You're Gonna Make Me Lonesome When You Go," or with "sick in" and the terminal word of a verse from "Tombstone Blues" for which at least one critic has not given Dylan a pass, "The sun's not yellow it's chicken."[97]

Antithesis, one of the major rhetorical devices of Sabina's lyrics, also appears frequently in Dylan's lyrics. He provides an exceptionally clever example, within a parallel syntactical structure, in his anthemic "The Times They Are A-Changin'." The portentous, almost millenarian vision of the song makes for extremely fertile conditions to produce antithesis, and Dylan does not disappoint. At the beginning of the final stanza, he reports that a "line it is drawn" and, in the next verse, a "curse" is "cast." While not antithesis at this point, the pairing of "line" with "cast" creates a template to relate those images positionally in the stanza, thus establishing the interlacing of antonyms that follows in a sustained, zigzag pattern: "slow" / "fast" from the third and fourth lines; "now" / "later" from the third and fourth, and also the fifth and sixth lines, before again returning to "And the first one now will later be last" and the final verse with its iteration of the song's title.[98]

Just as with antithesis, Dylan and Sabina are very skilled with poetic devices such as simile, metaphor, paradox, and discourse in the ironic mode, in which a singer can convey meaning without having to express it explicitly. With regard to simile, there are a myriad of examples in the hundreds of songs composed by both artists. Certainly, the American's most celebrated simile would have to be "like a rolling stone," but Dylan could also be whimsical with the device, as in "Leopard-Skin Pill-Box Hat," when he sings that the spotted accessory balances on his girlfriend's head, "Just like a mattress balances / On a bottle of wine."[99] Sabina has penned similes that breathe new life into the poetic depiction of loneliness—for example, "solo como un poeta en el aeropuerto" (*"alone like a poet in the airport"*)[100]—as well as other creative similes for emotions regularly expressed in literature. Sabina can also be playful with his similes, for example in "19 días y 500 noches" ("19 Days and 500 Nights") when he describes himself after being jilted: "De pronto me vi, / como perro de nadie, / ladrando a las puertas del cielo" (*"Suddenly I saw myself, / like an ownerless dog, / barking at the gates of heaven"*).[101]

With metaphor—arguably that most powerful resource of the poet—Dylan has conceived of a few that are as weighty as Melville's white whale: "chimes of freedom," "Desolation Row," "Highway 61," among many others. Sabina, too, excels at metaphor, as exemplified in an inspired definition of life from "Jugar por jugar" ("Play for Play's Sake"): "La vida no es un bloc cuadriculado / sino una golondrina en movimiento / que no vuelve a los nidos del pasado / porque no quiere el viento" (*"Life is not a square notepad / but [rather] a swallow in flight / that doesn't return to the nests of the past / because the wind doesn't permit it"*).[102] Both Dylan and Sabina express the paradoxical almost casually, as when the American sings of the "lonely crowd" of the penitentiary in "I Shall Be Released," or when the Spaniard mentions the "comunista en Las Vegas" in "La del pirata cojo" ("The One About the One-Legged Pirate").[103] Seeming to echo Rousseau, in "Ganas de..." ("In the Mood for...") Sabina comments on people believing in lies to the point where they forget they are free: "Y la mentira vale más que la verdad / y la verdad es un castillo de arena / y por las autopistas de la libertad / nadie se atreve a conducir sin cadenas" (*"And the lie is worth more than the truth / and the truth is a castle made of sand / and along the freeways of liberty / no one dares to drive without chains"*).[104]

Finally, Dylan and Sabina are both adept at the ironic mode of discourse, in which less is more: "The term irony... indicates a technique of... saying as little and meaning as much as possible, or, in a more general way, a pattern of words that turns away from direct statement or its own obvious meaning."[105] Ricks argues persuasively that in "Only A Pawn In Their Game," Dylan gives an unforgettable elegy to Medgar Evers, the murdered civil rights activist, by including his name twice in the song (and identifying him as a "king" in the last stanza), whereas the killer is relegated to historical anonymity because "He ain't got no name."[106] Ricks also asserts that Dylan manages to convey that most inflammatory word of the racist lexicon, which was used by poor whites and "the South politician" who exploits them; even though Dylan's righteous song "observes the decencies," writes Ricks, "it manages to intimate to us that the racists... didn't observe them."[107] The following example of Sabina's use of the ironic mode is nowhere near as cerebral or praiseworthy as Dylan's, although it is more humorous. In his early tongue-in-cheek song "Eh, Sabina," from *Ruleta rusa*, the album with which Sabina fully adopted his popular persona of the scoundrel troubadour and carouser, he devotes both a stanza and the variable chorus to a vice that he admits to enjoying— "nicotina" (*nicotine*), "Paternina" (a well-known brand of Spanish wine), and "Josefina" (a common name for a female)—in spite of all the people who tell him to stop indulging in them.[108] Each of these vices ends with "ina," of course, and thus forms true rhymes that give an additional unity to the cookie-cutter design of the song. But the ironic mode—that communication in spite of saying nothing—comes about with the not-so-subtle suggestion of yet another true rhyme, this time with the word for perhaps the cantautor's most notorious vice of the 1980s (and early nineties), "cocaína," which he does in fact sing about in other songs.[109]

DISSONANCE

After having considered some of the poetic resources and techniques that the two artists share, it is time to examine some of the important differences to be found among their song lyrics. First, to return briefly to the inelegant comparison between "Only A Pawn In Their Game" and "Eh, Sabina" that closed the previous discussion of ironic-mode discourse, Sabina is much funnier than Dylan. Joaquín Leguina, the Spanish politician and president of the Community of Madrid during a large part of the movida, notes that the cantautor's willingness to express the "politically incorrect" in his music is an important element of his appeal: "Sabina une en su arte dos características inconfundibles. La versatilidad musical, que consiguen con insultante facilidad él y sus colaboradores, y un discurso poético propio, personal y transferible, unas lecturas «políticamente incorrectas». Es decir, libres" (*"Sabina brings together two unmistakable characteristics in his art. The musical versatility, which he and his collaborators achieve with ridiculous ease, and a poetic discourse completely his own, personal and transferable,* [*with*] *some politically incorrect readings. Which is to say, free"*).[110] Much of Sabina's work is highly irreverent, a trait that is largely uncharacteristic of the American songwriter's work after his initial albums.[111] Carbonell also admires the humor in much of Sabina's music, which he believes distinguishes the Andalusian from the vast majority of young Spanish cantautors.[112]

In the vast ludic territory of Sabina's music, even the casual listener will appreciate that the recurrent topic of most songs is the cantautor himself. That is, Sabina makes the autobiographical the centerpiece of his repertoire, a subject matter which in Menéndez Flores' words serves as "carne de canción, y de la mejor letra" ("[*the*] *song meat, and* [*that*] *of the best lyrics*").[113] It is a relatively simple exercise to trace a few of the major events of Sabina's life by analyzing lyrics composed at or about the same time: "40 Orsett Terrace" (1978, about his days living as a squatter in London), "Carguen, apunten, fuego" ("Ready, Aim, Fire," 1980, about his period of obligatory military service), "Caballo de cartón" (1984, about living with his wife Lucía, who held a day job in Madrid), "Contigo" ("With You," 1996, about the deteriorating relationship with Isabel Oliart, the mother of Sabina's daughters), and "Rosa de Lima" ("A Rose from Lima," 1999, an affectionate song dedicated to Jimena Corona, whose romantic relationship with the cantautor was intensifying at the time), "Ay! Carmela" (2009, a song about his eldest daughter), and so on. Coupled with Sabina's wit and occasional instances of self-deprecation, the autobiographical generates the humor that not only delights his fans but helps to distinguish his work.

While Dylan has and continues to write autobiographical songs, it is much more uncommon in his catalog and he rarely refers directly to himself in his music. On those occasions when song content alludes to details about his life, Dylan is often quick to dismiss the possibility. The straightforward prose of *Chronicles: Volume One* (2004) stands in contrast to the depictions of his life as they appear in many of his most famous compositions.[114] However, just as an important part of the Spaniard's music is making the autobiographical explicit, part of Dylan's brilliance is the way he artistically obfuscates the same material in his songs, leaving the burden of interpretation to listeners. But while the autobiographical element is clearly more pronounced with the Spaniard, the wider variety of themes in Dylan's music is noted by Sabina's first biographer, Maurilio de Miguel, in his examination of the parallels between Dylan and Sabina:

> Sabina observa ciertos paralelismos entre su evolución musical y la de Dylan. . . . Sin embargo, algo más ancho que el Atlántico les separaba. Mientras Dylan llegó a defender casi todas las banderas (la del folksinger, la pacifista, la de la psicodelia, la del rock armado y, últimamente, la de evangelista), Joaquín Sabina llegó tarde a defender casi todas excepto la de su propia vitalidad . . . [n]o había sido nunca un líder generacional.
>
> [*With*] *Sabina certain parallels are observed between his musical evolution and that of Dylan . . . However, something wider than the Atlantic separates them. While Dylan came to champion almost every cause (that of the folksinger, the pacifist, that of psychedelia, that of politicized rock, and, more recently, that of evangelism), Joaquín Sabina was late to defend almost all of them except the cause of his own personal vitality . . . He never has been a generational leader.*[115]

Earlier it was explained that the disappearance of what little political or social commentary Sabina used to work into his songs was largely the result of the dramatic changes taking place in Spain in the late 1970s. With the battle for a more progressive and democratic country already won, serving as a voice for change became largely pointless. So, rather than being that "*generational leader,*" Sabina started singing more often about himself and his urban escapades. In hindsight, this shift in subject matter turned out to be a shrewd decision by Sabina because it contributed mightily to his eventual commercial success. That being said, Sabina and Dylan do have subject matter in common other than the infrequent correspondence of autobiographical or political topics. Apart from that most enduring of themes—what might be called those Faulknerian "problems of the human heart in conflict with itself"[116]—both Dylan and Sabina mine that richest vein of archetypal gold found in the Western literary tradition: the Bible. Songs by Sabina such as "Eva tomando el sol" ("Eve Sunbathing"), and "El capitán de su calle" ("The Captain of His Street"), and "Noches de boda" ("Wedding Nights") reference Biblical stories such as that of the Garden of Eden, Edith (the wife of Lot), and the Last Supper. The previously discussed "Siete crisantemos" features stark apocalyptic imagery among its dense symbolism. Even apart from material composed during his evangelical Christian period, Dylan's catalog shows an abundance of Biblical references, for example in "The Times They Are A-Changin'," "All Along the Watchtower," and "Shelter from the Storm." Regardless of their different nationalities and periods of development, the Bible has proven to be influential to both Sabina and Dylan.

But on the whole (and the point bears repeating) there is little in common between the fundamental musical traditions upon which they developed their respective styles. With regard to the American, beyond the blues one notes country, roots music, the Tin Pan Alley songbook, and folk, all of which taken together create an original concoction that has led some to identify Dylan as a "neo-troubadour."[117] The essence of the Andalusian is that of the classic Spanish cantautor, but hued with the patina of the French tradition of George Brassens and a *mélange* of Spanish American songwriters. Like his American counterpart, Sabina does not simply reinterpret the work of earlier models but creates new meaning in song. By his early thirties, Sabina's style was metamorphosized and electrified by classic English-language rock music. It is plausible that the blues could be seen as a musical tradition shared by both artists and featured in their songbooks—but Dylan is by far the better student of the genre. If not for Sabina's exile in London, there would be even less correspondence between his musical background and that of Dylan. Of his exile Sabina has said that if he had not experienced it—and, furthermore, if he had not abandoned the vestments of the classic cantautor in the late 1970s—he would have become a *"Frenchified singer"* like others of his generation.[118] And it is significant that the Spaniard discovered the music of Dylan near the beginning of his London exile, because it undoubtedly opened his ears during his six-year immersion to other English-language rock performers, not a few of which had been influenced themselves by Dylan.

A point that often goes unremarked in the discussions of Dylan's subject matter is that he has returned to the political or topical since the 1960s, although the fact that he has never been as earnest in this regard as he was early on may have something to do with the subsequent decades not being nearly as tumultuous.[119] When a prominent Black Panther activist and author was shot to death by guards at the San Quentin State Prison in 1971, during an attempted escape, Dylan released a single named for him, "George Jackson." In this song Dylan remarks bleakly, "Sometimes I think this whole world / Is one big prison yard." Then, just in case a few listeners still felt beyond the scope of his metaphor, he adds, "Some of us are prisoners / The rest of us are guards."[120] On *Desire* (1976), Dylan returned yet again to activism with the superb narrative ballad, "Hurricane" (cowritten with Jacques Levy), based on the murder conviction of middleweight boxer Ruben "Hurricane" Carter. In his music, Sabina has never exhibited the level of social activism that Dylan has and, as an exponent of *littérature engagée*, there truly is no comparison between the two. Dylan's prime-time appearance on *The New Steve Allen Show*, on February 25, 1964, where he gave a brilliant performance of "The Lonesome Death of Hattie Carroll," just about the time William D. Zantzinger was released from his six-month sentence, demonstrates more political activism (and *chutzpah*) than the Spaniard has demonstrated over the course of his entire career. But none of this should imply that Sabina cannot express profound sentiments or critique the state of the world in his own way. The utopian "Noches de boda" proclaims a series of richly symbolic wishes to benefit all those who are sincere of heart: "que el diccionario detenga las balas . . . que los que esperan no cuenten las horas / que los que matan se mueran de miedo" ("*let the dictionary stop the bullets . . . let those who wait not count the hours / let those who kill die of fear*").[121] "Noches de boda" is a song of which Sabina is especially proud, having selected it as one of his six personal favorites.[122]

While both artists may be equally skilled at some of the most common poetic devices—antithesis, anaphora, simile—Sabina is more proficient than Dylan in the use of *synesthesia*, a device favored by the French Symbolists and defined as "the description of one kind of sensation in terms of another," for example, the depiction of a "loud shirt" or of a color such as "hot pink."[123] In the following example from "Así estoy yo sin ti," Sabina uses the sensory adjective "amargo" ("*bitter*") first to describe wine, and then two distinct situations that invoke the loneliness and incongruity of the song's theme: "Amargo como el vino del exiliado, / como el domingo del jubilado, / como una boda por lo civil" ("*Bitter like the exile's wine, / like Sunday for the retiree, / like a civil wedding*").[124] Another striking example is noted by Menéndez Flores in "Ahora que" ("Now That"): "ahora que tocan los ojos / que miran las bocas / que gritan los dedos" ("*now that the eyes touch / that the mouths look / that the fingers shout*").[125] While Dylan's songs do feature examples of synesthesia, it is not as prevalent as it is in Sabina's work. Ricks draws attention to the device in "Precious Angel,"[126] from the album *Slow Train Coming* (1979), but an even more vivid and famous example would be the "chimes of freedom flashing" (they "toll" and "strike" in the other verses of the song), from "Chimes of Freedom,"[127] or perhaps what seems to be the deliberate extinction of synesthesia in "Mr. Tambourine Man." In this classic song, Dylan begins with the general and works his way down the body: "My senses have been stripped, my hands can't feel to grip." Then, moving toward the motif of the "dancing spell," the descent is continued to the feet: "My toes too numb to step / Wait only for my boot heels to be wanderin'."[128] Dylan's use of the device often seems unintentional, as suggested by the first stanza of "Joey," the highly romanticized ballad about mobster Joseph "Crazy Joe" Gallo, who was born in Brooklyn and, according to the lyric, first opened his eyes to the sound of an accordion.[129]

While Sabina and Dylan are unusually gifted at rhyme, it is the Spaniard who is the more careful observer of meter. Much of the American songwriter's work in this area is haphazard, perhaps closer to something one might call "rhymed free verse." In fairness, classic meter is more narrowly poetic than musical, and for Dylan and other singer-songwriters, the goal would be accentual-syllabic rhythm[130] which, as previously observed, is a minimum requirement for the completion of rhymes at the end of verses. Accentual-syllabic rhythm—which could also be understood as an element of versification—serves to make vocal performances fluid, whether in the recording studio or during concerts. All this is to say that Dylan, and to a lesser degree Sabina, concern themselves with meter to the extent that it enhances the musicality of their lyrics, and not because they wish to become deeply involved in a literary exercise. The question of meter is also less important—even irrelevant—in the songs where there is a torrential outpouring of verse, such as in Dylan's "Subterranean Homesick Blues," or Sabina's "Todos menos tú" ("Everyone But You") and "La del pirata cojo."

With those disclaimers, there are many instances where Dylan extends verses in order to accommodate a few extra syllables or to reach the stressed syllable required to complete a rhyme. Perhaps more than any other trait observed in his songs, this adaptation of lyrics to music reaffirms the priority he has given to words in the process of songwriting. In "Dear Landlord," for example, the syllable count of the concluding verse of each of the lyric's three stanzas number eleven, eleven, and eight. To correct this disparity, Dylan hurries through (but observes the meter by producing stress at intervals) the first, stanza-concluding verse, adds the "with things" to the end of the penultimate verse of the second stanza, and draws out the final "you" of the song until a relative balance is achieved between the three verses. The total of eleven syllables at the end of the first stanza is attained only by adding the largely superfluous "that you live" to the root of the verse ("Dependin' on the way you feel"), which would match the syllabication of the final verse, "I won't underestimate you."[131] (Because it conveys a poetic idea essential to the interpretation of the song, the concluding verse of the second stanza maintains the syllabic count of eleven.) In *No Direction Home*, Shelton seems to allude to the incongruity of "Dear Landlord's" accentual-syllabic rhythm, writing that Dylan matched "a textual phrase with a musical phrase," although in his opinion it was successful.[132] This matching is clearly something to which Dylan himself has devoted much time and thought, for he draws attention to "wrestling with lyric phrasing" as the first of several "problems" during the composition of new material.[133] But Dylan's phrasing is his talisman, at times his redemption. If he were not so talented in that area of his vocal ability, very likely he would not be as ambitious as a lyricist because, behind the mic, there would be nothing to help accommodate the occasional torrent of verse to the rhythm and melody of his music.

One may find another example of discordant accentual-syllabic rhythm in the seventh stanza of "Hurricane," the lengthy ballad that opens the album *Desire*. In the eighth verse of the seventh stanza, Dylan must solve the problem of the stress of "murder" being on its penultimate syllable (rather than on the "der"), or risk producing a false rhyme with the "stir" of the preceding verse.[134] So Dylan puts an inordinate amount of stress on the appropriate syllable, at the same time lengthening it, and thus contributes to the kinetic pace of the song, fueled by Scarlet Rivera's stirring *legato* strokes. Generally speaking, there is a more careful observance of accentual-syllabic rhythm in Sabina's songs. To be fair, composing in Spanish has certainly made this easier, but even in a randomly selected song with nearly uniform six-line stanzas[135]—"Esta boca es mía" ("This Mouth is Mine")—one sees a consciously observed consistency in the number of syllables per verse (usually between nine and eleven), as well as nearly the same number of stressed syllables in each (between three and four). Sabina, of course, has published hundreds of poems in the past forty years, many of which are sonnets. According to investigator Julio Neira, although he takes a few liberties with this poetic form with roots in thirteenth-century Italy, it is clear that Sabina thoroughly understands the conventions of the sonnet.[136] Carbonell shares an anecdote from 1998 concerning Sabina's publicized professional and personal disagreements with Argentinian musician Fito Páez. Upon breaking off their planned tour to promote their album *Enemigos íntimos* (1998), Sabina composed a lengthy poem of much eloquence, with octosyllabic verses and careful attention to meter, which was shared with media outlets around the Spanish-speaking world. Offended, Páez responded with a hastily composed poem of his own, described by Carbonell as brief, full of assonances, and generally "*of poor quality.*"[137] This anecdote goes to show that Sabina takes meter quite seriously, even when he is simply ending his collaboration with another musician.

Even Sabina's diction—now more generally understood as his choice of words—reveals more concern with precision and correct usage than what is generally observed in Dylan's lyrics, which tend to feature more examples of colloquial language. This observation, of course, is only demonstrable on a general level and apart from the occasions when Sabina and Dylan reproduce the discourse of someone else in their songs, for example when Sabina assumes the personae of criminal figures, such as that of the delinquent "el Jaro" in "Qué demasiao" ("Awesome!"), the three young muggers from "Pacto entre caballeros" ("A Pact Between Gentlemen"), or the thief "el Dioni" from "Con un par" ("Ballsy").[138] With the acknowledgment that the double negative is in fact grammatically correct in Spanish, it would be highly unlikely to hear Sabina sing a verse such as "When you ain't got nothing, you got nothing to lose," as Dylan sings on *Highway 61 Revisited*'s recording of "Like a Rolling Stone"[139] (although Sabina most certainly would have been delighted to have sung that particular verse). In addition to his excellent diction, the vast majority of Sabina's lyrics could also serve as a model of proper Spanish grammar. Being such an expert on the language, the Andalusian even plays with grammatical concepts in a few of his songs. In the lyric of "Es mentira" ("It's a Lie"), he explores meaning as it is shaped by the subjunctive mood; in "Siete crisantemos," Sabina builds suspense and then surprises listeners with a vivid example of syncretism—two or more grammatical functions associated with the same word—which may occur in the third-person singular of the imperfect: "Lo bueno de los años es que curan heridas, / lo malo de los besos es que crean adicción, / ayer quiso matarme la mujer de mi vida, / apretaba el gatillo . . . cuando se despertó" (*"The good thing about years is that they heal wounds, / the bad thing about kisses is that they create an addiction, / yesterday the love of my life wanted to kill me, / the trigger was being squeezed . . . when she woke up"*).[140] In the past few years, in order to impart the nuances of Spanish grammar to their students, a few imaginative educators have introduced Sabina's lyrics into their classrooms.[141]

Many of Dylan's songs most appreciated as "poetic" display an amazing, offhand complexity. According to Willis, by 1963 "Dylan became self-consciously poetic, adopting a neo-beat style loaded with images."[142] This is an important observation because the preponderance of imagery rarely serves as the basis of disciplined, thoughtfully composed verse, but rather more often becomes an embarrassment of imaginative riches. One of the most significant differences between Dylan and Sabina relates to the poetic (rather than musical) tradition that shapes the most inspired lyrics of each. Those who analyze Dylan's lyrics—especially those he composed during the zenith of his creativity in the mid-1960s—discern the influence of many important literary figures, everyone from Dante to Rimbaud. Recently, Richard F. Thomas argued at length that Dylan is a careful reader of classical literature.[143] The major influences on Sabina's poetic development have been detailed earlier, but Dylan's lyrics, especially on the albums of his great mid-1960s trilogy—*Bringing It All Back Home, Highway 61 Revisited*

(1965), and *Blonde on Blonde*—show a profound influence of Beat generation writers, several of whom were among the singer's friends.[144] While Dylan is often enigmatic during interviews about the matter of influence, he has been straightforward about the importance of Allen Ginsberg and Jack Kerouac.[145] Beyond the considerable importance of the Beats in American literature, their work represented an alternate, often dissident view of American life that fueled much of the counterculture in the 1960s. At the beginning of his career, Dylan was heavily into the folk revival scene, but this does not mean that his admiration for the iconoclastic, urbane writers of the literary movement was at odds with the musical community that nurtured him. As one investigator has insightfully observed, the Beats and the folkies "shared certain ancestral connections with the Depression-era Left."[146] This key connection is alluded to by Shelton when he wrote near the beginning of his authoritative biography, "[h]ow Dylan put the beats and Woody Guthrie on his own highway is one of the themes of this book."[147] Dylan's affinity with the Beats went even deeper than poetry. In an early interview with Shelton, Dylan identifies Ginsberg as the only true poet of whom he knows, and one of only two holy people.[148]

In the Martin Scorsese documentary, *No Direction Home* (2005), Ginsberg remembers that when he first heard Dylan's "A Hard Rain's A-Gonna Fall" in the early 1960s, he wept because he felt "the torch had been passed to another generation, from earlier bohemian or beat illumination and self-empowerment."[149] But Beat literature is a notoriously undisciplined and freeform movement. One of its leading figures, the novelist Jack Kerouac, penned a Beat literature "How-To" of sorts entitled "Essentials of Spontaneous Prose" (1953), which looked to the improvised and emotive notes from jazz musicians—even comparing punctuation to the moments when they draw their breath—as the ideal model for writing.[150] The poet Allen Ginsberg, the closest friend of Dylan's among the Beats, also emphasized spontaneous visions and inspiration as the source of his poetry.[151] In her brief discussion of the Beats and their relationship to Dylan, Willis makes an important observation with regard to poetic expression in that it "also requires economy, coherence, and discrimination, and Dylan has perpetrated prolix verses, horrendous grammar, tangled phrases, silly metaphors, embarrassing clichés, muddled thought."[152] A few aspects of Willis' assertion are illustrated, for example, in "Ballad of a Thin Man," in which Dylan adds numerous questions to the already impenetrable meaning(s) of the composition. The seventh stanza beginning "Now you see the one-eyed midget" is especially opaque, which may be why in the fifth verse of the same stanza (even) Dylan sings, "What does this mean?"[153]

Sabina, too, recognizes the important relationship between Dylan and the Beats.[154] With regard to that same influence, it cannot be said that he is completely free of it, either. Maurilio de Miguel observes that the young Sabina read avidly "la lírica del vagabundo en la literatura de la generación beat americana" ("*the vagabond poetry of the American Beat generation literature*").[155] Sabina himself invokes the "generación *beatnik*" when he discusses the recurrence of train imagery in his early songs.[156] On a few occasions Sabina has stated that song lyrics are not poetry,[157] yet in his article for *El País* praising the Swedish Academy for awarding the Nobel Prize in Literature to Dylan, he calls the Minnesotan "*the best American poet and the best contemporary poet of the English language*," concluding his introductory paragraph with: "*the gesture of the Swedish Academy makes all of us that dedicate ourselves to dignifying words in pop feel we share the award with him.*"[158] As has been discussed, there are commonalities between these two poets in song beyond their interest in Beat literature, and even beyond the solidarity implied by the Spaniard in *El País*. Their differences are not of kind but of degree for, just as there is so much more political message to be found among the American's songs, the influence of Beat literature also manifests itself to a much greater extent in his music.

Because he is such a well-read student of Spanish literature, with a deep reverence in particular for the discipline of poetry, Sabina is a welcome anachronism: a Golden Age poet who happened to spring out of the movida, ten years older and seemingly wiser than just about anyone else. Dylan, too, is an idiosyncratic modern figure, essentially an American roots singer—Willis' "fifth-columnist from the past"[159]—with a broad political consciousness and more steeped in the spontaneous excesses of Beat literature. After observing that Sabina is a "*doctor*" in popular music, Carbonell quotes a Spanish professor of literature who discerns in Sabina and his work "un compositor muy leído . . . son perfectamente rastreables en sus «poemas» las huellas y formas de autores muy importantes de la tradición literaria española, con los que concide en su forma de mirar la realidad, como Quevedo o Valle-Inclán" ("*a very well-read composer . . . in his «poems» the traces and forms of very important authors from the Spanish literary tradition are noticeable, those that with whom he shares his way of seeing reality, such as Quevedo or Valle-Inclán*").[160]

A song that exemplifies Sabina's poetic virtues vis-à-vis those of Dylan is "El blues de lo que pasa en mi escalera" ("The Blues of What Happens on My Stairway") from *Esta boca es mía*. The track begins inauspiciously, with an opening guitar riff reminiscent of the insipid hit single of the mid-1980s by Kenny Loggins, "Footloose." But the music improves tremendously with— what was in 1994—the attributes of contemporary hard rock or grunge, courtesy of the electric guitars of Antonio García de Diego and Rosendo (Mercado), as well as Óscar Quesada's propulsive drumbeat. Over these instruments, Sabina's roaring vocals share space with some quirky keyboard fills, also performed by García de Diego. The lyric of "El blues de lo que pasa en mi escalera" is autobiographical, highly irreverent, and ultimately a testament to the persistence of an individual working his way through a world overpopulated by fakes. In a meaningful way the song brings up to date the theme of the talented individual at the mercy of the hordes of unexceptional people who despise him, introduced in Sabina's "Gulliver" of *Malas compañías* (1980). But in this reimagining fourteen years later, persistence and talent triumph.

To draw the inevitable comparison with Dylan, "El blues de lo que pasa en mi escalera" may be viewed as Sabina's version of "Tangled Up In Blue," the Minnesotan's magnificent opening track from *Blood on the Tracks* (1975), a collection of songs more personal and self-referential than many (if not most) of his other albums. By examining the lyrics of these particular songs, one can see that within a similarly autobiographical context, Sabina creates a distinct poetic space for himself and even outdoes Dylan in some interesting ways. Both songs have a kinetic energy, a bounce in spite of their (at times) heavy subject matter, illustrating Shelton's observation that the "blues can be sprightly."[161] Dylan's song shows a basic structure of seven, thirteen-line stanzas, each ending with the song's title as a refrain, "Tangled up in blue." Similar structures were utilized in some of Dylan's earliest songs, when he worked more frequently in the folk and blues genres.[162] Each stanza provides a description of another incident in the traveling musician's life, establishing the tenuous appearance of a linear narrative, which is the manner of storytelling seemingly preferred by Dylan. The single-verse chorus of "Tangled Up In Blue" unites the stanzas, and the specific incidents concerning the red-haired woman provide an additional cohesion to the lyric. Like those words of the "Italian poet," every one of Dylan's rhymes rings true and his agile phrasing turns out a superb, accentual-syllabic rhythm throughout the song.

Sabina's song features a more complex and varied structure: three twelve-line stanzas, each recounting the fate of someone he used to know from his school days, with a three-line stanza at the end of each, offering the final impression of each person. This structure represents a more sophisticated, wide-lens style of narration than that which one discerns in Dylan's song. While Dylan is able to provide the semblance of a linear narrative and geographic sequencing, Sabina gives listeners three scathing portraits of colleagues from the past, each eventually contrasted with the mildly acerbic self-portrait of Sabina that serves as the song's chorus. "El blues de lo que pasa en mi escalera" concludes with a long, anaphoric outro invoking a dizzying variety of musical genres apart from the blues that are sung by the Spaniard.

The songs feature much imagery in common, particularly with regard to the depiction of the female body, whether it is Dylan looking at the side of the woman's face in the topless bar, or Sabina's scandalous description of the curvaceous *"seductress-witch"* who used to *"hide a calculator under her skirt.*"[163] There is also similarity on a general level as it seems both songs focus on the journey of life and its many chapters, both occupational and romantic. The genesis of Sabina's song, however, could have sprung from the final eleven verses of the last stanza of "Tangled Up In Blue." There, Dylan sings that all the people he used to know are "an illusion" to him now. After describing their diverse occupations—mathematicians and carpenters' wives—he admits, "I don't know what they're doin' with their lives."[164] But in his build up to the final iteration of the song's refrain, Dylan reveals that he's "still on the road / Headin' for another joint," and listeners sense no small amount of misery in his voice. Finally, Dylan puts his poetic finger on why so much of the idealism born in the 1960s simply faded away, why so many people find it impossible to get along with each other, and why so many lives are submerged in the blues: "We always did feel the same / We just saw it from a different point of view."[165]

In Sabina's song, after the three unflattering sketches of his old colleagues, he expresses something quite dissimilar to the sentiment listeners are left with at the conclusion of Dylan's classic. While the Nobel laureate reveals some anguish in spite of his general stoicism, the Spanish singer, in his derisive and irreverent manner, declares: "Y yo que no soy más / listo ni tonto que cualquiera, / a mis cuarenta y pocos tacos, / ya ves tú / igual sigo de flaco / igual de calavera / igual que antes de loco / por cantar, / por cantar el blues / de lo que pasa en mi escalera" (*"And I, who am not / smarter or more of a fool than anyone else / at my age of forty-something, / now you see / I'm just as thin / I'm still a rogue / I'm just as crazy as before / about singing the blues / of what happens on my stairway"*).[166] Here in Sabina's chorus, there is a celebratory and self-affirming message. Though marked by battle scars, he is a survivor because he did what he wanted to do with his life. Sabina rejoices not in that he has aged, but in that he has not matured. Considered in this manner, "El blues de lo que pasa en mi escalera," is a celebration of Sabina's vitality while he reflects on others who became inextricably tangled up in the blues. On the other hand, Dylan's autobiographical narrator drifts about, solitary, seemingly as desperate as the people he so memorably describes.

BOOTS OF SPANISH LEATHER

Sabina nearly met Dylan, on the Calle de Almirantes in Madrid, most likely on June 27, 1984. This was the day after Dylan, in the midst of a European tour, had given a concert in the Spanish capital. According to Maurilio de Miguel, Sabina was in a styling salon getting his hair cut when he saw his idol emerge from a vehicle and enter a small fashion boutique across the street. Stupefied, Sabina rose from his barber's chair and crossed the street to meet the American songwriter. When Dylan and his assistant exited the boutique and returned to their car, Sabina was no more than a meter from him. And he already knew what he wanted to say to Dylan, "¿Has comprado ya las botas de cuero español?" ("*Have you just bought your boots of Spanish leather?*"), cleverly referring to one of several classic songs from *The Times They Are A-Changin'* (1964). Sabina also wanted to see if he could trade his jacket for the *sombrero* Dylan was wearing. But in spite of his proximity to Dylan during that improbable encounter, not a word escaped his lips. It was as if Sabina were starstruck. In his defense, Miguel suggests that Sabina was "*unpresentable*" there in the street, with his hair wet and still wearing the blue barber's cape that extended to his feet. Nevertheless, "*He lost his golden opportunity.*"[167]

Throughout his legendary career in music, Joaquín Sabina has not simply written lyrics with literary qualities; rather, he has infused Spanish-language rock music with poetry of the quality usually associated with canonical poets. In terms of this achievement, it would have to be concluded that Sabina managed to do for Spanish rock music what Dylan did for rock in the English-speaking world: he injected poetry into a medium that had been largely illiterate, and thus gave listeners something much more meaningful to take to their hearts. This, perhaps more than any other verifiable facet of their work, makes the strongest case for Sabina and Dylan as poets. Before Dylan, the landscape of rock-and-roll was intellectually barren. This was not necessarily a bad thing, as the music belonged mostly to teenagers who were interested in dancing, partying, surfing, and drag racing. As Nik Cohn wrote, with Dylan's early albums the music "began to be something more than simple auto-noise, it developed pretensions, it turned into an art form, a religion even ... Dylan was writing verse and getting hits with it."[168] Prior to Sabina, there had been a vibrant tradition of Spanish cantautors, but the other element of his music—the rock-and-roll—was mostly derivative in Spain (some may argue that it continues to be). Musically, the two singer-songwriters have also composed hundreds of beautiful melodies for their fans to enjoy—one might be tempted to say "dance to," but neither Dylan or Sabina have pioneered much in that regard, although Sabina did write the wonderful verse, "bailar es soñar con los pies" ("*dancing is dreaming with the feet*").[169]

Joaquín Sabina's music represents an original development in rock music that is largely unknown in English-speaking countries where, of course, it emerged and saw its greatest development. If more people knew Spanish, they would come to appreciate that Sabina's achievements even exceed those of most English-language acts that have tried to combine solid musicianship, eclectic arrangements, and intelligent lyrics in their songs. By concentrating largely on timeless subject matter such as identity, passionate love and the dullness that often suffocates it, and even the creative process,

Sabina has skillfully employed rhetorical and poetic devices such as simile, antithesis, auxesis, synesthesia, as well as remarkably sophisticated narrative techniques, to convey the complexity of the world as he perceives it. And he has done all this with a wonderful sense of humor. His unusual obedience to rhyme and meter, as well as the other manifestations of his devotion to the discipline of poetry, show Sabina to be much closer to the literary figure of the poet than any other cantautor. This includes, of course, Bob Dylan, who was always reluctant to assume that mantle. As early as 1965, in the liner notes of the album *Bringing It All Back Home*, Dylan mused, "some people say that i am a poet,"[170] and fifty-two years later the same man began his Nobel Prize lecture wondering how his songs could be related to literature.[171]

While expressing his admiration for Dylan when he received his Nobel Prize, Sabina observed an important difference in terms of their respective literary development: "Sobra decir que Dylan me cambió la vida. Después llegó el estudio de su música. He leído sus letras a conciencia (aunque no diría que me han influido en la escritura; él es un poeta torrencial, un maestro del caos, yo soy más académico)" (*"Needless to say that Dylan changed my life. Then came the study of his music. I have read his lyrics conscientiously (although I wouldn't say they have influenced me in what I write; he is a torrential poet, a master of chaos, I am more academic))."*[172] In retrospect, it is not at all surprising that Sabina balked when he had such a beautiful opportunity to meet his idol and master of his craft on that street in Madrid. Had he gotten the American's attention and traded for his hat, it would not have changed much in the future of either musician. Such obeisance on Sabina's part—though only hypothetical—would not have been misguided; it would simply have been unnecessary. Sabina was not starstruck because he and Dylan are more dissimilar than they are alike. Dylan's sombrero would not have looked right on Sabina's head for, although Bob Dylan is the better singer-songwriter, Joaquín Sabina is the superior poet.

NOTES

1. *"The lyrics of Sabina, compared one by one with those of Dylan, are superior."* Quoted in Carbonell, *Pongamos que hablo de Joaquín* (Barcelona: Ediciones B, 2011), 169.

2. To learn more about the fascinating life and career of Bob Dylan, the following biographies are highly recommended: Daniel Mark Epstein, *The Ballad of Bob Dylan: A Portrait* (New York, NY: Harper Perennial, 2012); Robert Shelton, *No Direction Home. The Life and Music of Bob Dylan* (New York: Beech Tree Books, 1986); and, of course, Dylan's own *Chronicles: Volume One* (New York: Simon & Schuster, 2004).

3. Among the Andalusian's primary biographers, Javier Menéndez Flores generally concurs with Maurilio de Miguel about the strong similarities between Sabina and Dylan. Julio Valdeón, however, recognizes more similarities with Leonard Cohen because, in the origins of both the Canadian and the Spaniard, there are "*many qualities of a pure writer.*" Sabina. *Sol y sombra* (Valencia: Efe Eme, 2017), 35.

4. Guillermo Laín Corona examines that "*most extensive perception*" of Sabina as the sole author of his works in "Sabina ¿no? es poeta," in *Joaquín Sabina o fusilar al rey de los poetas* (Madrid: Visor, 2018), 64–69. Richard F. Thomas, in his investigation of references to classical literature in Dylan's lyrics, concludes that the singer-songwriter merely "mines" the work of predecessors to make it about "the here and now." *Why Bob Dylan Matters* (New York: Dey St. Books, 2017), 322.

5. Sabina has attended many Bob Dylan concerts, some of which were, in his words, "*marvelous*" while others "*irritated*" him. Joaquín Sabina, "Poeta torrencial, maestro del caos. Me atrevería a decir que el galardón llega tarde," *El País*, digital edition (October 14, 2016), https://elpais.com/cultura/2016/10/13/actualidad/147638 0406_964576.html (accessed May 20, 2020).

6. In his 2016 interview with Valdeón, Sabina clearly implies that he has never met Dylan by saying, "Sí, pero dicen que no es buena persona [risas]. La gente que conozco que lo ha tratado me cuenta que es intratable [más risas]" ("*Yes, but they say that he's not a good person [laughter]. The people I know that have dealt with him tell me that he's difficult to deal with [more laughter]*"). "Tirso de Molina, julio de 2016," Interview with Julio Valdeón, *Sabina. Sol y sombra* (Valencia: Efe Eme, 2017), 484.

7. "Sobra decir que Dylan me cambió la vida" ("*Needless to say that Dylan changed my life*"). Sabina, "Poeta torrencial, maestro del caos," *El País*, digital edition (October 14, 2016), (accessed May 20, 2020).

8. Sabina and Menéndez Flores, *Sabina en carne viva*, 103. Bruce Springsteen memorably compared the initial snare shot of "Like a Rolling Stone" to a kick that opens "the door to your mind." "The Rock and Roll Hall of Fame Speech," *Studio A: The Bob Dylan Reader*, ed. Benjamin Hedin (New York, NY: W.W. Norton & Company, 2004), 202.

9. Joaquín Sabina, "Mis juglares. Dos sonetos," *Esta boca es mía*, illus. Gustavo Otero (Barcelona: Ediciones B, 2010), 386.

10. *Las huellas de Dylan*, online film, directed by Fernando Merinero (2006; n.p.: Vendaval Producciones, S.L.), https://www.documaniatv.com/biografias/las-huellas-de-dylan-video_0e464c413.html (accessed January 4, 2020). Sabina seems to echo this sentiment when he says on another occasion, "Dylan . . . no es precisamente el mejor cantante del mundo, pero claro que lo es" (*Dylan . . . is not exactly the greatest singer in the world, but of course he is*"). Sabina and Menéndez Flores, *Sabina en carne viva*, 407.

11. Harold Bloom, *The Anxiety of Influence. A Theory of Poetry* (New York: Oxford University Press, 1973), 5. Bloom elaborates, "*Poetic Influence—when it involves two strong, authentic poets,—always proceeds by a misreading of the prior poet, an act of creative correction that is actually and necessarily a misinterpretation.*" Ibid., 30 (italics in the original).

12. The key phrase comes from Bloom's explanation of the first level of reaction of a poet—which he called *clinamen*—to his or her precursor. The term may be understood as a reactionary movement by which the later poet "swerves away from his precursor, . . . reading his precursor's poem . . . This appears as a corrective movement in his [the later poet's] own poem, which implies that the precursor poem went accurately up to a certain point, but then should have swerved, precisely in the direction that new poem moves." *The Anxiety of Influence*, 14.

13. Springsteen, "The Rock and Roll Hall of Fame Speech," *Studio A*, 203.

14. Thomas, *Why Bob Dylan Matters*, 322.

15. Ángel Antonio Herrera, "El Dylan de los que no sabemos inglés," in Javier Menéndez Flores, *Perdonen la tristeza (edición revisada y actualizada)* (Barcelona: Libros Cúpula, 218), 433.

16. "Nuestro Leonard Cohen con muchas horas de noche. Nuestro Johnny Rotten con lecturas. Nuestro golfo de oro en los altares." Menéndez Flores, *Sabina. No amanece jamás*, 9.

17. Valdeón, *Sabina. Sol y sombra*, 16.

18. See, for example, the lengthy discussion of the Andalusian's place among Spanish cantautors, in Sabina and Menéndez Flores, *Sabina en carne viva*, 119–25.

19. Maurilio de Miguel, *Joaquín Sabina* (Madrid: Ediciones Júcar, 1986), 45. See also Sabina and Menéndez Flores, *Sabina en carne viva*, 53–54.

20. Luis García Gil, "Joaquín Sabina: tras las huellas de Dylan," *Efe eme.com*, digital edition (February 9, 2019), https://www.efeeme.com/joaquin-sabina-tras-las-huellas-de-dylan/ (accessed September 18, 2019).

21. Sabina acknowledges the influence of "Talkin' New York" on "Pongamos que hablo de Madrid." Sabina and Menéndez Flores, *Sabina en carne viva*, 129.

22. Valdeón discusses the influence of "I Shall Be Released" on "Arenas movedizas." *Sabina. Sol y sombra*, 384.

23. Valdeón also explains that Dylan's "To Ramona" served as the inspiration for "Peces de ciudad." Ibid., 381.

24. See Menéndez Flores, *Perdonen la tristeza*, 147. Valdeón sees "¿Quién me ha robado el mes de abril?" as the "*daughter*" of the Dylan song and Neil Young's "Helpless" (1970). The chords and melody of the chorus of Sabina's song are quite similar to those of Dylan's song, and the tempo of all three songs is identical. *Sabina. Sol y sombra*, 169.

25. Sabina and Menéndez Flores, *Sabina en carne viva*, 131.

26. "I read *On the Road* in maybe 1959. It changed my life like it changed everyone else's." Dylan quoted at *BobDylan.com* (September 20, 1991), https://www.bobdylan.com/books/road/ (accessed May 22, 2020).

27. Joaquín Sabina, "¿Quién es Caín, quién es Abel?", *Con buena letra* (Madrid: Temas de Hoy, 2002), 277.

28. In Sabina's words, he wrote "El joven aprendiz de pintor" as if to "*take revenge on certain people*." Sabina and Menéndez Flores, *Sabina en carne viva*, 132.

29. Shelton, *No Direction Home*, 99.

30. Valdeón, for example, suggests that "Ring, ring, ring," from *Ruleta rusa*, is modeled on Dylan's "Idiot Wind," "Don't Think Twice, It's All Right," and "Like a

Rolling Stone" because its rhetorical occasion is that of one person—in each instance, the singer—rebuking his ex-girlfriend. Sabina. *Sol y sombra*, 93–94.

31. An estimate given by Sabina during the interview with Valdeón, "Tirso de Molina, julio de 2016," 486.

32. Sabina and Menéndez Flores, *Sabina en carne viva*, 359.

33. During part of his interview with Menéndez Flores, when Sabina is speaking so exuberantly about Jiménez and his songs, the cantautor pulls out a guitar and actually begins performing "Que te vaya bonito." Ibid.

To be fair, the original recording by Jiménez features changes of tempo that are not exhibited in "Noches de boda," though the melody and chords are very similar.

34. Eccles. 1: 9.

35. Dylan, for his part, is quite candid about how he used to approach songwriting by starting with an older melody. He explains that he "changed words around and added something of my own here and there." Dylan continues, "You could write twenty or more songs off that one melody by slightly altering it. I could slip in verses or lines from old spirituals or blues. That was okay; others did it all the time." *Chronicles: Volume One*, 228.

36. García Gil, "Joaquín Sabina: tras las huellas de Dylan," *Efe eme.com* (February 9, 2019).

37. Nik Cohn, *Awopbopaloobop alopbamboom: The Golden Age of Rock* (New York: Grove Press, [1970] 1996), 170.

38. A superb example of the kind of literary scholarship that Dylan's lyrics occasionally inspire is Christopher Ricks, *Dylan's Visions of Sin* (London: Penguin Books, 2003).

39. There are many instances of Dylan reacting negatively to perfunctory or shallow adulation, making it difficult to select a single example. One of his best quips may be what he said to an Australian reporter who had asked, "Some people call you a genius; do you agree?", to which Dylan responded, "People who call me a genius don't have any grandparents." Quoted in Shelton, *No Direction Home*, 365.

40. David Yaffe, *Bob Dylan. Like a Complete Unknown* (New Haven: Yale University Press, 2011), 129. By Dylan's own account, he has written "maybe a thousand songs." *Chronicles: Volume One*, 229.

41. The release of the new album was announced on the website, https://www.bobdylan.com/ (accessed May 24, 2020).

42. Greil Marcus, *When that Rough God goes Riding. Listening to Van Morrison* (New York: PublicAffairs, 2010), 85–86.

43. Lester Bangs, "Love or Confusion?" in *Studio A: The Bob Dylan Reader*, ed. Benjamin Hedin (New York: W.W. Norton & Company, 2004), 156.

44. Benjamin Hedin, introduction to "Self Portrait No. 25," in *Studio A: The Bob Dylan Reader*, ed. Benjamin Hedin (New York: W.W. Norton & Company, 2004), 73.

45. Menéndez Flores, *Perdonen la tristeza*, 215.

46. Quoted in Ibid., 408.

47. Sabina and Menéndez Flores, *Sabina en carne viva*, 43.

48. Quoted in Menéndez Flores, *Perdonen la tristeza*, 410.

49. Julio Valdeón, telephone conversation with the author, November 13, 2019.

50. Elijah Wald, *Dylan Goes Electric! Newport, Seeger, Dylan and the Night That Split the Sixties* (New York: Dey St. Books, 2015), 307.

51. Sabina, "Tirso de Molina, junio de 2016," Interview with Julio Valdeón, 489.

52. To mention a few differences apart from those found through the analysis of their lyrics, during interviews Sabina is usually gregarious and jovial while Dylan is often enigmatic and terse. In terms of musicianship, Dylan is a talented multi-instrumentalist while Sabina generally sings and plays guitar. Yet another difference is the fact that the Spaniard is nonreligious while his American counterpart experienced a very public Christian conversion. Finally, while Sabina has not directed film projects or written a partial autobiography as Dylan has, he has been the more prolific writer of the two, having penned several collections of poetry, an epistolary collection, a compilation of miscellaneous materials, and a book of his artwork.

53. The evidence of Dylan and Sabina's underwhelming album covers is extensive. In Dylan's case, he wears the same brown jacket in the photos of several album covers from the 1960s. For the cover art of what is arguably his greatest album, *Blonde on Blonde* (1966), Dylan selected a blurry, out-of-focus photograph of himself, grimacing in the Manhattan cold, with a nondescript brick wall behind him (the cover is now classic, of course, and could never be improved upon). (See "Bob Dylan—The Story of the *Blonde On Blonde* album cover (Digital Video)," *YouTube* (October 28, 2015), https://www.youtube.com/watch?v=A3qXRfHIeuY (accessed April 19, 2020)). For Sabina's part, the album covers of two of his finest studio efforts, *Física y química* and *Yo, mí, me, contigo*, seem amateurish, almost crude. On the cover of the first album, we see the cantautor holding a sign with the words "Física y química" (part of a celebrated aphorism by Spain's Nobel Prize-winning biochemist, Severo Ochoa); in the touched-up photo, inexplicably, Sabina has a heavy case of "5 o'clock shadow" reminiscent of Emmett Kelly. The cover of *Yo, mí, me, contigo* shows a simple caricature of Sabina sitting at a desk, in front of a blackboard, with the album's title scrawled in chalk behind him; again, inexplicably, we see that Sabina's legs are those of a woman wearing stockings. Sabina's best album cover is probably that of *Malas compañías*, which features an Octavio Colis painting of the interior of a bar, crowded with stylized figures of pastel colors.

54. For example, see the selection of photos from Miguel's *Joaquín Sabina*.

55. When asked if he is a fan of Winehouse, Dylan responded, "Yeah, absolutely. She was the last real individualist around." Bob Dylan, "Q&A with Bill Flanagan," Interview with Bill Flanagan (March 22, 2017), http://www.bobdylan.com/news/qa-with-bill-flanagan / (accessed May 24, 2020). Sabina dedicated a poem to the R&B singer, *"Amy's Song,"* about three years before she died. *Esta boca es mía*, 464.

56. Ellen Willis, "Dylan," in *Beginning to See the Light: Sex, Hope, and Rock-and-Roll* (Minneapolis: University of Minneapolis Press, [1992] 2012), 20.

57. Christgau, "Excerpt from 'Rock Lyrics are Poetry (Maybe)'," 63.

58. Sabina, "Tirso de Molina, julio de 2016," Interview with Julio Valdeón in *Sabina. Sol y sombra*, 486.

59. Richard Goldstein, *The Poetry of Rock* (New York: Bantam, 1969), 5–7.

60. During an early press conference, Dylan told reporters unequivocally that he starts with "the words" when he writes songs. See "Television Press Conference, KQED (San Francisco), December 3, 1965," in *Bob Dylan. The Essential Interviews*, ed. Jonathan Cott (New York: Wenner Books, 2006), 63. Sabina has also explained that he starts with "*a complete lyric*" when he composes a song. Sabina and Menéndez Flores, *Sabina en carne viva*, 108.

61. Shelton, *No Direction Home*, 65–74. Interestingly, in his brief biographical poem "My Life in a Stolen Moment" (1962), Dylan states that the only subject in which he did "OK" was Spanish, "though . . . I knew it beforehand." Ibid., 65.

62. Holman and Harmon, *A Handbook to Literature*, Sixth edition (New York: MacMillan, 1992), 408 (italics in the original).

63. Ibid., 313.

64. Ibid., 39.

65. All else being the same, most plural forms of nouns and adjectives may be paired with singular forms to complete a rhyme in Spanish, as with "colmillos"/"gatillo."

66. The *Oxford English Dictionary* features the meaning, history, and pronunciation of approximately 600,000 words. (2020) https://public.oed.com/about/ (accessed May 27, 2020). The latest edition of the Royal Spanish Academy of the Language's *Diccionario de la lengua española* (2014) has entries for 93,111 words and a total of 195,439 definitions for them. See the "Préambulo" of the *Diccionario*, (2014) https://www.rae.es/sites/default/files/Preambulo.pdf (accessed May 27, 2020).

67. Sabina says that he loves words, especially those that are "rancias, antiguas y en desuso" ("*rotten, ancient and in disuse*"). Sabina and Menéndez Flores, *Sabina en carne viva*, 337.

68. Ricks, *Dylan's Visions of Sin*, 32.

69. Quoted in Carbonell, *Pongamos que hablo de Joaquín*, 190.

70. Ibid.

71. Sabina, "Tirso de Molina, junio de 2016," Interview with Julio Valdeón, *Sabina. Sol y sombra*, 490.

72. Sabina and Menéndez Flores, *Sabina en carne viva*, 78, 81.

73. See Andrew Kirell, "'Desire': Bob Dylan's Sloppiest Masterpiece Turns 40," *The Daily Beast* (April 13, 2017), https://www.thedailybeast.com/desire-bob-dylans-sloppiest-masterpiece-turns-40 (accessed May 29, 2020).

74. "*Weird, like a duck in the Manzanares River, / clumsy like a reluctant suicide, / absurd like a Belgian singing flamenco, / empty like an island without Robinson.*" Sabina, "Así estoy yo sin ti," *Con buena letra*, 74.

75. "*When the city paints its lips [the color of] neon / you will climb aboard my cardboard rocking horse.*" "Caballo de carton," *Con buena letra*, 54.

76. Sabina, "Así estoy you sin ti," *Con buena letra*, 74.

77. In the medley that includes "Así estoy yo sin ti," from *Sabina y Cía. Nos sobran los motivos*, the cantautor sings "camarón," although those in attendance may be heard chanting "Robinsón."

78. "Seis tequilas" is one of only six songs on the album (of thirteen tracks) with lyrics written exclusively by Sabina.

79. Sabina, "Seis tequilas," *Alivio de luto*, Sony-BMG Music Entertainment, 8287 674202-2, 2005 (compact disc).

80. Spanish music critic Diego A. Manrique observed that around the time of Sabina's album *Vinagre y rosas*, he did not see evidence of music anywhere in the cantautor's home when he would visit, and "*the only thing he wanted to do was show you manuscripts and first editions*" of books. Manrique suggests that it may be a case when an artist suddenly gets the inspiration to become involved in another form of expression, like "*Dylan with movies, and Joaquín with verses and drawings*," but in both cases "*distancing themselves more and more from what they did best.*" Quoted in Valdeón, *Sabina. Sol y sombra*, 438–39.

81. For a very engaging exposition of Dylan's flair with rhyme, see Ricks, *Dylan's Visions of Sin*, 30–48.

82. Bob Dylan, "Shelter from the Storm," in *Lyrics 1962–2001* (New York: Simon & Schuster, 2004), 345–46.

83. Dylan, "Like a Rolling Stone," *Lyrics 1962–2001*, 167–68.

84. Sabina, "Siete crisantemos," *Con buena letra*, 137.

85. Dylan, "The Lonesome Death of Hattie Carroll," *Lyrics 1962–2001*, 96.

86. Dylan, "Just Like a Woman," *Lyrics 1962–2001*, 202.

87. Shelton, *No Direction Home*, 323. For what some have considered its unflattering description of women, "Just Like a Woman" is reminiscent of Sabina's "Aves de paso" ("Passing Birds") from the album *Yo, mí, me, contigo*.

88. Holman and Harmon, *A Handbook to Literature*, 236.

89. John Lennon and Paul McCartney, "Nowhere Man," *Rubber Soul*, EMI Records Ltd., 0946 3 82418 2 9, [1965] 2009 (compact disc).

90. Holman and Harmon, *A Handbook to Literature*, 169.

91. Sabina, "Calle melancolía," *Con buena letra*, 38.

92. Dylan, "My Back Pages," *Lyrics 1962–2001*, 125–26.

93. Dylan, "Fourth Time Around," *Lyrics 1962–2001*, 207.

94. Menéndez Flores, *Sabina. No amanece jamás*, 17.

95. See Genette, *Narrative Discourse*, 27.

96. Sabina, "Y nos dieron las diez," *Con buena letra*, 120. Writing about this particular verse, Emilio de Miguel Martínez calls it a "*glorious* ripio" that "*serves to transport the action to a year later,*" not with "*flourishes, but in the most pedestrian fashion.*" *Joaquín Sabina*, 187.

97. Dylan, "You're Gonna Make Me Lonesome When You Go" and "Tombstone Blues," *Lyrics 1962–2001*, 338, 169. About the line "The sun's not yellow it's chicken," see Bangs, "Love or Confusion?," 156.

98. Dylan, "The Times They Are A-Changin'," *Lyrics 1962–2001*, 82.

99. Dylan, "Leopard-Skin Pill-Box Hat," *Lyrics 1962–2001*, 201.

100. Sabina, "Así estoy yo sin ti," *Con buena letra*, 74.

101. Sabina, "19 días y 500 noches," *Con buena letra*, 186.

102. Sabina, "Jugar por jugar," *Con buena letra*, 155.

103. Dylan, "I Shall Be Released," *Lyrics 1962–2001*, 303; Sabina, "La del pirata cojo," *Con buena letra*, 127.

104. Sabina, "Ganas de . . . ," *Con buena letra*, 146.

105. Northrup Frye, *Anatomy of Criticism. Four Essays* (Princeton: Princeton University Press, [1957] 1990), 40.

106. Dylan, "Only A Pawn in Their Game," *Lyrics 1962–2001*, 90–91.

107. Ricks, *Dylan's Visions of Sin*, 171–78.

108. Sabina, "Eh, Sabina," *Con buena letra*, 56.

109. See Sabina's description of his drug use from the interview with Menéndez Flores, *Sabina en carne viva*, 73–81.

110. Joaquín Leguina, "Los amores perdidos," in Menéndez Flores, *Perdonen la tristeza*, 435.

111. Dylan is, perhaps, at his most gloriously irreverent during the final tracks of his second album, *The Freewheelin' Bob Dylan* (1963): "Honey, Just Allow Me One More Chance" and "I Shall Be Free." Yet, because of the prevailing opinion of Dylan as a "serious" artist, even his first biographer, Robert Shelton, dismisses these final songs as "almost inconsequential" and "anticlimax," concluding with "two of the weakest songs are tucked in at the end, like shirttails." Shelton, *No Direction Home*, 157.

112. Joaquín Carbonell, e-mail message to the author, May 24, 2020.

113. Menéndez Flores, "Sabina, el gran tema de Joaquín Martínez," 14.

114. Dylan scholar Mike Marqusee, in his review of *Chronicles: Volume One*, found the narrative a bit meandering, but described the author's prose as a "blend of luminous specifics and myopic vagueness." "Maximum Bob," *The Guardian*, online (October 15, 2004), https://www.theguardian.com/books/2004/oct/16/highereducatio n.biography (accessed May 30, 2020).

115. Miguel, *Joaquín Sabina*, 121.

116. William Faulkner, "Banquet Speech," (December 10, 1950), https://www .nobelprize.org/prizes/literature/1949/faulkner/speech/ (accessed May 24, 2020).

117. Shelton, *No Direction Home*, 226.

118. Sabina quoted in Menéndez Flores, *Perdonen la tristeza*, 43.

119. A tacit acknowledgment of the (over)abundance of 1960s source material is the lengthy song from Dylan's most recent album *Rough and Rowdy Ways*, "Murder Most Foul," which practically lists a myriad of cultural references centered around the JFK assassination.

120. Dylan, "George Jackson," *Lyrics 1962–2001*, 273.

121. Sabina, "Noches de boda," *Con buena letra*, 206.

122. Sabina and Menéndez Flores, *Sabina en carne viva*, 136.

123. Holman and Harmon, *A Handbook to Literature*, 468.

124. Sabina, "Así estoy yo sin ti," *Con buena letra*, 74.

125. Menéndez Flores, *Sabina. No amanece jamás*, 25.

126. Ricks, *Dylan's Visions of Sin*, 385.

127. Dylan, "Chimes of Freedom," *Lyrics 1962–2001*, 116.

128. Dylan, "Mr. Tambourine Man," *Lyrics 1962–2001*, 152.

129. Dylan, "Joey," *Lyrics 1962–2001*, 363. As with all but two of the songs from the album *Desire*, the lyrics of "Joey" were cowritten with Jacques Levy.

130. Holman and Harmon, *A Handbook to Literature*, 291.

131. Dylan, "Dear Landlord," *Lyrics 1962–2001*, 229.

132. Shelton, *No Direction Home*, 393–92. With this statement, Shelton appears to be echoing Willis' assertion that one of Dylan's greatest abilities is that of forging "a unity of sound and word that eludes most of his imitators." "Dylan," 20.

133. Dylan, *Chronicles: Volume One*, 160.

134. Dylan, "Hurricane," *Lyrics 1962–2001*, 356.

135. But not including the fifth stanza, which appears to be a coda with its shorter verses leading to the concluding "esta boca es mía."

136. Neira, "Los sonetos de Sabina," 268.

137. Carbonell, *Pongamos que hablo de Joaquín*, 438.

138. Dylan has also written his fair share of songs about outlaws, for example "Outlaw Blues," "John Wesley Harding," and "Joey."

139. Bob Dylan, "Like a Rolling Stone," *Highway 61 Revisited*, Columbia Records, CK 92399, 1965 (compact disc).

140. Sabina, "Siete crisantemos," *Con buena letra*, 137.

141. For example, see the article by Virginia R. Delgado Polo, "La música en el aula de E/LE: explotación de una canción de J. Sabina," *Foro de profesores de E/LE* 5 (2009): 1–7.

142. Willis, "Dylan," 13.

143. Thomas, *Why Bob Dylan Matters*.

144. Sean Wilentz has argued that the eleven-minute track "Desolation Row," from *Highway 61 Revisited*, owes a significant debt to Kerouac's late novel, *Desolation Angels* (1965). "Bob Dylan, the Beat Generation, and Allen Ginsberg's America," *The New Yorker*, online edition (August 13, 2010), https://www.newyorker.com/news/news-desk/bob-dylan-the-beat-generation-and-allen-ginsbergs-america (accessed May 10, 2020). In a 1969 interview with Jan Wenner, Dylan said that Ginsberg's "city poetry" was actually more of an influence on the song. See, "Interview with Jann S. Wenner, Rolling Stone, November 29, 1969," in *Bob Dylan. The Essential Interviews*, ed. Jonathan Cott (New York: Wenner Books, 2006), 148.

145. Bob Dylan, "Interview with Ron Rosenbaum," in *Playboy* (March 1978), reprinted in *Bob Dylan. The Essential Interviews*, ed. Jonathan Cott (New York, NY: Wenner Media, 2006), 202–3.

146. Wilentz, "Bob Dylan, the Beat Generation, and Allen Ginsberg's America" *The New Yorker*, online edition (August 13, 2010).

147. Shelton, *No Direction Home*, 138.

148. Bob Dylan, "Interview with Robert Shelton, from 'No Direction Home,' March 1966," reprinted in *Bob Dylan. The Essential Interviews*, 86–87.

149. "Allen Ginsberg on Bob Dylan," *YouTube* (November 16, 2014), https://www.youtube.com/watch?v=84bNaA-BV4Q (accessed October 10, 2019).

150. Jack Kerouac, "Essentials of Spontaneous Prose," in *The Portable Jack Kerouac*, ed. Ann Charters (New York: Penguin, 1995), 484–85.

151. Ginsberg states, "what I try to do is forget entirely about the whole world of art, and just get directly to the . . . fastest and most direct expression of what it is I got in heart-mind. Trusting that if my heart-mind is shapely, the objects or words, the word sequences, the sentences, the lines, the songs, will also be shapely." Quoted in Louis Simpson, "Souls in Symphony with One Another," in *On the Poetry of Allen Ginsberg* (Ann Arbor: University of Michigan Press, 1984), 115.

152. Willis, "Dylan," 19–20.

153. Dylan, "Ballad of a Thin Man," *Lyrics 1962–2001*, 175.

154. Sabina and Menéndez Flores, *Sabina en carne viva*, 132.

155. Miguel, *Joaquín Sabina*, 36.

156. Sabina and Menéndez Flores, *Sabina en carne viva*, 132.

157. See, for example, the cantautor's detailed description of his songwriting process, in *Sabina en carne viva*, 106–8.

158. Sabina, "Poeta torrencial, maestro del caos," *El País*, digital edition (October 14, 2016), (accessed May 20, 2020).

159. Willis, "Dylan," 6.

160. Carbonell, *Pongamos que hablo de Joaquín*, 188.

161. Shelton, *No Direction Home*, 441.

162. Because of the return to an earlier style, as well as the album's stripped-down arrangements, critic Robert Christgau initially viewed the album as "a sell-out to [Dylan's] pre-electric period." Cited in "Bob Dylan," *Robert Christgau. Dean of American Rock Critics* online (n.d.), https://robertchristgau.com/get_artist.php?name=Bob+Dylan (accessed May 31, 2020).

163. Sabina, "El blues de lo que pasa en mi escalera," *Con buena letra*, 143.

164. Dylan, "Tangled Up In Blue," *Lyrics, 1962–2001*, 333.

165. Ibid.

166. Sabina, "El blues de lo que pasa en mi escalera," *Con buena letra*, 142.

167. Miguel, *Joaquín Sabina*, 142.

168. Cohn, *Awopbopaloobop alopbamboom*, 171.

169. Sabina, "Jugar por jugar," *Con buena letra*, 155.

170. Dylan, liner notes, *Bringing It All Back Home*, Sony Music Entertainment, CK 92401, 1965 (compact disc).

171. Bob Dylan, "Nobel Lecture," *The Nobel Prize*, online (June 5, 2017), https://www.nobelprize.org/prizes/literature/2016/dylan/lecture/ (accessed June 1, 2020).

172. Sabina, "Poeta torrencial, maestro del caos," *El País*, digital edition (October 14, 2016) (accessed July 16, 2019).

Bibliography

Allinson, Mark. "The Construction of Youth in Spain in the 1980s and 1990s." In *Contemporary Spanish Cultural Studies*, edited by Barry Jordan and Rikki Morgan-Tamosunas, 265–73. London: Arnold, 2000.
Aristotle. *On Rhetoric*. Translated by George A. Kennedy. New York: Oxford University Press, 1999.
Barbero, Sonia Beatriz, and Cecilia Malik de Tchara. "La autoficción metapoética de Joaquín Sabina: el lugar desde el que se dice 'poeta'." *RECIAL: Revista del Centro de Investigación de la Facultad de Filosofía y Humanidades. Áreas Letras* 8, no. 11 (2017). https://dialnet.unirioja.es/servlet/articulo?codigo=6070550.
Benedetti, Mario. "Joaquín Sabina." In *Joaquín Sabina: Calle melancolía y otras canciones*, 5–7. Buenos Aires: Espasa-Calpe, 1995.
———. *El olvido está lleno de memoria*. Buenos Aires: Editorial Sudamericana, 1995.
Ben Slama, Mohamed. *El arte de asustar. Las caras de miedo en los relatos de Emilio Carrere*. Almería: Círculo Rojo, 2018.
Bloom, Harold. *The Anxiety of Influence. A Theory of Poetry*. New York: Oxford University Press, 1973.
Booth, Wayne C. *The Rhetoric of Fiction*, Second edition. Chicago: Chicago University Press, 1983.
Borges, Jorge Luis. "Partial Enchantments of the Quijote." In *Other Inquisitions, 1937–1952*, translated by Ruth L. C. Simms, 53–46. Austin: University of Texas Press, 1964.
———. *Borges on Writing*. Edited by Norman Thomas di Giovanni, et al. Hopewell, NJ: The Ecco Press, [1973] 1994.
Borges, Jorge Luis, and Roberto Alifano. *Twenty-four Conversations with Borges. Including a Selection of Poems*. Translated by Nicomedes Suárez Araúz, Willis Barnstone, and Noemí Escandell. Housatonic, MA: Lascaux Publishers, 1984.
Boyle, Catherine. "The Politics of Popular Music: on the Dynamics of New Song." In *Spanish Cultural Studies. An Introduction*, edited by Helen Graham and Jo Labanyi, 291–94. London: Oxford University Press, 1995.

Carbonell, Joaquín. *Pongamos que hablo de Joaquín. Una mirada personal sobre Joaquín Sabina*. Barcelona: Ediciones B, 2011.
Cardillo, Luis. *Los tangos de Sabina*. Buenos Aires: Editorial Olimpia, 2003.
Castro, Ruy. *Bossa Nova. The Story of the Brazilian Music That Seduced the World*. Translated by Lysa Salsbury. Chicago: A Capella Books, 2000.
Cattaneo, Simone. "A mitad de camino entre la canción y el cuento. Pongamos que hablo de Joaquín Sabina." In *Narrativas de la posmodernidad del cuento al microrrelato*, edited by Salvador Montesa Peydró, 421–429. Málaga: AEDILE, 2009.
Cohn, Nik. *Awobopaloobop alopbamboom: The Golden Age of Rock*. New York: Grove Press, [1970] 1996.
Colmeiro, José F. "Canciones con historia: Cultural Identity, Historical Memory, and Popular Songs." *Journal of Spanish Cultural Studies* 4, no. 1 (2003): 31–46.
———. "Review of How Political Singers Facilitated the Spanish Transition to Democracy, 1960–1982: The Cultural Construction of a New Identity, by Esther Pérez-Villalba." *Bulletin of Hispanic Studies* 86 (2009): 449–50.
Darío, Rubén. *Songs of Life and Hope/Cantos de vida y esperanza*, A Bilingual edition. Edited and translated by Will Derusha and Alberto Acereda. Durham, NC: Duke University Press, 2004.
Del Águila, Pablo. *De soledad, amor, silencio y muerte (poesía reunida 1964–1968)*. Edited by Jairo García Jaramillo. Madrid: Bartleby Editores, 2017.
Delgado Polo, Virginia R. "La música en el aula de E/LE: explotación de una canción de J. Sabina." *Foro de profesores de E/LE* 5 (2009): 1–7 (available online).
Dylan, Bob. *Chronicles: Volume One*. New York: Simon & Schuster, 2004.
———. *Lyrics 1962–2001*. New York: Simon & Schuster, 2004.
Epstein, Daniel Mark. *The Ballad of Bob Dylan: A Portrait*. New York: Harper Perennial, 2012.
Esteban, José, José María Kaydeda, et al. *Café Gijón. 100 años de historia: nombres, vidas, amores y muertes*. Madrid: Ediciones Kaydeda, 1988.
Franco, Jean. *César Vallejo. The Dialectics of Poetry and Silence*. London: Cambridge University Press, 1976.
Frye, Northrup. *Anatomy of Criticism. Four Essays*. Princeton: Princeton University Press, [1957] 1990.
Gallero, José Luis. *Sólo se vive una vez. Esplendor y ruina de la movida madrileña*. Madrid: Ediciones Ardora, 1991.
García-Castañón, Santiago. "Hacia una poética del perdedor: Joaquín Sabina o la escritura en los márgenes de la sociedad." *MIFLC Review. Journal of the Mountain Interstate Foreign Language Conference* 10 (Fall 2001): 64–84.
García Gil, Luis. "Joaquín Sabina: tras las huellas de Dylan." *Efe eme.com*, Digital edition, February 9, 2019. https://www.efeeme.com/joaquin-sabina-tras-las-huellas-de-dylan/.
García Jaramillo, Jairo. "Las huellas borradas de Pablo del Águila." In Pablo del Águila, *De soledad, amor, silencio y muerte*, edited by Jairo García Jaramillo, 7–68. Madrid: Bartleby Editores, 2017.
García Montero, Luis. "El mundo de Joaquín Sabina." In Joaquín Sabina, *Ciento volando de Catorce*, 7–15. Madrid: Visor, [2001] 2016.

Gascón-Vera, Elena. "Más allá de la Movida: España en los 90." In *Pespectivas sobre la cultura hispánica. XV aniversario de una colaboración interuniversitaria*, coordinated by John P. Gabriele and Andriena Bianchini, 161–81. Córdoba: Tipografía Católica, S.C.A., 1997.

Genette, Gérard. *Narrative Discourse. An Essay in Method*. Translated by Jane E. Lewin. Ithaca: Cornell University Press, 1980.

Goldstein, Richard, editor. *The Poetry of Rock*. New York: Bantam, 1969.

González del Pozo, Jorge. "La 'Princesa' de Joaquín Sabina: nostalgia a caballo entre el amor y el miedo." *Bulletin of Hispanic Studies* 87, no. 3 (2010): 353–370.

González Lucini, Fernando. *Veinte años de canción en España (1963–1983)*, 4 vols. Madrid: Grupo Cultural Zero, 1984–1987.

———. *Crónica cantada de los silencios rotos. Voces y canciones de autor, 1963–1997*. Madrid: Editorial Alianza, 1998.

———. *De la memoria contra el olvido: Manifiesto canción del sur*. Madrid: Junta de Andalucía/Iberautor Promociones Culturales, SRL, 2004.

Graham, Helen, and Jo Labanyi. "Editors' Preface." In *Spanish Cultural Studies. An Introduction*, edited by Helen Graham and Jo Labanyi, v–viii. London: Oxford University Press, 1995.

Hedin, Benjamin, editor. *Studio A: The Bob Dylan Reader*. New York: W.W. Norton & Company, 2004.

Holman, Hugh C., and William Harmon. *A Handbook to Literature*, Sixth edition. New York: MacMillan, 1992.

Jacobs, Michael. *A Guide to Andalusia*. London: Penguin Books, 1991.

Kerouac, Jack. "Essentials of Spontaneous Prose." In *The Portable Jack Kerouac*, edited by Ann Charters, 484–85. New York: Penguin, [1953] 1995.

Kloss, Jürgen. "Rhyming with Bob: About the Use of Rhyme in Bob Dylan's Songs." *...Just Another Tune*, May 2, 2007. http://www.justanothertune.com/html/rhymingwithbob.html.

Laín Corona, Guillermo, editor. *Joaquín Sabina o fusilar al rey de los poetas*. Madrid: Visor, 2018.

———. "Sabina ¿no? es poeta." In *Joaquín Sabina o fusilar al rey de los poetas*, edited by Guillermo Laín Corona, 29–88. Madrid: Visor, 2018.

León, Víctor. *Diccionario de argot español y lenguaje popular*. Madrid: Alianza Editorial, 1998.

Lichtmann, Maria R. *The Contemplative Poetry of Gerard Manley Hopkins*. Princeton: Princeton University Press, 1989.

Lord, Albert B. *The Singer of Tales*. New York: Atheneum, 1976.

Marcus, Greil. *Like a Rolling Stone. Bob Dylan at the Crossroads*. New York: PublicAffairs, 2005.

———. *When that Rough God goes Riding. Listening to Van Morrison*. New York: PublicAffairs, 2010.

Mendoza, Vicente T. *El corrido mexicano*. México, D.F.: Fondo de Cultura Económica, [1954] 1993.

Menéndez Flores, Javier. *Joaquín Sabina. Perdonen la tristeza (edición revisada y actualizada)*. Barcelona: Libros Cúpula, 2018.

———. "Sabina, el gran tema de Joaquín Sabina." In *Joaquín Sabina o fusilar al rey de los poetas*, edited by Guillermo Laín Corona, 13–28. Madrid: Visor, 2018.
———. *Sabina. No amanece jamás*. Barcelona: Blume Editorial, 2016.
Miguel, Maurilio de. *Joaquín Sabina*. Madrid: Ediciones Júcar, 1986.
———. *Joaquín Sabina. Eso será poesía. De los inicios a 'Joaquín Sabina y Viceversa.'* Las Palmas de Gran Canaria: El Ángel Caído, 2017.
Miguel Martínez, Emilio de. *Joaquín Sabina. Concierto privado*. Madrid: Visor, 2008.
———. "Sabina canta historias (técnicas y recursos de un narrador en canciones)." In *Joaquín Sabina o fusilar al rey de los poetas*, edited by Guillermo Laín Corona, 89–159. Madrid: Visor, 2018.
Muñoz Molina, Antonio. *Beatus Ille*. Prologue, bibliography, and notes by Cristina Moreiras Menor. México, D.F.: Fondo de Cultura Económica, 2007.
———. "Joaquín Sabina." In *Perdonen la tristeza (edición revisada y actualizada)*, edited by Javier Menéndez Flores, 440. Barcelona: Libros Cúpula, 2018.
Navas, Sara. "Un cóctel molotov en un banco y siete años de exilio en Londres: así fueron los inicios de Joaquín Sabina." *El País*, Online edition, November 9, 2019. https://elpais.com/elpais/2019/11/07/icon/1573135703_285643.html#comentarios.
Neira, Julio. "Los sonetos de Sabina." In *Joaquín Sabina o fusilar al rey de los poetas*, edited by Guillermo Laín Corona, 251–81. Madrid: Visor Libros, 2018.
Neruda, Pablo. *Veinte poemas de amor y una canción desesperada*. Edited by Hugo Montes. Madrid: Castalia, 1989.
Neyret, Juan Pablo. "Polvo enamorado. Quevedo y el Barroco español en la poética de Joaquín Sabina." *Espéculo: revista de estudios literarios* 27 (July–October 2004). http://webs.ucm.es/info/especulo/numero27/polvoen.html.
Ordovás, Jesús. *Historia de la música pop española*. Madrid: Alianza Editorial, 1987.
Ortuño Casanova, Rocío. "Atlas de lugares sabinianos." In *Joaquín Sabina o fusilar al rey de los poetas*, edited by Guillermo Laín Corona, 161–201. Madrid: Visor Libros, 2018.
Pérez Costa, Lola. "La melancolía en la obra de Joaquín Sabina." *Espéculo: revista de estudios literarios* 26 (March–June 2004). http://webs.ucm.es/info/especulo/numero26/sabiname.html.
Pérez-Villalba, Esther. *How Political Singers Facilitated the Spanish Transition to Democracy, 1960–82: The Cultural Construction of a New Identity*. Lewiston: Edwin Mellen, 2007.
Poe, Edgar Allen. "The Philosophy of Composition." *The Poetry Foundation*, n/d 2020. https://www.poetryfoundation.org/articles/69390/the-philosophy-of-composition.
Prado, Benjamín. "Cómo olvidar una canción de Joaquín Sabina." In *Con buena letra*, edited by Joaquín Sabina, 15–20. Madrid: Temas de Hoy, 2002.
Previtera, Roberta. "Entre la risa y el escalofío: la metaficción en los microrrelatos de Ana María Shua." *BRUMAL. Revista de investigación sobre lo fantástico* 6, no. 1 (Spring 2018): 91–103.

Rice, Miriam W. "Metaphorical Foreshadowing in La Regenta." *Hispanófila* 71 (January 1981): 41–52.
Ricks, Christopher. *Dylan's Visions of Sin*. New York: Penguin, 2003.
Roas, David, editor. *Teorías de lo fantástico*. Madrid: Arco/Libros, 2001.
———. "Hacia una teoría del miedo y lo fantástico." *Semiosis, Tercera época* 2, no. 3 (January–June 2006): 95–117.
Sabina, Joaquín. *De lo cantado y sus márgines*, 2ª edición. Granada: Diputación de Granada, [1986] 1999.
———. *Con buena letra*. Madrid: Temas de Hoy, 2002.
———. *Esta boca es mía*. Illustrations by Gustavo Otero. Barcelona: Ediciones B, 2010.
Scott, Carl Eric. "What Bob Dylan Means to Literature, and to Song. Was it a Mistake to Award Dylan a Nobel Prize?" *Modern Age* 59, no. 2 (Spring 2017): 75–82.
Shelton, Robert. *No Direction Home. The Life and Music of Bob Dylan*. New York: Beech Tree Books, 1986.
Thomas, Richard F. *Why Bob Dylan Matters*. New York: Dey St. Books, 2017.
Todorov, Tzvetan. *The Fantastic: A Structural Approach to a Literary Genre*. Translated by Richard Howard. Ithaca: Cornell University Press, [1973] 1975.
Torres Blanco, Roberto. "«Canción protesta»: definición de un nuevo concepto historiográfico." *Cuadernos de la historia contemporánea* 27 (2005): 223–46.
Uribe, Matías. *Polvo, niebla, viento y rock: cuatro décadas de música popular en Aragón: de Rocky Kan a Labordeta, Bunbury y Amaral*. Zaragoza: Ibercaja, 2003.
Valdeón, Julio. *Sabina. Sol y sombra*. Valencia: Efe Eme, 2017.
Valle-Inclán, Ramón del. *Luces de Bohemia. Esperpento*. Edited by Alonso Zamora Vicente. Madrid: Espasa-Calpe, 1987.
Valls, Fernando. "Sobre el microrrelato: otra filosofía de la composición." In *Mundos mínimos. El microrrelato en la literatura española contemporánea*, edited by Teresa Gómez Trueba, 117–24. Gijón: Llibros del Pexe/Cátedra Miguel Delibes, 2007.
Vázquez Montalbán, Manuel. *Crónica sentimental de España*. Prologue by Guillermo Heras. Madrid: Espasa-Calpe, 1986.
Wade, Graham. *Segovia: A Celebration of the Man and his Music*. London: Allison & Busby, 1983.
Wald, Elijah. *Dylan Goes Electric! Newport, Seeger, Dylan, and the Night that Split the Sixties*. New York: Dey St. Books, 2015.
Wilentz, Sean. "Bob Dylan, the Beat Generation, and Allen Ginsberg's America." *The New Yorker*, Online edition, August 13, 2010. https://www.newyorker.com/news/news-desk/bob-dylan-the-beat-generation-and-allen-ginsbergs-america.
Willis, Ellen. "Dylan." In *Beginning to See the Light: Sex, Hope, and Rock-and-Roll*, 2–25. Minneapolis: University of Minnesota Press, [1992] 2012.
Yaffe, David. *Bob Dylan. Like a Complete Unknown*. New Haven: Yale University Press, 2011.

DISCOGRAPHY

Beatles. *Rubber Soul*. EMI Records Ltd., 0946 3 82418 2 9, 1965 (compact disc).
Dylan, Bob. *The Freewheelin' Bob Dylan*. Columbia Records, CK 8786, 1963 (compact disc).
———. *The Times They Are A-Changin'*. Columbia Records, CK 8905, 1964 (compact disc).
———. *Another Side of Bob Dylan*. Columbia Records, CK 8993, 1964 (compact disc).
———. *Bringing It All Back Home*. Sony Music Entertainment, CK 92401, 1965 (compact disc).
———. *Highway 61 Revisited*. Columbia Records, CK 92399, 1965 (compact disc).
———. *Blonde on Blonde*. Columbia Records, CGK 841, 1966 (compact disc).
———. *John Wesley Harding*. Columbia Records, CK 9604, 1967 (compact disc).
———. *Nashville Skyline*. Sony Music Entertainment, CK 92394, 1969 (compact disc).
———. *Blood on the Tracks*. Sony Music Entertainment, CK 92398, 1974 (compact disc).
———. *Desire*. Sony Music Entertainment, CK 92393, 1975 (compact disc).
Reed, Lou. *Transformer*. RCA, PCD14807, 1972 (compact disc).
Sabina, Joaquín. *"Inventario"*. Fonomusic, 5046620142, 1978 (compact disc).
———. *Malas compañías*. CBS Spain, 2-462592, 1980 (compact disc).
———. *Ruleta rusa*. Sony Music, 462591900, 1984 (compact disc).
———. *Hotel, dulce hotel*. BMG-Ariola, 9A 258409, 1987 (compact disc).
———. *El hombre del traje gris*. BMG-Ariola, 259322, 1988 (compact disc).
———. *Mentiras piadosas*. BMG-Ariola, CDL-1146, 1990 (compact disc).
———. *Física y química*. BMG-Ariola, 3500-2-RL, 1992 (compact disc).
———. *Esta boca es mía*. BMG-Ariola, 74321 21432 2, 1994 (compact disc).
———. *Yo, mí, me, contigo*. BMG-Ariola, 74321 39565 2, 1996 (compact disc).
———. *19 días y 500 noches*. BMG-Ariola, 74321 69383 2, 1999 (compact disc).
———. *Dímelo en la calle*. BMG-Ariola, 74321 97509 2, 2002 (compact disc).
———. *Alivio de luto*. Sony-BMG Music Entertainment, 8287 674202-2, 2005 (compact disc).
———. *Vinagre y rosas*. Sony Music, 886976118327, 2009 (compact disc).
———. *Lo niego todo*. Sony Music, 889854133221, 2017 (compact disc).
Sabina, Joaquín, Javier Krahe, and Arturo Pérez. *La Mandrágora*. Sony Music, 085426900, 1981 (compact disc).
Sabina, Joaquín, and Cía. *Sabina y Cía. Nos sobran los motivos*. BMG-Ariola, 74321 81132 2, 2000 (two compact discs).
Sabina, Joaquín, and Viceversa. *Juez y parte*. BMG-Ariola, CDL-1145, 1985 (compact disc).
———. *Joaquín Sabina y Viceversa: En directo*. BMG-Ariola, 74321 40349-2, 1986 (two compact discs).
Los Secretos. *Grandes éxitos*. GEMA-BIEM, 0630 17065 2, 1996 (compact disc).

FILMS

Merinero, Fernando, director. *Las huellas de Dylan*. Vendaval Producciones, S.L., 2006.

Scorsese, Martin, director. *No Direction Home: Bob Dylan*. Paramount Pictures, 2005.

INTERVIEWS

Dylan, Bob. *Bob Dylan. The Essential Interviews*. Edited by Jonathan Cott. New York: Wenner Books, 2006.

Sabina, Joaquín. "Joaquín Sabina. Entrevista noctámbula." Interview with Carlos Boyero, *Rolling Stone*, Spanish edition, February 2000. https://www.taringa.net/+apuntes_y_monografias /entrevista-noctambula-joaquin-sabina_131ler.

———. "Tirso de Molina, julio de 2016." Interview with Julio Valdeón, in *Sabina. Sol y Sombra*, 481–99. Valencia: Efe Eme, 2017.

———. "Uno no puede mentirle a su gente y fingir que es un rockerito de 25 años." Interview with Carmen Lozano, *Diario Córdoba*, Online edition, April 15, 2018. https://www.diariocordoba.com/noticias/cultura/uno-no-puede-mentirle-gente-fingir-es-rockerito-25-anos_1218720.html.

———. "Joaquín Sabina: 'Me jodió mucho el gatillazo en Madrid'." Interview with Guillermo Abril, *El País Semanal*, Digital edition, November 29, 2018. https://elpais.com/elpais/2018/11/19/eps/1542640867_028138.html.

Sabina, Joaquín, and Javier Menéndez Flores. *Sabina en carne viva. Yo también sé jugarme la boca*. Barcelona: Ediciones B, 2006.

Index

Achebe, Chinua, 2
"Adiós muchachos" (poetic *tango* from 1928), 82, 91–92n83
"Adivina, adivinanza", 10, 22n54
Alarma!!!, 46
Alaska y Los Pegamoides, 42
Alberti, Rafael, 67
Alcover, Raúl, 30
The Alhambra, 29
Alivio de luto, 18, 52–54, 66, 81, 86, 136
"¡Al ladrón, al ladrón!", 123n39
"All Along the Watchtower" (Dylan), 150
Almodóvar, Pedro, 6, 113
"Amor se llama el juego", 29, 78
Anderson Imbert, Enrique, 129n145
Anthony, Marc, 49
"Arenas movedizas", 133
Aristotle, 67, 77, 88n17
"Así estoy yo sin ti", ix, 47, 74–75, 142, 151
Aute, Luis Eduardo, 2, 30, 32, 44–45, 134
"Aves de paso", 115, 166n87
"Ay! Carmela", 149

Baez, Joan, 4, 29
"Ballad of a Thin Man" (Dylan), xiii, 155
Banco de Bilbao, 5, 33
Banderas, Antonio, 60n100
"Barbi Superestar", 83
Basinger, Kim, 6
The Beatles, 1–2, 28, 57n22, 124n63, 133, 135, 144
Beat literature, 134, 155–56
Beatus Ille (novel by Antonio Muñoz Molina), 27
Bécquer, Gustavo Adolfo, 66
Belén, Ana, 5, 7
Benedetti, Mario, 8–9, 49
Berlin Wall, 6
Berro, Quique, 117
Berry, Chuck, 27–28, 102
Bill Haley and the Comets, 27
"Bird on the Wire" (Leonard Cohen), 74
Blake, William, 13
Blonde on Blonde (Dylan), 144–45, 155, 164n53
Blood on the Tracks (Dylan), 142, 157
Bloomfield, Mike, 143
BMG-Ariola label, 46
Booth, Wayne C., 95, 100, 116, 119, 121
"Boots of Spanish Leather" (Dylan), 159
Borges, Jorge Luis, 76, 94, 101, 114, 122n10, 129n145

Bound for Glory (autobiography by Woody Guthrie), 134
Brassens, George, 13, 32, 150
Brel, Jacques, 13, 32
Bridge, Wayne, 79
Bringing It All Back Home (Dylan), 139, 154, 160
"Bruja", 43
Buarque, Chico, 13, 141
Bukowski, Charles, 141

Caballé, Montserrat, 72
"Caballo de cartón", 39, 142, 148
Café La Mandrágora, xi, 43, 116, 139
Cale, J. J., 2, 37, 134
"Calle melancolía", 43, 69–70, 75, 145
Camacho, Hilario, 43
"Camas vacías", 52
"Cancíon de primavera", 88n23
"Canción para las manos de un soldado", 10
Canito Memorial Concert, 42
Cano, Carlos, 30
Cano, Teresa, 44
cantautor, 3–5, 17, 19n15, 31–32; "crisis" of, 40; definition of, 3–4; poeticism of, 66, 140; regional manifestations of, 31; relationship to protest songs, 5, 31
Capdevielle, Jean-Patrick, 13
Carbonell, Joaquín, xi, 34, 44, 50, 73, 79, 148
"Carguen, apunten, fuego", 148
Carrere, Emilio, 110
Carter, Ruben "Hurricane", 151
Cash, Johnny, 138
Castro, Fidel, 11
Catalonian independence (referendum of October 2017), 11
CBS España, 72
Cela, Camilo José, 72
Celaya, Gabriel, 30
Central Intelligence Agency (CIA), 5
"Cerrado por derribo", 85
Cervantes, Miguel de, 26

Chamberlain, Richard, 37
Chandler, Raymond, 128n130
cheli slang, x, 103
Chernobyl nuclear accident, 6
"Chimes of Freedom" (Dylan), xii, 147, 151
Christgau, Robert, 14, 139
Chronicles: Volume One (Dylan), 7, 149
"Churumbelas", 105
"Círculos viciosos", 43
City Lights Bookstore (San Francisco), 9
"Ciudadano cero", 95–98, 117, 121
Civil Rights Movement, 4
Club Antonio Machado, 37
Cohen, Leonard, 2, 13, 38, 49, 74, 134
Coleridge, Samuel Taylor, 101–2
Colis, Octavio, 164n53
Communist Party of Spain (PCE), 11, 31, 34, 72
"Como te digo una 'co' te digo la 'o'", 49, 52
"Como un dolor de muelas", 53
"Conductores suicidas", 51, 62n127
"Con la frente marchita", 48
Conservatism, 4
"Construção" (Chico Buarque), 141
"Contigo", x, 78–80, 148
"Continuidad de los parques" (micronarrative by Julio Cortázar), 114
"Con un par", 123n39, 154
copla / canción popular, 28, 57n18
Coronado, Jimena, 26, 50, 52, 55, 115, 148
Cortázar, Julio, 77, 114
"Crisis", 92n100
Cruella de Vil, 124n60
"Cuando aprieta el frío", 47
"Cuando era más joven", 46, 70, 81–82, 133
"Cuervo ingenuo" (song by Javier Krahe), 44
Curtis, Jean-Louis, 121

Danius, Sara, 2
Dante, 154
Darío, Rubén, x, 3, 68
Davies, Ray, 2
"The Dead" (short story by James Joyce), 133
"Dear Landlord" (Dylan), xii, 152–53
Defoe, Daniel, 142
Del Águila, Pablo, 29–30
Denny, Sandy, 122n14
"De purísima y oro", 25–26, 49–50, 83
Desire (Dylan), 151, 153
"Desolation Row" (Dylan), 147
Díaz, Aurelio ("el Buly"), 38
Dímelo en la calle, 52–53, 86
"Don't Think Twice, It's All Right" (Dylan), 73
"Do Right to Me Baby (Do Unto Others)" (Dylan), 144
"Dos horas después", 52, 53
Down in the Groove (Dylan), 136
Dúrcal, Rocío, 51
Dylan, Bob, 2, 7, 12, 14–15, 17, 32, 38, 48–49, 55, 66, 81–82, 93, 122n14, 131–60; allegations of plagiarism, 22n62; attitude toward the Vietnam War, 7; biblical references, 150; criticism of, 136–37; "Dylanology", 3; Newport Folk Festival of 1965, 7, 138; Nobel Prize, 2–3, 12–13, 15, 17, 133, 156, 160; poetry, 2–3; pre-electric phase, 4; Rolling Thunder Review, 139

"Eh, Sabina", 45–46, 147–48
"El blues de lo que pasa en mis escalera", 78, 81, 105, 112, 156–58
"El café de Nicanor", 124n50
"El capitán de su calle", 150
"El caso de la rubia platino", 83, 95, 99, 116–17, 119–21, 129n140
"El cromosoma" (song by Javier Krahe), 44
El Dúo Dinámico, 5, 28
"Eleanor Rigby" (The Beatles), 124n63

The Electric Prunes, 133
El Escorial, 86
El Hierro (island of the Canary Islands), 74
El hombre del traje gris, 47, 102, 105
Elígeme (concert venue), 101
"El joven aprendiz de pintor", 47, 70, 72–73, 134
Elliott, "Ramblin' Jack", 139
Ellroy, James, 128n130
El País (newspaper), 156
"El rocanrol de los idiotas", 15
El Sol (discotheque), 42
Elvis, 27–28, 133
Enemigos íntimos (collaboration with Fito Páez), 48, 153
Epic/CBS, 42
"Es mentira", 114–15, 154
Essentials of Spontaneous Prose (essay by Jack Kerouac), 155
"Esta boca es mía", 50, 153
Esta boca es mía, ix, 48–49, 52, 77, 143, 156
Esta boca es mía. Edición completa de los versos satíricos (collection of satirical poems), 125n63
Esta Noche (Spanish television program), 72
"Este adiós", 85–86
ETA (*Euskadi Ta Askatasuna*), Basque separatist group, 33
Eurovision Song Contest of 1968, 5
"Eva tomando el sol", 57n20, 150
Exile on Main Street (album by The Rolling Stones), 38

Falangist hymns, 27
"Family Snapshot" (Peter Gabriel), 96
Faulkner, William, 27
Felipe, León, 30
Ferré, Léo, 32
Física y química, ix, 6, 29, 48, 51–52, 70, 77, 93, 107, 114
flamenco music, 26
Fonsi, Luis, 2

"Fool in the Rain" (Led Zeppelin), 102
"Footloose" (Kenny Loggins), 156
"40 Orsett Terrace", 148
"Fourth Time Around" (Dylan), xii, 145
Franco, Francisco, 4–5, 10, 25, 28, 31–32, 38–40
Francoism / Francoist, 5, 10, 27, 30, 34, 40
The Freewheelin' Bob Dylan, 167n111

Gabriel, Peter, 96
Gallo, Joseph "Crazy Joe", 152
"Ganas de…", 50, 147
García, Charly, 51
García Candeira, Margarita, 30
García de Diego, Antonio, 17, 47–50, 53–54, 62n127, 80, 115, 156
García Lorca, Federico, x, 9, 13, 29, 31
García Márquez, Gabriel, 9
García Montero, Luis, 8, 65–66
Gardel, Carlos, 28, 48, 91n83
Gelman, Juan, 66
Genette, Gérard, 95–97, 114, 120
"George Jackson" (Dylan), xii, 151
Ginsberg, Allen, 155–56
Golden Age of Mexican Cinema, 80
Goldstein, Richard, 12, 15, 139
González, Felipe, 44
González Lucini, Fernando, 5
Good As I Been to You (Dylan), 136
"Gotta Serve Somebody" (Dylan), 144
Gran Café de Gijón ("el Gijón"), 9
Grupo Planeta, 9
Guerra, Pedro, 51
"Guerra Mundial", 45, 46
Guevara, Che, 69
"Güisqui sin soda", 46, 112
Gulf War, 11
"Gulliver", 70, 139, 157
Gutenberg, Johannes, 13
Guthrie, Woody, 4, 133, 139, 155

Hammett, Dashiell, 128n130
"A Hard Rain's A-Gonna Fall" (Dylan), 143, 155

Harris, Emmylou, 138
Harrison, George, 37
Hemingway, Ernest, 9
Heredia Maya, José, 30
Hierro, José, 27
"Highway 61 Revisted" (Dylan), 147
Highway 61 Revisited (Dylan), 154
Hitchcock, Alfred, 113
Hoffmann, E.T.A., 110
Holmes, Sherlock, 116
"Homeward Bound" (Paul Simon), 4
"Honey, Just Allow Me One More Chance" (Dylan), 167n111
Hopkins, Gerard Manley, 67
"Hotel, dulce hotel", 81
Hotel, dulce hotel, 6, 47, 74, 81, 99, 102
"Hurricane" (Dylan), xiii, 151, 153

Ibáñez, Paco, 140
"Idiot Wind" (Dylan), 73
"I'll Be Your Baby Tonight" (Dylan), 138
Inaugural address of John F. Kennedy, 14
Interviú (weekly news journal), 8, 54
"In the Garden" (Dylan), 144
Inventario, 6, 8, 10, 18, 30, 38–39, 43, 66, 68, 69, 136
Iron Curtain, 6
"I Shall Be Free" (Dylan), 167n111
"I Shall Be Released" (Dylan), xii, 133, 147
"It Ain't Me Babe" (Dylan), 73

Jara, Víctor, 5, 32
Jiménez, José Alfredo, 13, 134–35
Joaquín Sabina y Viceversa: En Directo (live album), 46, 134
"Joey" (Dylan), 152
Johnson, Robert, 139
John Wesley Harding (Dylan), 32, 133
Joyce, James, 25, 133
"Juana la loca", 45, 46
Juez y parte, 46–47, 70, 72–73, 96
"Jugar por jugar", 147, 159

"Just Like a Woman" (Dylan), xi, 144

Kaka de Luxe, 42
Kerouac, Jack, 134, 155–56
The Kinks, 102
Knocked Out Loaded (Dylan), 136
"Knockin' on Heaven's Door" (Dylan), 133
Krahe, Javier, 43–45, 116
Kurosawa, Akira, 98

"La, la, la" (El Dúo Dinámico), 5
"La canción de las noches perdidas", 52
"La canción más hermosa del mundo", 86
"La del pirata cojo", 52, 147, 152
"Lágrimas de mármol", 127–28n116
Laín Corona, Guillermo, 9
La Mandrágora, 10, 44
"A la orilla de la chimenea", 70–71
Led Zeppelin, 102
Leiva, 53, 54
Lennon, John, 102, 104, 144–45
León, Fray Luis de, 27
León, Víctor, *x*
"Leopard-Skin Pill-Box Hat" (Dylan), xii, 146
Levy, Jacques, 142, 150
Lewis, Jerry Lee, 51
Lhardy (Madrid restaurant), 47
"Like a Rolling Stone" (Dylan), xii, 73, 131, 143, 154
Literary pop / rock songs, 4, 6, 66
Little Richard, 28
Llach, Lluís, 31
"Lola" (The Kinks), 102
"The Lonesome Death of Hattie Carroll" (Dylan), xi, 144, 151
"Lo niego todo", 16
Lo niego todo, 8, 37, 53–55, 86, 93, 105, 127–28n116, 136
López Mondéjar, Publio, 35–36
Lord, Albert, 12
Los Brincos, 28
Los Llopis, 28

Los Secretos, 42, 46, 111
Loxa, Juan de, 30, 104

Machín, Antonio, 28
Magariños, María Ignacia, 9–10, 22n50
"Maggie's Farm" (Dylan), 138
Malas compañías, 42–43, 55, 69, 84, 139, 157
Manifiesto Canción del Sur movement, 30
Manolete, 72, 89n43
Manrique, Jorge, 27
Manuel, Víctor, 5, 7, 31–32
Marcuse, Herbert, 31
"Marieta" (song by Javier Krahe), 44
Marlowe, Philip, 117
Martin, Ricky, 49
Mary Magdalene, 84
"Más de cien mentiras", 67, 114, 125n72
Massiel, 69, 88–89n25
"Masters of War" (Dylan), 7
Mata, Antonio, 25, 30
McQueen, Steve, 104
"Me and Julio Down by the Schoolyard" (Paul Simon), 102
"Medias negras", 95, 102–4, 107, 112, 115
Melville, Herman, 147
"Memphis, Tennessee" (Chuck Berry), 102
Mendezona, Ramón, 72
Menéndez Flores, Javier (Sabina biographer), 3, 10, 17–18, 34–35, 53; *Perdonen la tristeza*, 34–35, 38; *Sabina en carne viva. Yo también sé jugarme la boca*, 9, 18, 34, 37, 53; *Sabina. No amanece jamás*, 34–35
"Mentiras piadosas", ix, 78
Mentiras piadosas, 6, 48, 52, 103, 114, 125n72
"Me pido primer", 33, 81
Mexican *corrido* genre, 111
Mexican *ranchera* genre, 48, 77, 111

"Mi amigo Satán", 43
Miguel, Maurilio de (Sabina biographer), x, 3, 6, 29, 34, 46; *Joaquín Sabina*, 3, 34
Miguel Martínez, Emilio de, 15–16
Milanés, Pablo, 11, 51, 83, 134
"Mi primo El Nano", 58n49
"A mis cuarenta y diez", 49, 81
"Mis juglares. Dos sonetos" (sonnet in *Esta boca es mía. Edicíon completa de los versos satíricos)*, 125n63, 131–32
Mitchell, Joni, 2
"Mi vecino de arriba", 10–11, 40
Molina, Miguel de, 28
Montiel, Sara, 28
Moraes, Vinícius de, 12
Moratalla, Enrique, 30
Morrison, Jim, 141
Morrison, Van, 18n5
Movida (Spanish cultural movement of the 1980s), 42
Movieplay, 39
"Mozambique" (Dylan), 142
"Mr. Tambourine Man" (Dylan), xii, 152
Muñoz Molina, Antonio, 26–27, 36, 93
Muñoz Romero, Tomás, 43
"Murder Most Foul" (Dylan), 167n119
Muriel, Antonio, 89n48
"My Back Pages" (Dylan), xii, 14, 145

Nacha Pop, 42
"Nebraska" (Bruce Springsteen), 96
"Negra noche", 45, 83
Neruda, Pablo, 8, 30, 66
"The New Steve Allen Show" (TV show), 151
"19 días y 500 noches", 83, 146
19 días y 500 noches, ix, 15–17, 26, 48–49, 51–52, 54, 78, 81, 83, 135–36
"1968", 30–31, 68
Nobel Prize Committee, 2
"Noches de boda", 83, 135, 150–51

No Direction Home (documentary by Martin Scorsese), 152, 155
North Atlantic Treaty Organization (NATO), 11
"Norwegian Wood" (The Beatles), 102, 104, 145
"Nos sobran los motivos", 85
"Nowhere Man" (The Beatles), 144

Ochs, Phil, 4
"Oiga, doctor", 91n65
"Ojos de gata" (Enrique Urquijo), 111
Oliart, Isabel, 51, 79, 148
Oliver, Antonio "Tony", 49
Olmos, Alberto, 12
Onassis, Christina, 6, 125n72
"Only A Pawn In Their Game" (Dylan), xii, 147–48
On the Road (novel by Jack Kerouac), 134
Otero, Blas de, 30
Out of the Past (film *noir* classic), 129n140

"Pacto entre caballeros", 95, 99–103, 107, 112, 154
Páez, Fito, 10, 18n3, 48, 50–51, 83, 153
"Paisanaje", 53
Parra, Violeta, 32
"Pasándolo bien", 43
"Pastillas para no soñar", 134
Paxton, Tom, 4
"Peces de ciudad", 133
"Peor para el sol", 95, 102, 107–9, 115, 120
Pérez, Alberto, 43–44
Pérez-Villalba, Esther, 7, 11
"Pero qué hermosas eran", 49, 102, 105
Picasso, 9, 72
Pinochet, Augusto, 5
Piquer, Concha, 28
"Pisa el acelerador", 60–61n100
"Pobre Cristina", 51, 125n72
Poe, Edgar Allen, 94, 110, 122n10, 122n16, 129n145

Poesía 70, 8, 30–31
poetic/literary/rhetorical devices, 17;
  alliteration, x, 14, 143; anaphora,
  14, 23n73, 67, 78, 86, 87n16,
  143–44, 151, 157; antanaclasis,
  67, 78, 81, 86, 87n16; antiphonal
  dialogue, 108, 125n78; antithesis,
  14, 25, 67–68, 146, 151, 160;
  lexical, 68–71, 82; of imagery,
  68, 72–78; structural, 68, 78–86;
  assonance, 14, 140, 145; auxesis,
  67, 86, 87n16, 105, 143, 160;
  chiasmus, 68; diegesis, 97–98, 103;
  of heterodiegetic and homodiegetic
  narrators, 97; enjambment, x, 14,
  145; fantastic narrative, 109–16;
  homonyms, 14; hyperbaton, 122n9,
  132, 144–45; irony/ironic mode,
  105, 132, 146–48; in medias res,
  94, 99, 107–8, 117; metafictional
  discourse, 108; metaphor, 14, 39,
  103, 106–7, 146–47; meter, 67, 132,
  138, 141, 144, 152, 160; narrative,
  94–121, 160; novela negra, 116–17,
  119, 121, 128n130; paradox, 146;
  parallelism, 68; poetic license, 101;
  polysyndeton, x; retruécano, 68, 82,
  88n24; rhyme, 14–15, 67, 132, 138–
  48, 152, 160; simile, ix, x, 67, 132,
  142, 146, 151, 160; syncretism, 154;
  synesthesia, x, 67, 132, 151–52, 160;
  vignette, 104–6, 121, 124n63
The Poetry of Rock (paperback by
  Richard Goldstein), 12
"Pongamos que hablo de Joaquín" (Luis
  Eduardo Aute), 134
"Pongamos que hablo de Madrid",
  43–44, 55, 69, 133
"Por el bulevar de los sueños rotos", 50,
  77, 80
"Por el túnel", 83
"Positively Fourth Street" (Dylan), 73,
  134
Prado, Benjamín, 47, 54, 94
Prado Museum, 27

"Precious Angel" (Dylan), 151
Premio Miguel de Cervantes, 9
Premios de la Música (awards
  ceremony), 83
"Princesa", 46, 51, 70, 73–74
protest song / *canción de protesta,* 5, 31
Proust, Marcel, 27
The Puerta del Sol, 70
Pulgarcito (*"Little Flea"*), 42–43
punk rock, 37
Punto . . . y seguido (compilation box
  set), 134

"Qué demasiao", 43, 123n39, 154
"¿Qué estoy haciendo aquí?", 37, 52,
  95, 105–6
Quesada, Oscar, 156
"Que se llama soledad", 75–76, 107–8,
  115
"Que te vaya bonito" (Jiménez), 135
Quevedo, Francisco de, 66
"¿Quién es Caín, quién es Abel?", 134
"¿Quién me ha robado el mes de abril?",
  x, 47, 95, 105, 133

Radio Futura, 42, 46
Raimon, 31
"Rainy Day Woman #12 & 35" (Dylan),
  134
Ramoncín, 10
"Rap del optimista", 60n78
Rashomon (film), 98
Reed, Lou, 2, 38, 124–25n63
reggae, 37
Ricks, Christopher, 19n9
Rimbaud, Arthur, 154
"Ring, ring, ring", 45, 83
Ríos, Miguel, 2
Rivera, Scarlet, 153
Rock and Roll Hall of Fame, 133
Rock-Ola, 42, 60–61n100
Rodríguez, Silvio, 13, 134
The Rolling Stones, 2, 28, 37–38,
  134–35
Román, Olga, 50

Romeo and Juliet (tragedy by William Shakespeare), 79
"Rosa de Lima", 50, 85, 148
Rosendo (Mercado Ruíz), 156
Rot, Ariel, 51
Rough and Rowdy Ways (Dylan), 136, 167n119
Rourke, Mickey, 6
Rousseau, Jean-Jacques, 147
"Roxanne" (The Police), 83
Royal Spanish Academy of the Language, 3, 9, 26–27, 41
"Ruido", 50, 52
Ruleta rusa, 45–46, 66, 96, 139, 147

Sabina, Joaquín: Andalusia, 25–26, 55; awards, 83; biblical references, 150; biographies of, 3, 34; bohemian and nocturnal activities as theme, 6; Carmela Juliana (daughter), 51, 149; "Chispa" (first girlfriend), 28, 57n20; collaborations with other musicians, 51, 83; don Jerónimo (father), 27, 31; doña Adela (mother), 27; don Rámon (grandfather), 27; drug use of, 51; Dylan, comparison to, 7, 131–60; Eighth International Congress of the Spanish Language, 9; Francisco (brother), 27; Granada, 8, 25, 29–33; isolation as theme, 74; Jimena Coronado (wife), 26, 50, 52, 55, 115, 148; London exile, 2–3, 5, 8, 11, 19n7, 25, 33–39, 148; love/the romantic relationship as theme, 6, 71, 74, 78–80, 102–9; Lucía Inés Correa Martínez (ex-wife), 39; Marxism, 11; Merry Youngs (first band), 28; Mexico, 11, 48; Molotov cocktail incident, 5, 20n26, 33–35, 59n66; musical styles of, 52–53; as narrator-agent, 100, 102–3, 107, 111–13, 117–20; *No es fácil ser joven* (first collection of poems), 8; nostalgia as theme, 6; obligatory military service of, 34, 39, 148; personal freedom and pleasure as theme, 6; persona of, 45–46; political activism of, 5–7, 10–12; prostitution/prostitutes as theme, 80–81, 83–85, 119; published works (poetry, sonnets, drawings and paintings), 2–3; *Ciente volando de catorce* (collection of sonnets), 8, 65; *Con buena letra* (compilation of song lyrics), 8, 22n65, 56; *De lo cantado y sus márgenes* (second book of poems), 8; *Esta boca es mía. Edicíon completa de los versos satíricos* (book of satirical poems), 125n63; *Esta boca sigue siendo mía* (book of satirical poems), 8; *Garagatos* (book of drawings and paintings), 8; *Memoria del exilio* (first published book of poems), 8, 38; *Muy personal* (book of drawings and paintings), 8; recurring themes of songs, 6, 150; relationship to Madrid, 25, 39–56; relationship to *Poesía 70*, 30–32; relationship to the movida, 5, 7, 41–42, 44, 46, 61n101, 73, 99, 139, 148, 156; Rocío (daughter), 51; transition to "electrified cantautor", 42–43, 139; Ubeda, 25–29

Sabina y Cía. Nos sobran los motivos, 50, 85, 111, 139
sabinero, ix, xiiin1
Sabines, Jaime, 79
sabinista, ix, xiiin1, 3
Sánchez Ferlosio, Chico, 44
Sánchez Muros, Carmelo, 30
Sanz, Alejandro, 2
Sartre, Jean-Paul, 121
Savater, Fernando, 10
Saved (Dylan), 136
Seeger, Pete, 29
Segovia, Andrés de, 26
"Seis tequilas", 142
Self-Portrait (Dylan), 136–37
Senante, Caco, 51
Serrat, Joan Manuel, 2, 5, 8, 11, 13, 18n3, 31–32, 45, 55, 58n49, 134

Shakespeare, William, 13, 79
Shakespeare and Company bookstore (Paris), 9
Shakira, 2, 49
"Shelter from the Storm" (Dylan), 142, 150
Shelton, Robert, 15, 157, 167n111
"Siete crisantemos", 77, 143, 150, 154
Silber, Irwin, 134
Simon, Paul, 4, 102
Slow Train Coming (Dylan), 151
Smith, Patti, 1–2
Sony Music Entertainment, 1, 40
Spanish Constitution, 5, 32, 40
Spanish Golden Age, 10, 66, 156
Spanish Transition, 5, 20n23
Springsteen, Bruce, 96, 133
Starkweather, Charles, 96
Stinus, Jaime, 46
Stivel, Alejo, 49, 117
Street-Legal (Dylan), 136
Subcomandante Marcos, 53
"Subterranean Homesick Blues" (Dylan), 152
Swift, Jonathan, 70

"Talkin' New York" (Dylan), 133
"Tangled Up in Blue" (Dylan), xiii, 157–58
"Tango del quinielista", 30, 40
"Tan joven y tan viejo", 81–82
tauromaquia, 11
Taylor, Elizabeth, 37
Tena, Manolo, 10, 45–46
Tequila (band), 49
Thomas, Richard F., 15
"The Times They Are A-Changin'" (Dylan), xii, 146, 150
The Times They are A-Changin' (Dylan), 159
Tin Pan Alley, 150
Todorov, Tzvetan, 95, 109–10, 112–14, 116, 119
"Todos menos tú", 152
"Tombstone Blues" (Dylan), xii, 146

"To Ramona" (Dylan), 133
Tourneur, Jacques, 129n140
"Tratado de impaciencia (número 10)", 40, 102

Última Hora (newspaper), 8, 39
"Una canción para la Magdalena", 83–85
"Una de romanos", 57n20, 90n53
Unamuno, Miguel de, 9
Under the Red Sky (Dylan), 136
Universal Music Group, 1
University of Granada, 29
University of La Rioja, 3
University of Minnesota, 140
University of Salamanca, 3
Urquijo, Enrique, 111
Ussía, Alfonso, 10

Valdeón, Julio (Sabina biographer), x, 3, 32, 34, 38, 43, 45–46; *Sabina. Sol y sombra*, 3, 34
Valle-Inclán, Ramón María del, 39, 156
Vallejo, César, x, 30, 38, 66
Vargas, Chavela, 51, 77, 80, 135
Varona, Francisco "Pancho", 17, 47–50, 53–54, 101
Vázquez Montalbán, Manuel, 28, 128n130
Vega, Antonio, 42, 46
Vega, Lope de, 3
Velázquez, Diego, 27
Verlaine, Paul, 16
Viceversa, 18n3, 46–47, 70, 96
"Vinagre y rosas", 81
Vinagre y rosas, 18, 53–54, 66, 86, 136
"Viridiana", ix, 80–81, 83, 102
"Viudita de Clicquot", 91n78

Waits, Tom, 1–2
"Walk on the Wild Side" (Lou Reed), 124n63
Warner Music Group, 1
Welles, Orson, 9

Why Bob Dylan Matters (book by Richard F. Thomas), 15
Williams, Big Joe, 139
Winehouse, Amy, 139, 164n55
written versus sung poetry, 12–16
Wyman, Bill (music critic), 13

"Y nos dieron las diez", 48, 77, 95, 102, 111, 113–15, 121, 145
Yo, mí, me, contigo, 48–49, 52, 78, 81, 83, 114–15
"Yo me bajo en Atocha", 48
"Yo quiero ser una chica Almodóvar", 48
Young, Neil, 162n24
"You're Gonna Make Me Lonesome When You Go" (Dylan), xii, 146
"Y sin embargo", 50, 79–81
Yupanqui, Atahualpa, 29, 32

Zamarro, Justo, 19n13
Zantzinger, William, 144, 151
zarzuelas, 26, 28, 56n5
Zola, Émile, 2
Zugasti, Mariano, 33

About the Author

Daniel J. Nappo is professor of Spanish at the University of Tennessee at Martin. He earned his PhD (Spanish Language and Literature) at Michigan State University under the direction of Professor Javier D. Durán. In 2001, Dr. Nappo was awarded a García Robles Fulbright Fellowship for dissertation research. Dr. Nappo's areas of scholarship include Spanish American literature, Mexican cinema, and the history and phonetics of the Spanish language. Since he started teaching at the University of Tennessee at Martin, Dr. Nappo has received the Coffey Outstanding Teaching Award (2012) and the UT Alumni Outstanding Teaching Award (2016). Dr. Nappo's most recent article, "Rubén Darío, lo fantástico y la Revolución mexicana," was published in the journal *Ístmica. Revista de estudios centroamericanos y caribeños*. In his free time, Dr. Nappo enjoys cycling, listening to music, playing guitar, reading, and spending time with his family.

www.ingramcontent.com/pod-product-compliance
Lightning Source LLC
Chambersburg PA
CBHW050906300426
44111CB00010B/1401